From Outlaw to Classic

The Wisconsin Project on American Writers

Frank Lentricchia, General Editor

From Outlaw to Classic

Canons in American Poetry

ALAN GOLDING

The University of Wisconsin Press

The University of Wisconsin Press
2537 Daniels Street
Madison, Wisconsin 53718

3 Henrietta Street
London WC2E 8LU, England

Library of Congress Cataloging-in-Publication Data
Golding, Alan.
    From outlaw to classic: canons in American poetry / Alan Golding.
    264 p.   cm. — (Wisconsin project on American writers)
    Includes bibliographical references (pp. 211–234) and index.
    ISBN 0-299-14600-6   ISBN 0-299-14604-9 (pbk.)
    1. American poetry—History and criticism—Theory, etc.
    2. Canon (Literature) I. Title. II. Series.
    PS303.G6   1995
    811.009—dc20   94-24157

For my mother,
Dorothy Margaret Golding,
and in memory of my father,
Charles Golding (1904–1994)

No one is ahead of his time, it is only that the particular variety of creating his time is the one that his contemporaries who also are creating their own time refuse to accept.

The things refused are only important if unexpectedly somebody happens to need them.

The creator of the new composition in the arts is an outlaw until he is a classic, there is hardly a moment in between.

Beauty is beauty even when it is irritating and stimulating not only when it is accepted and classic.

—Gertrude Stein, "Composition as Explanation"

Contents

Acknowledgments

The completion of any book depends on various forms of support, and I now face the pleasant task of acknowledging that. I have been helped considerably by grants from the Universities of Mississippi and Louisville, and by my respective departmental chairs at those institutions, Evans Harrington and Bob Miller. I am grateful also to those who have contributed crucial feedback as this project evolved: Charles Altieri, Rae Armantrout, Charles Bernstein, Cid Corman, Clayton Eshleman, Norman Finkelstein, Dana Gioia, Gerald Graff, Barbara Hanrahan, Langdon Hammer, Hank Lazer, Margaret Lynch, Steve McCaffery, Jerome McGann, Cristanne Miller, Bob Perelman, Kenneth Price, Joan Retallack, Kit Robinson, Lawrence Rothfield, Jeffrey Rubin-Dorsky, Ron Silliman, Harvey Teres, and Barrett Watten. I want to extend special thanks to three people who read the bulk of the manuscript at various stages—Tom Byers, John Taggart, and Robert von Hallberg; and to two who encouraged the project early, helped along the way, and finally read all of it—Lynn Keller and Marjorie Perloff. Don Rapp's word-processing expertise and diligence in the library facilitated the book's final stages and averted more than one last-minute crisis. I thank my wife, Lisa Shapiro, for her love, her fortunately-not-quite-interminable patience, and her brilliance with guided imagery: K.O.S. got me through. Chase and Jordan remain the center in relation to which almost everything else is marginal.

Charles Bernstein's "The Age of Correggio and the Carracci" is reprinted with the editors' and author's permission from *American Poetry Review* (Sept.–Oct. 1989): 14. "Freud's Butcher" is reprinted from *The Nude Formalism* (Los Angeles: Sun & Moon, 1989), unpaginated, © Charles Bernstein, 1989, by permission of the publisher. Unpublished material by Brad Westbrook and Bob Perelman is used by permission of the authors. A version of Chap. 1 appeared in *Canons*, ed. Robert von Hallberg (Chicago: U of Chicago P, 1984), © 1984 by The

University of Chicago. All rights reserved. Parts of Chap. 3 appeared in *Sagetrieb* and in *Publications of the Mississippi Philological Association* and are used by permission of those journals' editors. A version of Chap. 4 appeared in *American Literary History* 2 (1990): 691–725 and is used with the permission of Oxford University Press. A paragraph in Chap. 5 is reprinted from *Contemporary Literature* 35 (1994), © 1994, by permission of the University of Wisconsin Press.

Introduction

In the Peanuts cartoon on my desk, Sally says to Charlie Brown, "We've been reading poems in school, but I never understand any of them . . . How am I supposed to know which poems to like?" Charlie's reply: "Somebody tells you." This book, then, is about who has told and tells whom which poems to like; about how, where, why, and on what grounds they have done and do so; and about who and what gets left out in the process.

In the last decade's widespread critical and theoretical grappling with questions of canonicity, little sustained attention has been paid specifically to canon formation in American poetry. One striking exception is Cary Nelson's anatomy of "what we no longer know we have forgotten" (3) about modern American poetry, *Repression and Recovery*. Although they focus on individual poets rather than on poetry generally, I should also mention John Timberman Newcomb's reception history *Wallace Stevens and Literary Canons*, and Michael Bérubé's chapters on Melvin Tolson in *Marginal Forces/Cultural Centers*. Far more common, however, are studies of canonicity concentrating on fiction: John Rodden on Orwell, Leonard Schwartz on Faulkner, Richard Brodhead on Hawthorne, Jane Tompkins' *Sensational Designs*, Janice Radway's *Reading the Romance*. At the same time, much of what Frederick Crews has dubbed the "New Americanist" scholarship in American Studies is methodologically suggestive but has little to say on canonicity per se. Information-rich and theoretically sophisticated as it is, this scholarship nevertheless tends to reflect two widespread forms of intellectual narrowness in the academy. One is the oft-noted tendency of "radical" theorists to conceive revisionism in terms of rereading canonical texts—something that aligns them with putatively more "conservative" colleagues who are also likely to see the business of criticism as producing new readings of the "classics." The other involves the critical neglect of poetry in favor of prose forms (usually fiction) that have a superficially more "direct" connection to social and historical reality.

In *Boundary 2*'s 1990 New Americanist special issue, supposedly a key revisionist document, nine of the eleven essays (excluding editor Donald Pease's introduction) are devoted to nineteenth-century American prose, mainly fiction. The authors receiving most attention are Melville, Twain (both in two essays), Emerson, Howells, James, and those "official representatives of the excluded" (Peter Carafiol's term) Chopin and Douglass.[1] DuBois is the closest that the issue gets to the present. Susan Mizruchi's claim that "New Historicists who reassess the claims of historical reality upon literary works are drawn to American realism" (272) may yield an appealing coherence of focus, but it also means that the New Americanist canon remains mostly the same as the Old Americanist canon, except for the excision of Whitman, Dickinson, and the whole genre of poetry.

Conversely, another dominant line of work on canons is highly theoretical but often insufficiently grounded in material, historical specifics. Paul Lauter divides contemporary criticism into "formalist" and "canonical" approaches (*Canons* 133–53), thus offering a revised version of Edward Said's division between "theory" and "history" (1–30). But to the extent that these oppositions are viable, they describe not so much canon studies and its other(s) as the enterprise of canon studies itself, which includes both the "formalist"/"theoretical" and the "historical" strains. In a recent essay John Timberman Newcomb argues for "the potential productivity of a discourse on canonicity resituated on more concretely historical grounds" than those on which many recent arguments about canons rest, inviting an approach to canon studies "demonstrating the theoretical principle of the contingency of value in specific instances of cultural activity" ("Canonical Ahistoricism" 4, 6). In this study, then, I have sought to reconstruct a number of such "specific instances" in one area, that of American poetry.

Let me mention a few things that I do not do in this book. First, I have not set out systematically to address individual reputations, to make the case for particular inclusions or exclusions as if a writer or group of writers could unproblematically be considered "in" or "out." I know that I have betrayed my biases in passing: a little deflation of Berryman here, a little inflation of Olson and Creeley there. My last chapter, on Language writing's address to canonizing institutions, is where I come closest to promoting particular writers. But at no point are promotion and relegation my main purpose.

Second, I do not offer a canonical master-narrative, a theory of canon formation that claims broad generalizability to other genres, other periods, other cultures, on the assumption that such a theory would inevitably have inadequate explanatory power when applied to the specifics of widely differing social and literary-historical circumstances. While I disagree with Gayatri Spivak's commonly repeated claim that it is possible to jettison the very notion of canonicity, that we should (and can) "dethrone canonical method," I share her conviction that "there can be no general theory of canons" (790, 794). And third, on a related point, I have not felt compelled to choose among apparently competing models for understanding or theorizing canonicity. Rather, in Chapter 2 I argue for a *synthesis* of two dominant models in current debates over poetic canons, the aesthetic and the institutional: the view that writers make canons (the aesthetic model) and the view that critics, teachers, and the academy do so (the institutional model). Even there, however, I propose that this synthesis is most useful for discussing canons in a particular genre (poetry), time (the twentieth century), and place (North America). I make no universalizing claims for it, even if I do think generally that movement among different models offers the best possibility for a multifaceted understanding of how canons develop.

I make substantial use of the institutional model because it applies especially well to a century during which poetic production and (especially) consumption have increasingly been centered in one institution—the university. "Increasingly," but not exclusively: hence I have tried throughout to take seriously the claims of the aesthetic model and thus of poets themselves. Much of my discussion, then, ends up concentrating on the complex relationships—of difference, conflict, and symbiotic connection—between poets and the academy: for example, on the reluctantly academic poet-professors who founded New Criticism and promoted one modernist canon; on the canonizing force of a self-consciously marginal little magazine, *Origin*, that defined itself against an academic center; on the relationship of a contemporary poetic avant-garde (Language writing) to the academy. The influence in shaping canons of poets situated outside or on the margins of the academy makes monolithic adoption of an institutional model of canon formation untenable.

A few words on my method, which I am afraid I must define negatively. Since I am wary of applying an institutional model of canonicity exclusively, despite its usefulness and relevance, I distance myself from such approaches as John Guillory's privileging of the "school" (which includes the university) in his understanding of canon formation, and even from Michael Bérubé's more historically grounded "case-study reception history" (14) of Tolson and Pynchon. Bérubé writes:

I assume throughout that academic reception is both the determinant and measure of canonicity and the single most salient characteristic of the literary climate in which Tolson and Pynchon have produced their work. (18)

I prefer the indefinite article: academic reception as *a* determinant and measure, though admittedly a crucial one, of canonicity. Nor have I attempted Cary Nelson's broad survey of a period. And I have remarked already that, while I depend on theoretical work such as Barbara Herrnstein Smith's *Contingencies of Value* throughout, I am more interested in analyzing how such contingencies work at particular sites and moments of practice. Finally, while I applaud Newcomb's stress on the "concretely historical" and his effort to move beyond a purely academic context for reception and canonization, I am not engaged in reputation study.

My objective is to analyze some of the main forces within the system of literary production and consumption that have shaped, and continue to shape, the canons of American poetry. Although at a general level contemporary critics take the place of conflict in canon formation as axiomatic, few systematically trace particular *kinds* of conflict over an extended period or map the multiple conflicts within a literary-historical moment. Like all canons, those of American poetry have been and remain characterized by a series of conflicts: for example, between anthologists, between the aesthetics of different magazines and their editors (and *within* the pages of certain magazines), between schools of critical thought in university English departments, between canon-making institutions and individual writers or groups of writers. By reconstructing and analyzing some representative conflicts, we can understand more fully the complex processes by which canons in poetry are continually being made and remade. Chapter 1 offers a history of American poetry anthologies; Chapter 2 tests the claims of the two competing models for poetic canon formation that I have mentioned, the aesthetic and the institutional; Chapter 3 reconstructs the moment of the New Critics' entrance into the academy, emphasizing the implications for the American poetry canon of these critics' status as practicing poets, of their antinationalist reading of American poetry, especially Whitman, and of Brooks and Warren's landmark textbook *Understanding Poetry*. In Chapter 4 I examine the canonizing effects of a representative experimental little magazine, *Origin*; and Chapter 5 comes up to the present by discussing how the Language poets address, in both their theory and their practice, the canonizing institutions and canonical assumptions of the age.

I do not claim exhaustiveness for a moment, and I am acutely aware of what I might have done differently. Questions of race and gender inform parts of the study, as they must, but by no means constitute its central focus; the place of creative writing in the academy, and its relation to "theory," deserve a substantial treatment that I have not attempted here; so too does the interaction between modernist avant-garde and mainstream nonacademic periodicals (between the *Little Review* and the *Dial*, for instance); a case study along the lines of Bérubé's and Newcomb's would have its place. But a critical book, like a canon, is a highly selective construct. To end this preface with some examples of (in John Ashbery's phrase) "this leaving-out business" (*Rivers and Mountains* 39) is to invoke my central subject, and thus perhaps an appropriate way to launch a study of canons in American poetry.

From Outlaw to Classic

1

A History of American Poetry Anthologies

**Anthologies and the American Poetry Canon:
A Historical Overview**

In *Kinds of Literature*, Alastair Fowler distinguishes three main kinds of literary canon: the potential, the accessible, and the selective (213–16). He defines the potential canon as consisting of all extant literature, all the literature that, simply because it exists, any reader could potentially read. By the accessible canon, Fowler means that part of the potential canon to which readers have fairly easy access in the form of scholarly reprints, affordable paperbacks, or anthologies. His third category, the selective canon, covers those works in the accessible canon that trained readers have selected as especially worthy of attention. Fowler's categories describe the narrowing-down process by which a selective canon is achieved. They do not fully reveal, however, the complexity of that process. For instance, selection precedes as well as follows the formation of the accessible canon, affecting the form that "accessibility" takes. Some texts are considered worth keeping in print in a readily available form, while others survive only in the darker corners of university libraries. One way this process of selection works, one fundamental means by which the selective canon is formed and transformed, is through the poetry anthology. Examining the often conflicting standards that American anthologists have brought to bear on the problem of selection, then, illuminates more general issues of canon formation. It helps us understand how an anthology can reflect, expand, or redirect a period's canon; what literary and social principles regulated the poetry canon at different points in American literary history; and how those principles have changed over the years.

3

Conflicting principles of selection have marked American poetry anthologies from their beginning. When Elihu Hubbard Smith edited the first such anthology, *American Poems, Selected and Original* (1793), he hoped both to preserve poems published in periodicals and newspapers, which might otherwise be lost, and to invite evaluation, "a more certain estimation," of his poets' "comparative merit (iv).[1] Preservation, logically the first step in canon formation, gathers an initial accessible canon on which later anthologies can build or from which they can select. At the same time, placing the poems of the accessible canon side by side in one publication invites comparison and evaluation by readers, which eventually narrows the accessible canon. This sequence looks simple and logical: from preservation to evaluation to a more limited preservation. But evaluation actually occurs at two points, performed first by an editor and then by readers, making the sequence more complex than it first appears. Even in the earliest stage of canon formation, in which one would expect a broad, catholic preservation, evaluation governs the anthologist's work. An editor inevitably makes evaluative judgments in compiling an anthology, deciding that some poets and poems deserve preservation and others do not. The evaluation by readers that takes place after an accessible canon has been preserved confounds the preservative impulse that led the editor to gather the accessible canon. Preservation, the historian's goal, presumes the value of breadth, of collecting as much poetry as possible; it discourages further comparative evaluations that extract a more selective canon from the whole accessible canon. The preservative impulse assumes the value of a broad, inclusive canon, while evaluation produces a narrowed, exclusive canon. A long-term goal, preservation makes poems available as lasting documents of a literary period. But evaluation determines how long any work, once preserved, receives attention and, consequently, how long it is kept accessible.

Given these conflicts, any editor, whether interested, like Smith, in preserving the beginnings of American poetry or, like many later anthologists, in presenting its historical range, has an especially difficult task in weighing historical inclusiveness against evaluation and exclusiveness. The basis on which editors solve such dilemmas will often stay submerged. Thus an anthologist's stated goals may contradict not only each other, as Smith's do, but also the unstated biases on which the selections are founded. Again Smith provides a test case. Personal, regional, and political loyalties all underlie his work. To represent American poetry, he compiled a book dominated by his friends, by Connecticut poets, by Federalists. Much of the poetry he gathered consists of topical, Federalist satires on the dangers of unbridled populism. Like his stated goal of inviting evaluation, Smith's unstated ideology, which favors occasional poems devoted not to posterity but to the short-term goal of solving immediate political problems, conflicts with his long-term goal of preservation. Smith wanted to gain his poets "a more universal attention" (iii). But his ideological motive for winning readers was stronger than his altruistic desire to foster awareness of American poetry, and it limited the amount and kind of poetry he made available.

Smith's Federalism underlies what he saw as the use of his anthology: to build America's sense of identity by gathering an independent national literature to match and strengthen the country's newly achieved political independence. The particular political identity that Smith wanted that literature to embody is not what actually evolved, of course. Nevertheless, his and the other early American poetry anthologies, Matthew Carey's *Beauties of Poetry British and American* (1791) and *The Columbian Muse* (1794), did share this common goal. The term "American literature," rarely used before the 1780s, became commonplace after the 1783 Treaty of Paris. Magazines opened their pages to a flood of American writing, as their editors sent out crusading pleas for the creation of a "national" literature. The early anthologies supported this campaign: in *The Beauties of Poetry*, for instance, Carey reprinted large portions of his magazine the *American Museum*.

The literary nationalism fostered in eighteenth-century anthologies became even more programmatic as America moved into the nineteenth century. The country still felt an urgent need to assert that it had an indigenous poetry recognizably different from English poetry. Benjamin Spencer points out that "virtually every major and minor author between 1815 and 1860 felt obliged to expound some version of a national literature" (77). Emerson's "American Scholar," in which he famously asserts that "we have listened too long to the courtly muses of Europe," is only a highlight of an already widespread movement. Some critics and journals, like the *Monthly Anthology* and *Boston Review*, held out against this inflation of America's literary efforts. But on the whole, American critics until the mid-nineteenth century repeatedly called for a national literature and indiscriminately praised it.[2]

In the 1820s and 1830s, as the push to create a national literature gathered a momentum fueled by Washington Irving's success in England and William Cullen Bryant's example at home, the preservative and nation-building impulses behind the early anthologies branched off in two directions. In one direction, anthologists presented the historical range of American poetry (a "range" that continued to have its selective limits), to preserve the poetry that Americans had written so far and thus convince British skeptics that a national literature, an American poetry, was developing. At the same time, "nationality" acquired a moral edge, an alternative to perceived European decadence. A moral Adamism accompanied the literary Adamism, and as a result the nation-building motive for anthologies led directly to an inspirational one: now that its political institutions were established, America's citizens needed to have them justified and to be told how to live within them. Americans of the time looked to their poets for advice on these matters. Poetry's function, in this view, was to provide a national identity and morality. A poetry that is asked to instruct and inspire needs some degree of ideological conformity to succeed, and American poetry displayed just this conformity. The poetry that stood the best chance of being collected and widely disseminated through anthologies offered comforting and homely truths and affirmed the culture's sense of itself.

These two motives behind nineteenth-century anthologies, the historicizing and the inspirational, were closely related. The logical corollary of the historicizing impulse was to define the distinctively "national" characteristics of the poetry that had been preserved, and anthologists in the first half of the nineteenth century claimed, with some accuracy, that American poetry's defining characteristic was its moral purity. Consequently, since an anthologist like Rufus Griswold could find for The Poets and Poetry of America (1842) enough morally orthodox verse to provide both spiritual inspiration and historical breadth, the potential conflict between historical preservation and moral mission (which acts as a force of exclusion) did not arise. Nevertheless, just as evaluation precedes as well as follows preservation, so moral criteria for canonizing poetry not only describe what has been preserved—they also precede and govern the act of historicizing and preserving. Thus the typical anthology of the years 1830–60 included in its historical range only that poetry which fulfilled the book's moral mission. It excluded minority work such as Phillis Wheatley's and nonconformist poems by otherwise popular women poets, and ignored (at opposite ends of the historical and ideological spectrum) both Puritan poetry and Whitman.[3]

While America struggled for literary independence, a poem's, or indeed the whole canon's, claim to excellence rested on its embodiment of national characteristics. Once the debate over what constituted these characteristics seemed to be resolved and the need to extol only poetry that supported America's cultural identity had diminished, however, we might expect claims for transhistorical excellence, excellence judged by universal and international standards, to follow. This is exactly what happened, beginning with Charles A. Dana's *Household Book of Poetry* (1858) and Emerson's *Parnassus* (1874), both of which set American and English poems side by side, and continuing through Edmund Clarence Stedman's *American Anthology, 1787–1900* (1900) to the high modernist period. Like the earlier stages of canon formation, however, this later stage is not easily isolated. Even Smith had avowed universal, not national, standards of taste (although before 1815 and the end of the second war with England, "universal" meant "English," for all practical purposes). Heavily influenced by the critical tenets of the British Lord Kames and Hugh Blair, Smith, according to Spencer, considered "the belles-lettres of all nations as agents of universal taste uniting mankind in 'one vast brotherhood / In equal bonds of knowledge and of right' " (37).

Just as Smith had used supposedly universal standards in preserving an initial accessible canon, some modernist anthologists claimed to use them in revising the canon. Once an accessible canon develops, preservation becomes a less urgent motive for anthologizing. Once a stable literary and political culture is established, literary nationalism and political orthodoxy also become less urgent. Continued revision is the logical and ongoing final stage, but any revisionist editor who invokes universal standards in his or her defense walks on shaky ground. That editor may use the principle of transhistorical excellence to propose a new canon: the established poetry, in this view, does not meet universal standards. A more conservative editor, however, can use the same principle to justify the established canon. In this view, the "best" work rises to the top. A good poem or poet, once recognized, will always be, and will always be considered, good. Both anthologists, then, face a contradiction in this late stage of canon formation: if transhistorical excellence can be invoked to justify two different kinds of poetry, it offers neither the revisionist nor the more conservative editor a sound basis for a canon.

In recent decades, the American poetry canon has become especially open to revision and expansion. The diversity that has always been an unacknowledged part of American literary culture, manifesting itself since the mid-nineteenth century in politically partisan anthologies, women's anthologies, minority anthologies, and regional anthologies, has become more visible. One feature of the increased acknowledgment of this diversity has been a number of revisionist anthologies. These collections are all intended to shift an academic canon defined mostly by teaching anthologies like *The Norton Anthology of Poetry* or, particularly in the 1980s, texts such as *The Morrow Anthology of Younger American Poets*. To a large degree, however, these revisionist anthologies themselves also comprise the body of literature from which the academic editor selects. For the editor of the teaching anthology, the old question of what contemporary work to preserve takes a new but still problematic form. Today preservation usually means selecting from abundance, not protecting from oblivion. Due to the lack of general consensus on literary and social values and the sheer number of poets writing, however, the editor must sift multiple, conflicting claims to poetic worth, making that selection an arduous task.

Because they involve contradictory, often ideologically based definitions of "excellence," these claims undermine the tenability of any single dominant standard for "good" poetry. Evidently excellence is historical, *not* transhistorical. Once a putative canon is formed, it exists in a state of constant flux. The guests in the canonical house are continually shuffled from room to room. Broadly, of course, any canon is defined by what it excludes; so changes in the canon look like parts of a larger cycle of inclusion and exclusion. In practice, the cycle's nature is somewhat different. We rarely exclude a poet completely once he or she has been included for any length of time. A reputation may fluctuate wildly, but rarely collapse entirely. Once in, a poet tends to stay in, if only in a small corner of the attic. Getting in is another matter—a matter of meeting the historically specific standards that each literary generation has so easily thought "universal" (and including the standards that would deny the category of the "universal"), the standards exercised powerfully by each generation's anthologists.

Preservation: Elihu Hubbard Smith

When Smith set out to "offer a stronger, and more durable security" to poems otherwise fated to the short life of newspaper clippings, and to win an audience for "many poems, written by the most eminent American Authors . . . known only to a few of their particular acquaintance, and unheard of by the generality of their Countrymen," he was responding to publishing circumstances that made the anthology a genre particularly appropriate to American literature of the period (iv, iii). In the late eighteenth and early nineteenth centuries, most poetry appeared only in magazines, and those magazines had short lives. Only two eighteenth-century periodicals, the *New York Magazine* and the

Massachusetts Magazine, lasted eight years; the average life of an American magazine in that century was fourteen months. Widely dispersed readership; inadequate supply of affordable, high-quality printing materials; distribution difficulties; lack of advertising support; overdependence on subscriptions that were rarely paid promptly: all these circumstances explain why the early magazines appeared and disappeared at such alarming speed. As the nineteenth century progressed, distribution became easier. Roads and mail service improved, and postal routes were extended. Since subscription lists and income from advertising remained small, however, magazines continued to blossom and die quickly. Hence, as Fred Lewis Pattee puts it, in "the land of ephemeral periodicals" "there came early the thought of preserving the best of the writings in permanent form" ("Anthologies" n.p.).[4]

This attempt to preserve a national literature simultaneously with its creation distinguishes the early American anthologists from their British contemporaries. In America, unlike in England, the survival of the national poetry canon depended largely on the anthologists' success in preserving poetry. Some English anthologies, like Thomas Percy's *Reliques of Ancient English Poetry* (1765), did have preservation as a goal. But Percy wanted to preserve specimens of a particularly ephemeral genre, the ballad; the rest of English poetry was already taken care of. When George Ellis edited *Specimens of the Early English Poets* (1790) and sought to preserve "what is most valuable from the scarcest and least accessible compositions," he had in mind poetry of the tenth century, not of his own (2:v). And even Ellis's and Percy's aims were as much historicizing as preservative. Ellis wanted to illustrate "the rise and progress of our language" (1:iv); Percy wanted to "shew the gradation of our language, exhibit the progress of popular opinions, display the peculiar manners and customs of former ages, or throw light on our earlier classical poets" (ix). In America, however, a progressive literary history was something to argue for and something in which to participate in the present, not something to observe about the past. While British editors used their anthologies to review the historical development of an established body of poetry, American editors used theirs to preserve contemporary poems and to record their nation's literary progress as it occurred.

When Smith set out to "preserve" American poetry, however, he faced a conflict of interests. From today's perspective, preservation should have meant including Puritan poetry and a more representative range of Philip Freneau's and Joel Barlow's work. But the Puritans' social ideals conflicted with those of post-Revolutionary America, which saw itself as making its own social pattern, not following a God-given pattern. The Declaration of Independence presumed a doctrine of works, not of grace—a conflation, not a separation, of sacred and secular history (Pearce 34). Smith had to ask himself this question: Should he choose an eclectic thoroughness, or should he present an ideologically and poetically coherent canon in the service of the Federalist cause? The political situation was volatile enough, and perhaps the pressure (real or imagined) from his friends intense enough, that Smith chose the latter course. Consequently the American poetry canon began to be formalized in a rather surprising way. Instead of preserving a wide and representative accessible canon, which later selections might winnow, Smith began with a narrow, already rigidly selected canon. Preservation was fine, so long as it was the preservation of ideologically acceptable poetry. Whether the later volumes that he planned—cut off by his death in 1796—would have expanded this canon, we cannot know. As it was, America had to wait until Samuel Kettell's *Specimens of American Poetry* (1829) for a historically representative anthology. The conflicts that Smith faced make it clear that "American poetry" has been from its beginnings a socially constructed and contested rather than a natural category. Smith equated "American" with the United States, which began in 1776, whereas Kettell and many later anthologists thought of America as a *Geist* first manifested in the Puritan migration to the New World.

Apparently Smith did not have enough confidence in the nation's stability to make a broad selection that embraced conflicting ideologies. His own poetry expressed typical Federalist fears of Jeffersonian democracy, and the other Connecticut Wits, the poets and friends of Smith whom the anthology most fully represents, shared these fears. In one selection Smith made from *The Anarchiad*, a satirical long poem written jointly by Joel Barlow, David Humphreys, John Trumbull, and Lemuel Hopkins to influence the Constitutional Convention in favor of Federalism, the "anonymous" poet warns of

> the certain woe that waits
> The giddy rage of democratic states;
> Whose pop'lar breath, high-blown in restless tide,
> No laws can temper and no reason guide.
>
> (Smith 214)

To control this "giddy rage," the poet offers the Federalist solution of a strong central government: "One potent head, / Must rule your states"

(Smith 216).[5] Smith reinforced this bias by excluding any politically liberal or anti-Federalist poetry. Freneau, the most politically inflammatory poet of his age and an anti-Federalist, is represented by one apolitical poem, while Barlow is represented by early work written before his alienation from the Connecticut group in the late 1780s.

American Poems also founds the early American poetry canon on regional biases, biases that again suggest a hidden agenda on Smith's part. Although Smith says he intends otherwise, both his collection and Carey's *Beauties of Poetry* amount to regional anthologies. Most of Smith's 250 subscribers came from Connecticut, and both collections heavily favor the Connecticut Wits. Carey gives half his American section to Trumbull, Humphreys, Barlow, and Timothy Dwight, while Smith adds Hopkins and Richard Alsop to this group and similarly gives them half his space.

Smith's and Carey's anthologies were regional or provincial in the sense that all early American poetry was provincial: self-consciously nationalist but lacking indigenous standards, with, in Matthew Arnold's terms, "no centre, no intellectual metropolis." Arnold's essay "The Literary Influence of Academies" is relevant here, because Smith's regional bias can be explained as an attempt to set up Connecticut as an indigenous cultural center with a coherent, authoritative voice. He hoped Connecticut would take over London's role and serve, as Boston did later, an academy's function for the rest of America: "a supposed centre of correct information, correct judgment, correct taste" (Arnold 269). Thus he used his anthology to try to establish not only a politically narrow canon but also a source of standards by which future poetry might be evaluated. Like any anthology editor, Smith performed silent criticism through what he included and excluded, and, like any editor, he performed that criticism consciously. Even when, like Smith, the editor is mainly preserving an accessible canon, his or her critical judgment is deliberate and value-laden, not innocent and neutral.

Historicizing and Moralizing: Samuel Kettell, Rufus Griswold

During the 1820s America's rampant literary nationalism brought a huge explosion of poetry. In 1822 a British anthology, *Specimens of the American Poets*, featured only eight poets, with additional fugitive verse, in a book of 283 pages. By the end of the decade, in 1829, Kettell's hugely ambitious *Specimens of American Poetry* comprised three volumes and included the work of 189 poets from Cotton Mather to John Greenleaf

Whittier. Kettell faced a monumental task. No complete list of authors was available (Kettell remedies this by recording 429 books of American poetry published since the 1640 Massachusetts Bay Colony versification of the Psalms); texts were not yet collected in public libraries and were therefore hard to get. In gathering this material, he expanded the limited range of the accessible canon more than any anthologist before him and created the first scholarly anthology.

Kettell's goals resemble those of the earlier anthologists: furthering the cause of national literature, gaining an audience for the poetry, preserving texts. He also introduced a new goal to American anthologizing, by claiming historical inclusiveness for his text: "a general and comprehensive view" of what American poets have accomplished. As part of this "general view," Kettell redeems much Puritan poetry. His introduction reviews American poetry from the Bay Psalm Book to the Revolution. In his introduction and his text, he rescues over twenty pre-Revolutionary poets, and grants Benjamin Tompson, born in 1642, "the distinction of being the first native American poet" (1:v, xxxvii). In discussing Puritan poetry, Kettell permanently broadened the boundaries of what constituted "American" poetry and created a precedent that later anthologists could not ignore, even if they dismissed most of the poetry. Griswold's historical introduction to *The Poets and Poetry of America*, for instance, discusses the same pre-Revolutionary poets as Kettell, in exactly the same order.

Kettell's insertion of Puritan poets into the national canon reflects the changes in political thinking that had occurred since Smith's time. In 1829 most American writers were still obsessed with achieving literary independence from Britain. But as Freneau pointed out, "political and . . . literary independence . . . [are] two very different things—the first was accomplished in about seven years, the latter will not be completely effected, perhaps, in as many centuries" (44–45). Kettell himself, like many of his contemporaries, bemoaned America's continued reliance on English models: "The cultivation of literary talent has . . . been retarded by the state of dependence as to literature, in which we have continued, to the writers of Great Britain" (1:xlvii). But about affairs of state, Americans felt in 1829 what they had felt less confident of in the 1790s—that their republican experiment had succeeded, that political independence was assured. Given this confidence, Kettell did not feel compelled, as Smith had in 1793, to define American poetry by the political principles it adhered to. He could comfortably accord the Puritans, geographically Americans but politically English, a place in American literary history.

To compile not a critical but a historical anthology, covering the whole of American poetry, became a typical approach for the mid-nineteenth-century American anthologist, and one that contrasts sharply with the British tendency to select only the best poems.[6] In a historical collection, literary merit is not the overriding criterion for including a poem. Kettell included certain pieces because they afford "some insight into the spirit and temper of the times (1:iv). Inevitably, dozens of poets appear who have since been consigned to oblivion. But canon formation is a reductive process, especially in the stage of moving from an accessible to a selective canon, a process of narrowing down an initially large number of "accessible" poets, and Kettell's anthology made these many poets more available both for contemporary readers and for later editors.

Kettell's ambitions were matched by Griswold, America's first professional anthologist, in *The Poets and Poetry of America* (1842). Griswold, an opportunistic but talented synthesizer, combined all the best features of previous anthologies in his text: a wide range of poets (183 by the time R. H. Stoddard supervised the 1872 edition), lengthy selections, and thorough, although sometimes inaccurate, biographical and critical notices. By 1842 the American public was ready for another major poetry anthology. The collections that had appeared in the thirteen years since Kettell's anthology were limited in range,[7] and during those years some important new poets had arrived. Longfellow, James Russell Lowell, and Oliver Wendell Holmes had all published their first books of poetry; Poe, his second; and Whittier, a mixed book of poetry and prose.

Griswold's goals follow Kettell's: to present poetry that is otherwise not easily available and to "exhibit the progress and condition of Poetry in the United States." That condition was one of plenitude, and Griswold exhibited it amply. In doing so, Griswold, like Kettell, faced a conflict between historical range and literary merit. As if to anticipate charges that he lacked discrimination, he writes in the preface to the first edition that "the judicious critic will be more likely to censure me for the wide range of my selections than for any omissions" (6). This "wide range" derives from the impulse to include, for the sake of historical representativeness, work of extremely variable quality. Commenting on the first edition in the preface to the eighth, Griswold writes that he "did not consider all the contents of the volume genuine Poetry" and that he "accepted more that was comparatively poor" than good (5). Exhibiting the historical range of American poetry meant exhibiting it at less than its best.

The acceptable limits of this historical breadth were defined by the conviction that American poetry should be represented by specimens of the utmost moral purity, that poetry's function is inspirational. Such moral rectitude became one principle of selection in many nineteenth-century anthologies.[8] Certainly it propels most of Griswold's work. In his *Gems from American Female Poets* (1842), the first anthology of solely American women poets, Griswold asserted that "nearly all American poetry . . . is of the purest moral character" and that it showed "propriety and beauty of thought." A year later, in his school text *Readings in American Poetry*, he reminded his young readers that "a distinguishing characteristic of our poetry is its freedom from all licentiousness" (3). And in *The Poets and Poetry of America*, his most important book, he argued that "the office of the poet" is to create beauty and that "the sense of beauty, next to the miraculous divine suasion, is the means through which the human character is purified and elevated." Hence, although his critical notices counted Freneau the best of the Revolution-era poets, he excluded Freneau's political verses because they lacked "chasteness" (8th ed. 7, 31). (That Griswold meant moral, not stylistic, chasteness, we can infer from the anthology's moralizing tone and from the formally conventional, or stylistically "chaste," nature of Freneau's work.) The principle that American poetry "is of the purest moral character" delayed the acceptance of any poet who appeared to violate it, as Whitman later did, and thus it effectively controlled the moral and intellectual range of subject matter in canonical poetry. No poetry was admitted to the burgeoning canon unless it supported the moral status quo.

Other idiosyncratic biases besides morality propelled Griswold's shaping of the canon. His dislike of the South led him to include only two southern poets and to weight his canon heavily toward New England. This led, appropriately, to charges of sectionalism. The second charge most frequently leveled at Griswold, again appropriately, was that of partiality to personal friends. Griswold's friend Charles Fenno Hoffman, for instance, was for years the most fully represented poet in the anthology. Although he included a substantial amount of Emerson's work, Griswold's distaste for transcendentalism probably turned him away from Thoreau, whose poetry Emerson had recommended in a letter. And his conviction that "the literature of women . . . is, for the most part, sauzle" (*Passages from the Correspondence* 224) caused him largely to neglect women poets who, as a group, were producing a body of work quite as "representative" as that of their male contemporaries.[9] This combination of tastes meant that Griswold proposed an extremely homogeneous canon. His work suggested that American poetry had no tolerance of eccentric philosophies, that it was primarily written by men, and that it was created solely in New York and New England.

Read widely, Griswold's anthology became very influential. It went through seventeen editions in fourteen years, and Stoddard was still refining it in 1872. Frank Luther Mott counts it one of the best-selling books of the 1840s (*Golden Multitudes* 307). The anthology achieved this popularity and influence through its combination of nationalist fervor and moral weight—a combination that captured precisely what its readers looked for in their poetry—and through Griswold's ability to reflect both popular and critical taste. By repeating the poets gathered in earlier anthologies, his anthology perpetuated whatever canon had been established so far. Griswold selected familiar names from among the early poets of the republic, deriving this part of his canon from the 1790s anthologies. He began with Freneau and otherwise limited his eighteenth-century selections to works by Dwight, Trumbull, Humphreys, and Barlow, and one poem by Alsop. In his historical introduction, however, he flattered his readers by privileging contemporary American poetry. The representative historical impulse would not allow him to exclude the early poets, but he still asserted that no poetry before Freneau's was worth preserving in bulk. Thus Griswold offered an early version of the now traditional view that each generation of American poets begins anew—a position guaranteed to appeal to readers who held devoutly the doctrines of manifest destiny and of the westward course of empire.

In his selection of early American poetry, Griswold supported these doctrines by preserving the canon of names while radically altering the canon of individual poems. For example, he contrived to make Smith's Federalists look like solid nineteenth-century Democrats. Smith prints thirty poems by the eighteenth-century poets I named above. Griswold, in his 1847 edition, prints thirty-two poems by the same group, but with only one overlap, Dwight's "Columbia." He excludes any poem that suggests a remotely anti-Democratic politics (Dwight's "Address of the Genius of Columbia," Humphreys' "Mount Vernon: An Ode" and "The Genius of America," all of which Smith included) and supplements his selections with work that foregrounds America's independence from England. He selects from Dwight's "Greenfield Hill" a passage that sets England and America at odds, and, to stress the point, he titles the passage "England and America."

Any anthologist who seeks historical breadth includes much of the ephemeral; Griswold is no exception. A turn-of-the-century reader of Griswold's early editions would have disagreed with his equal ranking of then-forgotten writers alongside the Fireside Poets Longfellow, Bryant, Lowell, Holmes, Whittier—poets who themselves look minor today. Yet while Griswold rarely expands his selections for the lesser poets, the Fireside Poets all enjoy increased representation through his successive editions, so we can sketch an emerging nineteenth-century canon from his work. And while we should be wary of granting our contemporary sense of canon too much weight, Griswold deserves credit for raising his estimate of two poets whom recent critics would rank above the Fireside group: Emerson and Poe.[10] The selection from Emerson, as he produced more poetry and published his first complete volume in 1846, jumped from five poems in 1842 to fifteen in 1855, and Poe's showing jumped from three poems in 1842 to sixteen in 1855—this despite Poe's feud with Griswold and the editor's posthumous character assassination of him.

Universal Excellence: Bryant, Emerson, Whittier

After the Civil War, anthologists began to operate more and more on two assumptions: that a stable canon of American poets, complete with greater and lesser lights and reflected in the evolving editions of *The Poets and Poetry of America*, was emerging as a natural product of "time" and "history," and that an undefined community of readers agreed upon that canon. Although anthology editors rarely discussed how this consensus on the canon had been reached, they assumed it to rest on an important new criterion of selection introduced to American poetry anthologies by Charles A. Dana in his well-received *Household Book of Poetry*, first published in 1858 and still being reprinted in 1919. That criterion was the exercise of absolute rather than historically relative critical judgment. Dana attempts "to judge every piece by its poetical merit solely, without regard to the name, nationality, or epoch of its author" (v), a new step for an American editor and a major shift from Griswold's willing inclusion of much "that was comparatively poor." Earlier British anthologists had exercised absolute judgment as their main selective principle; Americans had not. Dana felt, however, that American literature no longer had to have its very existence questioned or be excused in the company of British literature with the argument that its interest was merely historical. Yet even when judged by "poetical merit," his canon of nineteenth-century American poets follows closely the path that the relative reputations of the period were already taking. It consists, in descending order of representation, of Longfellow, Bryant, Emerson, Whittier, and Lowell. Like most anthologists, except Griswold, Dana places Poe well below the New England poets and does not include Whitman in his 1858 or 1868 texts. (Whitman's Civil War poetry was accepted into the 1882 edition, presumably because of its subject matter.) In 1919 the text still did not include Melville or Dickinson.

To justify his canon, Dana appealed to an invisible network of civilized readers, to "the unanimous verdict of the intelligent" (vi). The same appeal, stated in similarly vague terms, underlies three other anthologies gathering both American and English works that were edited within a few years of each other by three of the important Ne.v England poets: Bryant's *Library of Poetry and Song* (1870), Emerson's *Parnassus* (1874), and Whittier's *Songs of Three Centuries* (1875). Bryant—whose text, advertised as the most complete poetry anthology ever published with its four-hundred-plus poets and over 1,500 poems, went through twenty editions in less than six months—includes all poets "acknowledged by the intelligent and cultivated to be great" (iii). Whittier bases his selections on "the verdicts of Time" and of "critical authorities" (iv). Emerson's title assumes an achieved canon, and his preface only mystifies the process by which a poet reaches the Parnassian peak. "The world" selects the "best" poems, "and we select from these our best" (v). Who "we" are remains unidentified. But this mystification does not obscure the fact that, since Griswold first compiled *The Poets and Poetry of America* in 1842, a significant change has occurred in how the American poetic canon is being shaped. By the mid-1870s, editors wanted not merely American poems but the best American poems, poems to stand alongside the best British poems.

What constituted the "best," however, contained no surprises. Because their own status was so great, the judgments about the "best" that Bryant, Emerson, and Whittier made in their anthologies had great influence. And those anthologies kept the canon stable, self-perpetuating. Bryant, Emerson, and Whittier all agree that the six most important poets in America are themselves, Longfellow, Lowell, and Holmes. They rank Poe below even minor, now-forgotten figures, and all exclude Whitman and Melville—despite the fact that in 1855 Emerson had been one of the few people to herald the achievement of *Leaves of Grass*, and that selections from *Leaves of Grass* and *Battle-Pieces* had appeared in the 1872 edition of *The Poets and Poetry of America*.[11]

The consensus on the American poetry canon that these poet-anthologists and Dana assume did not rest merely on assertion. In part it took the form of literate conversation: critics, poets, publishers, and magazine editors all knew each other and formed a tight-knit literary community around Boston and, secondarily, New York. The consensus also had some history to back it up and a sound basis in the critical opinion and popular taste of the time. In the 1840s, the early years of the *Democratic Review*, different critics on four separate occasions had ranked Bryant as America's leading poet.[12] While some reviewers had carped at Griswold's catholicity, few had argued with his opinion of the period's major names. In *Harvests of Change*, Jay Martin has documented thoroughly the high popular regard in which the New England poets were held, and as their careers progressed, critical opinion supported further their view of themselves. Assessing American poetry in 1866, the *Nation* considered Emerson, Bryant, Longfellow, and Lowell the four best living American poets, followed by Whittier, with Holmes part of a somewhat lesser but still worthy group. In 1885 a *Critic* plebiscite suggested that the popular canon had shifted to favor Holmes as the leading living poet, followed by Lowell and then Whittier. The relative ranks had changed temporarily but not the names. Predictably, Whitman ranked only twentieth.[13]

That these poets used their anthologies to preserve or enhance their own reputations is hardly surprising. That they showed such a narrow sense of what they would admit into the canon that their anthologies reflected is somewhat more surprising but still explicable: their claims to transhistorical excellence actually rested on historical grounds. To offset the disorienting effects of the Civil War and of rapid economic expansion, the postbellum reading public wanted a stable, ordered art. In *Parnassus* Emerson talked of "the necessity of printing in every collection many masterpieces which all English-speaking men have agreed in admiring" (iii), a necessity perhaps felt most powerfully in a restless time. Both formally and in their conservation of the European literary tradition (Longfellow translated the *Divine Comedy*, Bryant the *Iliad* and *Odyssey*, Emerson the *Vita Nuova*), the New England poets fit this bill; Whitman's radical experimentation did not. As Martin puts it, these poets "refused to threaten their culture with the new in literature, since Americans were, as they believed, too distracted by the new in life" (13). The New England poets stood for continuity in a disrupted time.[14]

Early Revisionism: Edmund Clarence Stedman

One stage of canon formation in American poetry had culminated in the Bryant, Emerson, and Whittier anthologies. At the same time, another stage had already slowly begun, as the claims of Poe and

Whitman began to be recognized. In *American Poems: A Collection of Representative Verse* (1872), the English editor William Michael Rossetti proposed a very different balance of reputations from that which had obtained previously, by representing Whitman—whose English reputation far outstripped his American one—as easily the most important American poet of his time.[15] Poe also receives more attention than ever before, while, with the exception of Emerson and Whittier, the New England poets are relegated to minor status (with Longfellow absent entirely). In *Poetry of America* (1878), another English editor, W. J. Linton, grants Whitman as much space as all the New England poets, or more; a portrait of Whitman forms his frontispiece. With the appearance of these texts in America, then, the first successful challenges to the nineteenth-century canon came not from the poets who might legitimately claim to have been neglected unfairly, nor from their American apologists, but from two editors who were distant from American literary debate.

The appeal of Poe's aestheticism to the Pre-Raphaelite Rossetti is clear. And when George Santayana coined the term "genteel tradition" in 1911, he explained why an English editor, working outside America's genteel literary circles, might value Whitman so highly. This editor "is looking for what may have arisen in America to express, not the polite and conventional American mind, but the spirit and the inarticulate principles that animate the Community" (52). It is not surprising that, at the height of the genteel tradition, English opinion should carry such weight in America. When a history of the genteel tradition characterizes "the genteel endeavor" by its reaction to New England Brahminism and by its Romantic literary program, its desire for a literature "more inclined to self-expression than to self-restraint" (Tomsich 271), one can see why Whitman began to receive a hearing. But the influence of gentility also explains why the limits on that hearing took some years to be lifted. Gentility can tolerate only a certain amount of barbaric yawping about the great "En-Masse," and by most genteel criteria Whitman was just what Santayana described him as: "the one American writer who has left the genteel tradition entirely behind" (52).

This gradual revaluation of Whitman, and to a lesser extent Poe, constitutes the anthologies' main contribution to canon formation in the last quarter of the nineteenth century. It was forcefully confirmed by Stedman, one of the period's most influential critics, in his voluminous *American Anthology, 1787–1900* (1900). Just as it needs its own literary history, every generation needs its own anthology. Stedman's was the first large anthology by a prestigious American editor since 1875, and the first of solely American poetry since Griswold's 1872 edition. This,

combined with Stedman's reputation as a critic, assured the book sub-
stantial influence. Despite Longfellow's popularity, Stedman says, it
is Emerson, Poe, and Whitman "from whom the old world had most
to learn," and he gives them appropriately full coverage. He writes
prophetically that "years from now, it will be matter of fact that their
influences were as lasting as those of any poets of this century" (xxiv).

Underlying Stedman's judgment is a radical shift from earlier anthol-
ogies in the criteria used for canonizing poets. By Stedman's time the
tendency to politicize and moralize poetry (explicitly, at least) had
largely dropped out of American anthologies. The country's sense of
political and literary accomplishment no longer needed the support of
anthologies documenting the unique national characteristics and moral
purity of American verse. The last collection to use moral virtue as a
selective principle was Henry T. Coates's *Fireside Encyclopedia of Poetry*
(1878). In that same year, Linton wrote that "hymns and 'religious'
poems . . . have been purposely excluded as out of place in such a col-
lection as [*Poetry of America*]" (x). Those whom Stedman saw as the best
American poets did not define or confirm their culture's dominant
values but revolted against them. Stedman preferred "Poe's renaissance
of art for beauty's sake, and Whitman's revolt against social and liter-
ary traditions" to Lowell's "homiletic mood." He may, indeed, have
derived this suspicion of the didactic from Poe, who he thought "gave
a saving grace of melody and illusion . . . to English didactics" (xxv,
xxiv). Hence, although he still considers Bryant the "progenitor" of
American poetry and represents the whole New England group equally
and more thoroughly than we would today, Stedman brings Whitman
and Poe to the fore of his canon. The earlier rebel Freneau, after suf-
fering from many anthologies that considered poetry before Bryant
merely a historical curiosity, also enjoys what has become a lasting
resuscitation. And Dickinson gets the space she would not receive again
for years. In the absence of easily available editions of Dickinson's
work—none appeared in America between 1896 and 1924, a factor that
delayed her entrance into the canon—Stedman did much to remind
later readers of her existence and importance. Except for a predictable
overrepresentation of his contemporaries, then, Stedman's choices
reflect more closely than any previous anthology our contemporary
sense of the American poetry canon through the late nineteenth
century.[16]

Stedman's praise for Whitman's "revolt against social and literary
traditions" foreshadowed the split between cultivated and popular taste
that came to characterize high modernism. Since the mid-1870s, fiction

had come to dominate the book market at poetry's expense. Stedman saw that this situation showed the "public indifference to the higher forms of poetry" (xxxi). He and most subsequent anthologists responded by emphatically separating popular and cultivated taste. In 1865 the best poetry was defined largely by popular taste: John W. S. Hows used for his *Golden Leaves from the American Poets* "poems that have, by general acceptance, become identified in the hearts of the People as the choicest and noblest specimens of American National Poetry" (v). In 1912, by contrast, Thomas R. Lounsbury defied in his *Yale Book of American Verse* "the wretchedness of taste displayed by the average man" (xliii).

Texts such as Lounsbury's *Yale Book, The Chief American Poets* (1905) edited by Curtis Hidden Paige of Dartmouth, and *American Poems* (1905) edited by Augustus White Long of Princeton show teachers of literature becoming more responsible for overseeing the canon in the two decades after 1900. The power to direct taste began to shift from individual editors to an institution—the university. These texts suggest that Stedman's revaluations took some time to catch on. Whitman's reputation still fluctuates, and Dickinson does not yet consistently hold a high place. Other names, however, have become relatively fixed: the New England poets and Poe form the core of the canon. These academic anthologies paradoxically embrace Stedman's values while ignoring his canon. Far from reaffirming popular values and taste, like most earlier anthologists, an editor like Long contrasts the often commercial and popularizing purpose of a nineteenth-century anthology with a book that can "serve as an introduction to the systematic study of American poetry" (3). Yet these anthologists, while demeaning popular taste, generally accepted the canon of poets which that taste had established. They did not significantly change the nineteenth-century canon's makeup; they had simply found a new way to validate the old poetry.

Revisionism Continued: Bliss Carman vs. F. O. Matthiessen

This establishment of the pre-twentieth-century canon left modern anthologists free to concentrate on gathering contemporary poetry, often in narrowly specified areas. However much they looked down on most earlier American poetry, still for anthologizing purposes they considered Stedman to have taken care of poetry before the twentieth century. Many modernist anthologies were coterie texts that mainly influenced other poets: Ezra Pound's *Des Imagistes* (1914), Amy Lowell's three-volume *Some Imagist Poets* (1915, 1916, 1917), Alfred Kreymborg's *Others* (1916, 1917, 1919). Used in this way, anthologies can become tools of a poetic program, defining a movement, promoting ideas that are also contained in critical essays, like Pound's Imagist manifestos, and thus helping to shift critical thought. Other anthologies of the period— Harriet Monroe and Alice Corbin Henderson's *The New Poetry* (1917, with three editions through 1932 and multiple printings through 1946), Conrad Aiken's *Modern American Poets* (1922), even Louis Untermeyer's quite populist (and certainly popular) *Modern American Poetry: An Introduction* (1919, with seven editions through 1950)—gathered a wider range of poets but shared assumptions similar to the smaller, coterie texts.[17] The central assumption was one that Stedman had introduced to thinking about the American poetry canon, an assumption that has become almost a critical article of faith: that the best American poets react against rather than support the poetic and cultural values of their times. These modernist anthologies typically collected poets who wrote against contemporary poetic trends, poets who later became canonized as the major modernists: Pound, Eliot, William Carlos Williams, Marianne Moore, Wallace Stevens.

Stedman's and the modernist anthologies, then, heralded a profound shift in the evaluation of American poetry—a shift in the principles by which a canon is selected. Nineteenth-century anthologies praised poetically conservative work; after Stedman, editors began increasingly to value the poetically innovative. Whereas nineteenth-century anthologies tended to reflect and even celebrate popular taste, the modernist anthologies programmatically deviated from it. Kreymborg takes his combative title *Others* from a terse epigraph that opposes new to familiar styles: "The old expressions are with us always, and there are always others." Earlier anthologies stressed how American they were; twentieth-century anthologies stress how up-to-date they are (even while, given the historical association of America with ideas of newness and modernity, this emphasis on the new could be seen as itself a veiled claim to a certain sort of Americanness). "New" or "modern" becomes a polemical as much as a temporal category in titles like *The New Poetry, Modern American Poets,* and *Modern American Poetry,* and later in *The New American Poetry* (1960), *The New Poetry* (1962), *The New Modern Poetry* (1967)—all a long way from George B. Cheever's humbly calling his 1831 collection *The American Common-place Book of Poetry.*[18]

Despite this stress on newness over Americanness, questions of literary nationalism did not disappear entirely from modern anthologies. In particular, the traditional drive to validate American literary produc-

tion in the face of British skepticism resurfaced. In the first edition of
The New Poetry, Monroe had remarked that American poetry, with its
nationality assured, could speak internationally. That poetry now
showed "a more enlightened recognition of the international scope . . .
of the great art of poetry," and its contributions were making poetry
in English "less provincial, more cosmopolitan" (xii). A few years later,
however, "Mr. J. C. Squire . . . asserted the general English attitude by
including not a single American poet among the forty-six British in his
anthology *Selections from Modern Poets*" (3d ed. li). In her second and
third editions (1923 and 1932), therefore, Monroe combatively revived
the old war with English poetry, claiming that the traditional relation-
ship between American and English poetry was now reversed so that
"as American poetry ceases to be colonial, much British poetry seems,
by comparison, provincial":

At last [American poetry] begins to be continental in scope; to express the
immense differences of climate, landscape, and racial and cultural environ-
ment, in this majestically vast and bewilderingly mixed nation. Compared with
this variety and spaciousness, so to speak, much of the recent English poetry
seems cribbed, cabined and confined in scope and range, and monotonous in
feeling and style. (3d ed. li)

Enlarging *Modern American Poets* into the 1944 *Twentieth-Century Amer-
ican Poetry*, Conrad Aiken similarly finds that America's achieved
national identity in poetry opens the way to the internationalism that
Monroe discusses. Modern American poetry can acknowledge its ties
with England rather than deny them: "For the first time, American
poetry is assured, mature and easy, in an unforced awareness of its
wonderful bilateral tradition, its unique inheritance of two separate but
complementary cultures" (xx). England, however, apparently felt more
reluctant to acknowledge its ties with America, for Aiken confesses that
he had edited *Modern American Poets* in 1922 "in the pious hope of
enlightening that country, then singularly uninformed about Ameri-
can literature, as to the state of contemporary American poetry" (xix).

   On the whole, however, modernity was a more central concern than
nationality for editors of this period, and many influential modern
anthologists were revisionists. Pound, Lowell, Kreymborg, Monroe,
Aiken: all used their anthologies to propose a canon written in defi-
ance of inherited poetic norms. (This spirit of defiance partly accounts
for the modernist tendency to choose not Freneau or Bryant but Whit-
man and Dickinson as the progenitors of American poetry.) Since they
no longer had to prove the existence of a national literature or set up

a national canon from scratch, they could move canon formation into its next stage, that of reevaluating the received body of texts. They agreed that the literary category "American poetry" was safely established, while they also shared a sense that that established poetry did not speak to modern social or aesthetic concerns. This shared view gave the modern anthologists some common ground and helps explain their revisionist impulse. But their common ground aside, these editors pursued their revision of the poetic canon from a variety of positions. In *American Poetry 1671–1928* (1929), for example, Aiken dismissed "purely historical considerations" and asserted that "the aesthetic judgment . . . is the only sound basis for [editorial] procedure." While he admits the difficulty of evaluating his contemporaries, Aiken does not admit that aesthetic judgment itself is a "historical consideration" (v). Monroe, on the other hand, who leans heavily toward American poetry in her transnational anthology, views that poetry as much from a historical as from an aesthetic angle. While she founds modern poetry on the aesthetic revolution of Whitman's and Dickinson's prosodic experiments—a view of these poets that did not receive wide currency until surprisingly late, in the 1930s—she does not claim to assess what parts of American poetry's subsequent experimentation will have lasting value.[19] It is all temporarily useful, she says, as "an assault against prejudice" (Monroe and Henderson xii). Here she aligns herself with the earlier anthological tradition of viewing poetry historically rather than absolutely. Her view recalls the assumption behind Griswold's nationalist anthologies: if the poetry serves the anthologist's purpose at a particular point in cultural history, its transhistorical quality is secondary. But while Griswold risked collecting ephemera because he wanted a representative anthology, Monroe risked doing so as part of an attack on the inherited canon, on the very poetry that Griswold had gathered. (In this sense, Monroe's approach can perhaps be more accurately described as *selectively* historical, insofar as she uses the mask of covering the present to promote modernist innovation.)

Since a tradition makes an inert antagonist if it has no defenders, revisionist editors thrive on live conservative opposition. No debate on the canon would arise, nor would anthologies compete, if the revisionist editor did not have a more centrist opposite number. The stage of canon formation that I have called revision actually involves an ongoing conflict between revision and conservation. This conflict produces difficult choices for the anthologist, who will usually feel compelled to come down on one side or the other. After a selective canon has been formed, every anthologist faces the choice of maintaining or trying to change the canon. In the first half of the twentieth century the conflict plays itself out most vividly in two successive editions of *The Oxford Book of American Verse*, the first edited by the Canadian poet Bliss Carman and the second by F. O. Matthiessen.

Carman's *Oxford Book of American Verse* appeared in 1927. Since no inclusive historical anthology had received wide circulation since Stedman's and no anthologist had attempted to combine the established canon and the new poetry, Carman's was an important publication. Carman does not try to be as encyclopedic as Stedman was, nor as thorough as Monroe and Henderson were for the modern period in *The New Poetry*, but he does claim to skim the whole field. The modernist rejection of nineteenth-century verse, however, made it almost impossible for a historical anthologist like Carman to cover both past and present representatively. If he accepted the established nineteenth-century canon, he accepted a poetry that conflicted with contemporary critical taste. If he changed the earlier canon, he failed in his goal of historical inclusiveness. Carman made the former choice. Although he did accept Whitman and Dickinson as central to nineteenth-century American poetry, he refused to rank them any higher than Longfellow or Bryant. He relegated Holmes, Lowell, and Whittier somewhat to suit twentieth-century tastes. But these changes simply juggle with an established body of poetry. They subtly modify rather than change the canon. Generally, Carman does not participate in the modernist shuffling of nineteenth-century reputations. As a predictable corollary, by today's standards he spectacularly underestimates modernist poetry. With critical opinion and other anthologies to guide him, he nevertheless includes no Eliot, Williams, Moore, Stevens, Hart Crane, or e. e. cummings; only one Pound poem; and no black poets beyond Paul Laurence Dunbar. Carman's surprising view of what differentiated the new from the old poetry also contributed to his critical myopia. He saw nineteenth-century American poetry as "imbued with a doleful spirit, or with a desperate resignation at best," while more recent work showed a "valiant and joyous spirit" (v). To consider the spirit of the age as valiant and joyous left little room for *The Waste Land* or *Hugh Selwyn Mauberley*.

Against Carman's more conservative tendencies, Matthiessen set the revisionism of the second *Oxford Book of American Verse* (1950), which brought one of the most radical redefinitions ever of the American poetry canon. As an academic editor, Matthiessen was in a position to institutionalize the canonical revisions proposed by the nonacademic modern anthologists like Monroe, Aiken, and Pound. His anthology

made the revised canon that the New Critics had already been ener-
getically promoting for some years acceptable for broad public con-
sumption. He redefined the canon in almost every way imaginable: the
canon of individual poems, of genres, of subject matter, and of names.
That redefinition, by diminishing many nineteenth-century reputations
in ways consistent with the practice of Matthiessen's poetic and New
Critical contemporaries, helped shape the nineteenth-century canon
that we hold today. Matthiessen added 28 poets to Carman's selection
and cut a remarkable 147. He demolished the nineteenth century,
cutting 91 poets between Lowell and William Vaughn Moody and
reducing selections from Bryant, Holmes, Lowell, and Whittier to a
mere handful.[20] He increased the representation of those poets on
whom he had centered *American Renaissance* (1941): Emerson (8 poems
added), Poe (10), Thoreau (4), and Whitman (24). He also bolstered
Dickinson (27 poems added), Edwin Arlington Robinson (18), Edgar
Lee Masters (15), Robert Frost (33), Carl Sandburg (14), and Pound (18).
The names that Matthiessen added to Carman would make a strong
anthology in themselves: Anne Bradstreet, Jones Very, Melville, Eliot,
Crane, Moore, Stevens, cummings.

Thus Matthiessen manipulated the canon of names, considering Poe
and Whitman the pivotal nineteenth-century figures and confirming
the modernist reputations established in Monroe and Henderson's,
Untermeyer's, and Aiken's anthologies. His preface corroborates the
revisionist impulse implied in all this surgery. Of Longfellow he says,
"my one aim was to smash the plaster bust of his dead reputation, to
eliminate the hackneyed inflated one-time favorites" (xviii) and to res-
cue some decent poetry. From Lowell and Holmes he also cut traditional
anthology pieces that he considered more popular than good. Like
Pound's *Des Imagistes*, but on a larger, more influential scale, Matthies-
sen's *Oxford Book of American Verse* pushed a critical program, further-
ing the modernist imperative to wring the neck of rhetoric.

Along with cutting the merely popular, Matthiessen tried to use
longer poems, to combat the effect he believed anthologies have of
persuading readers that poetry consists solely of lyrics. On this point
Matthiessen withstood a strong tradition. Generally, anthologies
defined not only what poets but also what *kind* of poem should be can-
onized, and they defined poetry as lyric. The first critical overview of
the American long poem did not appear till the third chapter of Roy
Harvey Pearce's *Continuity of American Poetry* in 1961. The British *Speci-
mens of the American Poets* (1822) and Horace E. Scudder's *American Poems*
(1879) were early exceptions to the lyric emphasis. But Francis Turner

Palgrave's *Golden Treasury,* perhaps the most widely read poetry anthology ever, used only lyrics. In *Songs of Three Centuries* Whittier had suggested that "brief lyrical selections" formed the most appropriate reading for the " 'snatched leisure' " of busy Americans (vi). Many gift-book anthologies presented poetry as something to be dipped into rather than read carefully, while Poe's famous dictum circulated the idea that a genuine poem could have no more than a hundred lines.

Matthiessen, however, adhered to a rule of "not too many sonnets" and thus redeemed a number of subgenres that require length for their effect. He included long narrative poems (Whittier's "Snow-Bound" and Robert Penn Warren's "Ballad of Billie Potts"), philosophical meditations (Stevens' "Comedian as the Letter C"), and spiritual autobiographies (Whitman's "Song of Myself"). Palgrave, by contrast, had excluded narrative, descriptive, and didactic poetry. Matthiessen's commitment to length also reintroduced historical and social subjects to the canon. He excerpted Melville's neglected *Clarel* for its "searching thought upon the dangers threatening American society" and used lengthy extracts from *Hugh Selwyn Mauberley* and *The Bridge* to contrast and supplement the vision of America history contained in "Song of Myself" (x, xiii).

Despite the thorough revisionism of Matthiessen's *Oxford Book,* William Cain is right to note one glaring lacuna: Matthiessen "did not include a single poem by a black man or woman. In fact, he omitted Paul Laurence Dunbar, the one black poet whom Bliss Carman had included in the 1927 edition" (*F. O. Matthiessen* 197). The "anthologies" decade of the 1840s had also seen the first two anthologies of poetry by black Americans: Armand Lanusse's *Les Cenelles* (1845) and William G. Allen's *Wheatley, Banneker, and Horton* (1849). *Les Cenelles,* what Henry Louis Gates calls "the first attempt to define a black canon" (*Loose Canons* 24) by gathering the work, in French, of seventeen free blacks born in New Orleans, seeks the end of racism through apolitical poems, and implicitly defines "black poetry" as any poetry written by blacks. Allen's anthology, however, defines black poetry by its racial themes. Thus opposing definitions of "black poetry" were in place by 1849, Gates shows, definitions that shaped such subsequent debate over black poetry's relation to the Anglo-American mainstream as that between Langston Hughes and Countee Cullen in the 1920s.

This background serves as a reminder that Matthiessen's *Oxford Book* followed a hundred-year history of black poetry anthologies, and in particular it followed a twenty-five-year period of visible and easily accessible anthologies. Given the extent to which later anthologies are made up of earlier ones, one would expect some cumulative effect on mainstream anthologies to derive from such publications as James Weldon Johnson's *The Book of American Negro Poetry* (1922), Alain Locke's *The New Negro* (1925), Countee Cullen's *Caroling Dusk* (1927), V. F. Calverton's *An Anthology of American Negro Literature* (1929), Sterling Brown, Arthur Davis, and Ulysses Lee's *The Negro Caravan* (1941), and Langston Hughes and Arna Bontemps's *The Poetry of the Negro, 1746–1949* (1949)—a number of which represented the efforts of black anthologists to formulate a racial canon as a way to combat their continued exclusion from "American" canons. W. S. Braithwaite's popular annual anthologies of contemporary magazine verse had contained mainly white but also some black poets. While Matthiessen's blindness on this point can be explained (though not excused) as generational and cultural, it still seems worth stressing that black poets' work *was* widely available, so mainstream editors could hardly use ignorance of its existence as an excuse.

Teaching and the Contemporary Canon: *Norton*s and Others

The tug-of-war that Carman and Matthiessen act out between opposing principles for canonizing poetry has become a prominent fact of post–World War II literary life. In the best-known variation of this opposition, Robert Lowell made this now notorious comment in 1960 on the state of American poetry:

Two poetries are now competing, a cooked and a raw. The cooked, marvelously expert, often seems laboriously concocted to be tasted and digested by a graduate seminar. The raw, huge blood-dripping gobbets of unseasoned experience are dished up for midnight listeners. There is a poetry that can only be studied, and a poetry that can only be declaimed, a poetry of pedantry and a poetry of scandal.

Lowell added coyly, "I exaggerate, of course" (quoted in Kunitz, "New Books"). But exaggeration or no, critics of the period accepted Lowell's division of American poetry into "raw" and "cooked," and his distinction was highlighted by the infamous "cold war" (Eric Torgersen's term) between two competing anthologies: the "cooked" *New Poets of England and America* (1957) edited by Donald Hall, Robert Pack, and Louis Simpson, and the "raw" *New American Poetry* (1960) edited by Donald Allen. The names had changed since Carman and Matthiessen; the dynamics of the debate had not.

The thirty-odd years since Allen's collection have seen the publication of a vast number of what could be called "identity-based" or "identity politics" and theme-based anthologies, along with a related proliferation of critical methods, aimed at opening the accessible canon to historically disenfranchised groups.[21] These trends should warn us against holding rigidly to separable "stages" in canon formation, fixed in a sequence long since complete. The impulses I have described in this chapter—preservation, nationalism and historicizing, the belief in transhistorical excellence, revisionism as a reaction to an established canon—chart accurately how the American poetry canon developed. At the same time, some of these impulses still fuel debate over both the received and the contemporary canon. Even in an age of mass reprinting, Allen assumed that texts can be lost in ephemeral little magazines and need to be preserved.[22] And at least since the Harlem Renaissance, some anthologists of black poetry have wanted to preserve black culture's early poetry, trace its generally ignored historical development, and encourage a racial pride that resembles mid-nineteenth-century nationalism.[23] The historical debate over the relationship of African-American poetry to Anglo-American tradition and current practice has also inevitably been reflected in anthologies, with Arna Bontemps asking in the preface to his *American Negro Poetry* (1963), "Is American Negro poetry a part of American literature or isn't it?" (xviii).

The suppression of African American poetry gives special weight to the preservative, historicizing, and "nationalist" ambitions of twentieth-century black anthology editors. In 1970 Robert Morsberger documented with chilling thoroughness the absence of black writers in widely used general and genre-specific American literature anthologies of the 1960s. While this absence is now hardly news, specific documentation of its pervasiveness remains an important part of the historical record. Morsberger cites seven multivolume American literature anthologies with either zero or at best one percent black representation. Two classroom anthologies of American poetry from the period, Karl Shapiro's *American Poetry* (1960) and Gay Wilson Allen, Walter Rideout, and James Robinson's *American Poetry* (1965), include no black poets in 1,307 total pages of text; neither does the 1968 edition of Hyatt Waggoner's critical history *American Poets from the Puritans to the Present*. Louis Untermeyer's 690-page *Modern American Poetry* (1962) includes six pages of poetry by blacks. As Morsberger puts it, "the implication of these texts . . . is that Negro poetry does not exist" (5). A National Council of Teachers of English Task Force echoed this observation about the Allen, Rideout, and Robinson anthology, and expressed a justified incredulity at Waggoner's work, "pursued to completion during the highest peak of integrationist consciousness in history—namely, the period between the March on Washington and the assassination of Dr. Martin L. King, Jr." (Kelly 9, 13) while still not referring to a single minority writer.

Two main kinds of anthology have emerged both as part of and in response to the developing pluralism of recent decades. One is the teaching anthology, to which I will return later. The other continues the tradition of the revisionist anthology designed to increase awareness of particular noncanonical poetry.[24] In its tone this anthology may recall the polemics of *The New American Poetry* or Pound's *Des Imagistes*. Unlike the teaching anthology, it is not necessarily or by definition intended for the classroom, even though it may be used there. The editors usually (though not always) minimize the scholarly apparatus of notes, essays, and bibliographies. They are sometimes scholars or critics, but often poets—poets aiming not at the aesthetic and social orthodoxy that Bryant, Emerson, and Whittier promoted, however, but at heterodoxy. From their inception, American poetry anthologies have usually pushed a political or literary program, so the contemporary revisionist anthology is not a new *kind* of anthology. Only recently, however, have the revisionist programs that reached a wide public become so many and so vocal, and their number reflects the nonacademic anthologists' increased power to shift the canon.

The category of the contemporary revisionist anthology can itself be subdivided into two kinds of collection: the identity-based anthology mentioned above, and the aesthetically revisionist anthology of which *The New American Poetry* is the definitive post-World War II model. These are not mutually exclusive kinds of text. I do not mean to suggest that the identity-based anthology, which typically gathers the work of a particular social group on the basis of ethnic, class, gender, or sexual identity, ignores questions of aesthetics or cannot include aesthetically innovative work. Nor is it the case that the anthology of experimental writing cannot be socially inclusive. At the same time, depending on the anthology's intended function, the editor will foreground principles of aesthetics or of social identity; the issue is one of emphasis. (Admittedly, to the extent that the goals and contents of these anthologies do *not* overlap, both kinds of text could be said to reinscribe the very separateness between the aesthetic and the social that some of their editors claim to collapse.)[25] A long list of recent identity-based or issue-based anthologies appears in note 21. Recent examples of revisionist anthologies that stand consciously in the *New American Poetry* line include Michael Lally's often overlooked *None of the Above* (1976); Ron Silliman's *In the American Tree* (1986); Douglas Messerli's *"Language" Poetries* (1987) and *From the Other Side of the Century: A New American Poetry, 1960–1990* (1994); Paul Hoover's *Postmodern American Poetry: A Norton Anthology* (1994); and Eliot Weinberger's *American Poetry since 1950: Innovators and Outsiders* (1993).

Weinberger is the one editor of an aesthetically innovative anthology actively to dismiss the validity of identity-based selective criteria. In a surprising twist of logic (not to mention history), Weinberger argues that creative writing programs have produced a literary multiculturalism under which "poets, especially bad poets, tend to distinguish themselves from the mob not by aesthetic beliefs and practices, but according to extra-literary categories such as ethnic background and sexual preference" (405). His point that "varied backgrounds can lead to the same poems" is well taken, for as Charles Bernstein similarly remarks, "too often, the works selected to represent cultural diversity are those that accept the model of representation assumed by the dominant culture in the first place" (*A Poetics* 6). However, Weinberger's related suspicion of a poetic diversity "based on ethnicity, not poetry" (406) reaffirms the structural opposition of "ethnicity" and "poetry" and, along with his chosen time frame, leads him to repeat traditional defenses of a predominantly white male canon: "Those who count heads according to gender and race should first consider how many poets genuinely qualify within these chronological limits" (xiii).

In response to this challenge, a quick race-and-gender-based head-counting of other "innovators and outsiders" within Weinberger's limits—poets born before 1945 and publishing after 1950—might include Anne Waldman, Diane di Prima, Diane Wakoski, Joanne Kyger, Barbara Guest, Melvin Tolson, Clarence Major, and Lorenzo Thomas. But for Weinberger's anti-Language animus, it would also include Beverly Dahlen, Kathleen Fraser, Lyn Hejinian, and Hannah Weiner.[26] In his defense, Weinberger does acknowledge that "a subsequent selection of the innovators from the post–World War II generation would probably contain a majority of women, with a greater number of nonwhite poets, male and female" (xiii). But the (presumably unintended) *effect* of Weinberger's editorial principles is to suggest that, except for Susan Howe, no woman or minority poet later than Levertov or Baraka has contributed to innovations in "American poetry since 1950."

One virtue of Weinberger's anthology, however, is that it interestingly shows both the continuities and the differences possible within the revisionist anthological minitradition deriving from *The New American*

Poetry.[27] Like Allen, and as his subtitle suggests, Weinberger depends on a center-margin or mainstream-tributary model. His governing metaphor is that of "ruling and opposition parties," with the former governing the "channels of recognition" (xi), although he is more willing than Allen—and given the current ambiguous relations of avant-gardists to the academy, more obliged—to admit the fuzzy boundaries between the two. One goal, then, becomes to counter the "ruling party" and offer "an alternative to the existing anthologies" (xiii). As with Allen again, though less directly, Olson is central to Weinberger's view of the period. A manuscript page from *The Maximus Poems* makes up Weinberger's frontispiece, while his 1950 starting date is "the date of the magazine appearance of Charles Olson's 'The Kingfishers,' the first major work by a new writer in the postwar American poetry renaissance" (xii). At the same time, Weinberger's fierce resistance to Language poetry leads him to exclude most of the writers who dominate Silliman's anthology and Messerli's 1987 collection and who continue in various ways, even as they deviate from, the Objectivist–Black Mountain–New American poetics that Weinberger otherwise represents so thoughtfully. His chronological principle of selection (no poets born after 1945) gives him a convenient excuse for this exclusion, while his historical overview of the period's poetry provides a forum to repeat familiar, tired complaints about Language poetry: its alleged humorlessness (399), confusion of poetry with theory, infatuation with theoretical jargon, and suspicious coziness with the academy (406).[28]

The very need for an anthology like Weinberger's defines the limits of the New American and related poets' assimilation. Nevertheless, it remains the case that many polemics from editors outside the academy have succeeded. Anthologists like Allen have gained their favored poets canonical status. Allen's "raw" poets are represented almost equally with Hall, Pack, and Simpson's "cooked" poets in the major academic anthologies today.[29] Yet in one sense these poets enter the canon as the victims of a Catch-22. Much of the interest and vigor of a book like *The New American Poetry* lay in its extracanonical status. The book's tone and contents assailed the walls of the academically established canon, eventually broke them down, and Charles Olson, Robert Creeley, and such were admitted. But when these poets became tentatively canonized, their combative rhetoric was assimilated by the cultural institution it assailed and lost much of its point. As numerous theorists of the avant-garde argue, this is the likely fate of any extracanonical group or individual seeking the acknowledgment of serious attention. The more positive implications of this process, involving the potential to address and affect, from within, the institutions with which an extracanonical poetics is nominally at odds, form the subject of my final chapter.

The near future should provide an unusual opportunity to assess the anthologizing of alternative poetic practices and traditions, given the recent publication of Weinberger's text; of the Hoover and Messerli anthologies mentioned above; of Dennis Barone and Peter Ganick's anthology of "post-Language" poets, *The Art of Practice: 45 Contemporary Poets* (1994); and given Jerome Rothenberg and Pierre Joris's work on their projected two-volume international anthology of twentieth-century avant-garde writing, *Poems for the Millennium.* The superficial resemblance between Weinberger's *American Poetry since 1950* and Hoover's *Postmodern American Poetry* as collections of experimental work makes it worth detailing some of the similarities and differences between them. The anthologies differ immensely in the *scale* of their coverage of the same period. Weinberger includes 35 poets in 390 pages of poetry, with each poet getting around 10–11 pages each. Hoover includes 103 poets in 609 pages, with much greater range (from 3 pages to 20) in the representation of each individual. While 21 of Weinberger's poets also appear in Hoover—a predictable degree of overlap—that means that Hoover's anthology contains 82 poets *not* represented in Weinberger.

Differences in purposes and in chronology explain many of the differences in content. Beginning earlier than Hoover, Weinberger includes first- and second-generation modernists; Hoover includes many writers born after 1945, Weinberger's cutoff date. While Weinberger seeks to provide a sense of historical roots for the post–World War II work that interests him—and in that sense is engaged in the active (re-)construction of a tradition—Hoover is more concerned to bring his material up to the present. If we discount the earlier modernists whom Weinberger includes as not fitting Hoover's schema, the two anthologies overlap most significantly in their sense of the mid-century "alternative" canon. Starting with Olson, 21 of Weinberger's 26 poets also appear in Hoover. The major differences lie, as I have said, in their sense of "period" and the scale on which they try to reflect it. Applying to Hoover Weinberger's criteria (poets born before 1945, writing after 1950), Hoover still includes 52 poets whom Weinberger does not, occupying a total of around 261 pages. Clearly, Hoover goes for breadth, Weinberger for depth. (This difference could be dictated by economics as well as purpose, with Hoover's publisher, Norton, the larger and more established commercial house, being able to put more money into permissions and production costs because it can expect a larger return.)

At the same time, both anthologies show the impossibility now of what once could be imagined: the all-inclusive anthology of recent countercanonical American poetry, an impossibility evident since at least the late 1970s and since the move toward more aesthetically or politically focused anthologies. (The idea of a historical American poetry anthology, meanwhile, seems even more quixotic. Can there ever be another *Oxford Book of American Verse, New* or otherwise, in this situation?) In 1960 Donald Allen could at least claim to represent the margin thoroughly, although even in *The New American Poetry* gender-based exclusions have become more evident with time. But in 1994 even the margins—and I stress the plural—as represented by Hoover have 103 poets in them. An anthology like Anne Waldman's *Out of This World,* a collection of work first published through the St. Mark's Poetry Project from 1966 to 1991, shows how large an anthology can be constructed out of one location for Hoover's avant-garde: 593 pages of poetry, around 230 (mostly American) poets including translators. Hoover's is the first Norton anthology that I know to use the indefinite article in the title—*A Norton Anthology*; this is not just a sensible but an almost inevitable gesture.

Hoover's use of the term "postmodern" provides another angle of approach to these issues. He appears to overlook the conflict between the historical or periodizing and the aesthetic uses of that slippery term. Early in his introduction he writes: "As used here, 'postmodern' means the historical period following World War II. It also suggests an experimental approach to composition. . . . Postmodern poetry is the avant-garde poetry of our time" (xxv). The point is simple: "postmodern" as a period term includes hundreds of poets whom the criterion of the "experimental approach to composition" excludes from consideration, from Wilbur, Lowell, Bishop, and early Rich through *The Morrow Anthology of Younger American Poets* to the New Formalists. But how could Hoover possibly have compiled an anthology that genuinely considers the postmodern inclusively and historically? He couldn't. As he puts it, quoting Lyn Hejinian, " 'The (unimaginable) complete text, the text that contains everything, would be in fact a closed text. It would be insufferable' " (xxxv).

How does Hoover's collection relate to or complement other anthologies published by Norton? Volume 2 of *The Norton Anthology of American Literature* (4th ed. 1994) contains thirty-four American poets born after Hoover's foundational figure, Charles Olson; *The Norton Anthology of Poetry* (3d ed. 1983) contains forty-six; Richard Ellmann and Robert O'Clair's *Norton Anthology of Modern Poetry* (2d ed. 1988) contains eighty-one. The number of poets overlapping between these texts and *Postmodern American Poetry* is nine, twelve, and twelve respectively. The fact that a core of nine poets overlap across all four anthologies suggests some consensus about a countercanon of poets launching their careers in the decade after World War II: Olson, Creeley, Levertov, Duncan, Ginsberg, Ashbery, O'Hara, Snyder, and Baraka.[30] (While these poets' appearance in all four Norton anthologies raises legitimate questions about the "countercanonical" status of their work, I would add that only two of them—Ginsberg and Levertov—appear in all seven of the current major trade textbook anthologies of American literature, while Olson, Creeley, and Duncan appear in only four, three, and two of these texts, respectively.)[31] The very publication of *Postmodern American Poetry* indicates the power of alternative poetries to diffuse or redefine the center, and it might remind us to consider difference "within" as well as "from" a mainstream that is becoming increasingly harder to locate. Harder: but perhaps not impossible. For at the same time, the very limited overlaps between Hoover's and the other Norton texts (especially *The Norton Anthology of American Literature*, the timing of which must have allowed for some inclusion of Hoover poets) suggests not so much the assimilation of poetic tributaries into the mainstream as the continued tendency of editors and publishers to map the poetic landscape by reference to parallel but separate rivers.

The pluralism that has created the impossibility of broadly inclusive or representative collections has also brought a sharp increase in a second main category of anthology, the teaching anthology. In the 1970s and 1980s, this category, like that of the revisionist anthology, fell increasingly into two parts: the mainstream contemporary survey and the textbook anthology. The mainstream survey does not present itself as a textbook in the way that *The Norton Anthology of Poetry* does, but it is most likely to be used in the classroom. It differs from the *Norton* in various ways, ways that make it resemble in format—though not in tone, purpose, or content—the revisionist collection. It usually has only one or two editors, who are often poets themselves—Dave Smith and David Bottoms; Jack Myers and Roger Weingarten; J. D. McClatchy; Robert Pack, Sydney Lea, and Jay Parini; Daniel Halpern.[32] It keeps apparatus to a minimum, often just to a biobibliographical note on each author. And it limits its representation to the contemporary (that is, mid-1970s on) scene. Frequently the mainstream survey draws on and addresses the MFA/Creative Writing program circuit for its contents and audience.[33]

The canonization of outsider poets that I have discussed, however, is represented and furthered more by the textbook anthology, so the revisionist collection and the textbook anthology depend on each other. The revisionist editor needs the teaching canon to react against; the teacher-editor needs to accommodate extracanonical work if he or she is to represent the current state of poetry with any accuracy. When a textbook anthology such as *The Norton Anthology of Poetry* canonizes poetic outsiders, however, it renders their work culturally and intellectually harmless. What one might call this detoxification of potent work has its sources in the interpretive community's survival instinct, and the fact that if a pluralist literature is to be taught, it must be systematized. The academy ensures its own survival and that of "literature" by adopting a more pluralist canon. A revised canon provides new texts for exegesis and helps keep alive the whole interpretive enterprise. The textbook anthology is one tool of systematization and of the literary academy's self-perpetuation.

In what follows, I will focus on *The Norton Anthology of Poetry*, for two reasons. The first has to do with what Norton anthologies symbolize, with the cultural heft and associations that the Norton name carries. As Michael Bérubé puts it, "Nortons are almost by definition 'central' anthologies; . . . as central anthologies, they represent the consolidation of movements rather than their announcement (as was the function, for example, of Donald Allen's 1960 *New American Poetry*, or, for that matter, *Des Imagistes*)" (138).[34] Second, the *Norton*'s very centrality, combined with its implied claims to inclusiveness, makes it more useful than the mainstream survey for discussing center-margin relations in recent anthologies.

What problems in selection do the editors of a textbook like *The Norton Anthology of Poetry* face in trying to adopt a pluralist canon? More, I suggest, than the polemically minded editors of an extracanonical anthology face. The latter include what fits their ideological, poetic, or intellectual program. That program simplifies editorial choices by narrowing them. This is less true of the editors of the textbook anthology. If they want to create an inclusive, representative text, a useful teaching tool, that goal complicates editorial choice. They must respond to heterogeneous audiences with conflicting literary and political interests. They also face the conflict, which dates back at least to Griswold, between representativeness and quality, in a time when to be representative means to include not just many poems but many different kinds of poems. Simultaneously they face heavy pressure to expand the canon and heavy pressure to mount a "defense of the classics" against the incursions of what some critics as recently as 1982 could luridly describe as "feminist *vers libre*" and "obscene black anti-ve&se" (Wellek, "Respect for Tradition"; Burgess). And whereas a nineteenth-century editor like Griswold shared with his age a limited range of aesthetic and ideological criteria for judging poetry, the editors of the contemporary textbook anthology have no such consensus on which to lean.

The *Norton*'s editors have responded to these problems by embracing a heterodoxy that incorporates but also defuses previously extracanonical poetry. In updating the anthology in 1975 from its 1970 edition, they self-consciously announce their text's liberal, pluralist credentials: "Four new black poets amplify the presentation of that tradition," and "there are now twice as many women poets as before" (xlv). But this inclusiveness has its limits, especially when we examine the *Norton*'s third (1983) edition. We face the extraordinary claim that "there are more Afro-American poets than before" when by my count there are actually *fewer*: Audre Lorde and Frank Marshall Davis are added, but Haki Madhubuti (Don Lee), Nikki Giovanni, Margaret Walker, and Claude McKay are cut. The only nod in the direction of increased ethnic diversity is the addition of three Leslie Marmon Silko poems. American modernism looks a less thoroughly male affair with the addition of Louise Bogan, Edna St. Vincent Millay, and Dorothy Parker. To represent British modernism, meanwhile, Cecil Day Lewis and Isaac Rosenberg are added, but the far more daring Edith Sitwell and Basil Bunting are cut. With the latter's replacement by Ogden Nash, the *Norton*'s erasure of the entire Objectivist tradition on both sides of the Atlantic is complete.

Whatever surface diversity the Norton anthologies do have hides a deeper homogeneity. The 1983 edition of *The Norton Anthology of Poetry* includes forty-five American poets born after Olson in 1910, many of them still alive and working. The second edition of Ellmann and O'Clair's *Norton Anthology of Modern Poetry* (1988), while its focus on a specific historical period leaves it more room for eclecticism, still reprints thirty-seven of those forty-five; Ellmann and O'Clair's second edition of *Modern Poems: An Introduction* (1989), also published by Norton, reprints thirty-four. For Norton editors, unlike many readers of contemporary poetry, the canon of names is not so diverse that it can't be agreed upon. Some of the poets anthologized in *The Norton Anthology of Poetry*'s various editions—Langston Hughes, Amiri Baraka, Lee, Giovanni, Lorde, Adrienne Rich—have written poetry sharply and openly critical of American culture. But reading the *Norton*, no one would know it. The book uses poems that stay within acceptable limits of vitriol and thus serves the same function as many nineteenth-century anthologies: maintaining the cultural status quo. A gesture like the inclusion of "four new black poets" partially responds to social pressures to open the canon while fundamentally preserving the canon's hegemonic function—especially when that "openness" contracts again a few years later.

The tendency even of more recent anthologies produced under the aegis of multiculturalism to exclude socially as well as aesthetically antagonistic work should not be ignored. As Cary Nelson observes, "the dominant pattern for many years for general anthologies of American literature [and, I would add, poetry anthologies] has been to seek minority poems that can be read as affirming the poet's culture but not mounting major challenges to white readers ("Multiculturalism" 49). Recommending an approach to anthologizing that openly acknowledges social conflict (Nelson focuses on race, but his point extends to issues of gender, class, sexuality) by including texts that explicitly reflect it, Nelson notes the exclusion even from racially diverse anthologies of "texts making aggressive attacks on injustice and urging revolutionary change" (52).

This evasion of disruptive cultural energies is served further by the quality the *Norton* has of being produced not by people but by a corporation. Because it has not one or two editors but six (all male), it bears the stamp of no individual's personality. This oracular, *ex vacuo* quality, typical of many textbook anthologies with multiple editors, lends the collection much of its authority and reduces the likelihood of debate. The anthology alchemically both "broadens and refines that cultural tradition" represented in its earlier editions (3d ed. xi). The editors never suggest, however, that these simultaneous processes of inclusion and exclusion might be problematic, and they never discuss what governs their choices. On the second edition's dust jacket, distinctions between "major poets" and "their interesting contemporaries" are assumed to be clear and not open to question. Barbara Herrnstein Smith summarizes the effect of this assumption: "One of the major effects of prohibiting or inhibiting explicit evaluation is to forestall the exhibition and obviate the possible acknowledgment of divergent systems of value and thus to ratify, by default, established evaluative authority" (24).

Nor do the *Norton*'s editors admit as problematic the limited sense that a textbook anthology provides of what kind of poem the canon includes and how to read it. Admitting new work to the canon often requires new ways of reading. But the structure and purpose of the textbook anthology limit these new ways of reading, perpetuating old ways of reading the new poetry. By definition the textbook anthology contains poetry that can be readily discussed in university classrooms. That usually means short poems teachable alongside other poems in busy fifty-minute class periods and made more teachable by the scholarly apparatus of footnotes, glossaries, biographical notices, and historical introductions. Conversely, despite their claim to "a collection representative not merely of the lyric and the epigrammatic, but of the entire range of poetic genres in English" and their inclusion of some longer work ("Crossing Brooklyn Ferry"), the *Norton* editors still find it "impossible" to include something as hard to digest in a class period as "Song of Myself" (3d ed. xii). (Recall that Matthiessen did not find this so in 1950, when he inveighed against anthologies of solely lyric poetry.) By this principle of teachability, the *Norton* systematizes a potentially chaotic pluralist canon.

As a compromise that can help them rescue their claims to generic inclusiveness, the editors include "representative and self-sufficient selections" from long poems (3d ed. xii). But this can mean that even long poems end up being discussed according to criteria more applicable to lyrics. Thus the *Norton* carries, built into its selections, a set of critical assumptions about how poetry should be read. As in many pre-twentieth-century anthologies, the work least likely to appear is that which is least susceptible to accepted methods of reading: for example, the Native American pieces in Jerome Rothenberg's *Technicians of the Sacred* and *Shaking the Pumpkin*, which cannot even be defined as texts in the traditional Western sense.[35] In times when readers shared narrower definitions of poetry and how to read it, and when form and style carried moral overtones, exclusion on this basis was not surprising; in a pluralist time it is much more so. By continuing to exclude this work, the editors of the *Norton* sidestep the problems of selection raised by extreme cultural fragmentation.

On close scrutiny, then, we see that even an apparently inclusive teaching anthology does not adequately represent today's pluralist literary climate. But perhaps, finally, it cannot. Teaching literature requires systematization; pluralism resists it. Since the power of different anthologies to affect the canon is increasing, albeit slowly, and given the wide range of anthologies addressed to different audiences and different needs, it is unlikely that any single anthology will again dominate a period's reading and direct a period's sense of the canon as Griswold's did. While the poetry canon remains largely an academic institution, its boundaries are more flexible than in the past because countercanons are frequently thrust forward for consideration. The important forces behind canon formation in the last two decades have made themselves felt less in individual anthologies than in the relationship between the revisionist collection and the canonical teaching text. Each kind of anthology gains its identity in contrast to the other. While texts like the *Norton* define a limited teachable canon, anthologies of noncanonical work continue to lead toward the pluralization of that canon into canons.

2

Poets Canonizing Poets

John Berryman's "Homage to Mistress Bradstreet"

Institutional and Aesthetic Models of Canon Formation

This book is occupied with proposing certain (local and partial) answers to the global questions "Who makes canons in American poetry, and how?" I am concerned mainly to provide historical accounts of specific canonizing forces: anthologies, magazines, critical practice. But at a more general level, it can be said that two models or schools of thought govern recent critical thinking about canon formation in American poetry, and in this chapter I want to explore the relative strengths and weaknesses of these models. One school holds that the process of canon formation, at least in this century, is governed by academic institutions. According to this view, teacher-critics shape canons through their criticism, reviewing, and teaching, while anthologies, the publishing industry generally, grant-giving agencies, and the structuring of English studies according to "field" all make up related parts of what one might call the institutional model for understanding canon formation. The other, which I shall call the aesthetic or poet-based model, holds that poetic canons are mainly the creation of poets themselves. The most useful model of canon formation in American poetry is one that draws on and synthesizes these two models.

"In practice, the institution with which we have to deal is the professional community" (*Art of Telling* 168): so observes Frank Kermode, whose version of the institutional theory of canon formation can stand for that of most critics.[1] Kermode summarizes the characteristics of the literary institution of the academy as follows: "a professional community which has authority (not undisputed) to define (or indicate the limits of) a subject; to impose valuations and validate interpretations" (169). What he calls "institutional control of interpretation" includes institutional control and shaping of canons: "the literary institution . . . controls the choice of canonical texts" (176). However changes in the canon originate (whether from movements inside or outside the academy), "there is still a rule which says that the institution must validate texts before they are licensed for professional exegesis" (180). (Conversely, professional exegesis is also itself a *form* of institutional validation.) Kermode ends up stating his position as a kind of creed: "I believe that institutions confer value and privilege upon texts, and license modes of interpretation" (183). One can argue that Kermode holds a rather narrow definition of critical activity (the professional exegesis of particular texts), and that canons are more than simply lists of texts. He does not explicitly extend his discussion to include canonical authors, genres, themes, periods, and so on. These objections, however, do not affect Kermode's main point: that whatever we mean by a canon, it is an institutional creation.

From a different political stance, Terry Eagleton holds essentially the same position. For Eagleton too, the "institution" in question is the academy. Criticism cannot justify its enterprise by appeal to a canon of intrinsically valuable works, Eagleton argues, because "criticism is part of a literary institution which constitutes these works as valuable in the first place." Eagleton puts the matter with useful bluntness: "Shakespeare was not great literature lying conveniently to hand, which the literary institution then happily discovered: he is great literature because the institution constitutes him as such" (*Literary Theory* 202). This view is held widely enough that it has become virtually axiomatic in much recent critical theory. One early version of it comes from Jonathan Culler, whose theory of "literary competence," defined as control of "a set of conventions for reading literary texts," implies a view of literary value as institutionally determined. His theory, he claims, "leads one to reformulate as conventions of literature and operations of reading what others might think of as facts about various literary texts" (118, 128). These conventions of reading "are the constituents of the institution of literature" (116), and are mainly exercised within what Stanley Fish later came to call an "interpretive community." In laying out this influential notion, Fish is interested in "the power of an interpretive community to constitute the objects upon which its members (also and simultaneously constituted) can then agree" (338). As Fish puts it, "insofar as the system (in this case a literary system) constrains us, it also fashions us, furnishing us with categories of understanding, with which we in turn fashion the entities to which we can then point" (332). But my point here is not simply the commonplace that canons are always "constructed." Rather I mean to raise the issue of *how*, or *by whom*, they are constructed.

Like Eagleton, Culler, and Fish, Jane Tompkins uses an institutional model in an attempt to refute the ideas of "intrinsic value" and "genius," and like them, the institution she has in mind is the academy. If the academy cannot be credited (or blamed) for creating the long-standing reputation of a writer such as Hawthorne, who enjoyed canonical status long before the academy had any influence on canons, Tompkins argues, it *can* be credited with maintaining that reputation.[2] In this view, literary value again is best understood in institutional, not aesthetic, terms. It is according to this premise that Tompkins titles one chapter of *Sensational Designs* "The Institutionalization of Literary Value." *Sensational Designs* has itself become a canonical source for the argument that texts and authors remain canonical not because of what they are but because of how they are used: "When classic texts are seen not as the ineffable products of genius but as the bearers of a set of national, social, economic, institutional, and professional interests, then their domination of the critical scene seems less the result of their indisputable excellence than the product of historical contingencies" (xii).

While Barbara Herrnstein Smith does not accord the academy such central status as Tompkins does, still it remains an important variable affecting what she calls "contingencies of value." In fact, Smith argues rightly that long-term canonical survival *cannot* be explained solely by the power of established institutions, that to attribute to these institutions an "objectively (in the Marxist sense) conspiratorial force" (47) is to oversimplify. It is also to risk, I think, an ahistorical explanation for a historical process—at least if one's "institution" is the academy. Eagleton, for instance, in turning to the example of Shakespeare, falls into the trap of ahistoricity to which proponents of an institutional model are often prone. For could it not be argued that many readers *did* find Shakespeare "great literature" long before the "literary institution," in the academic sense that Eagleton apparently means the term, existed as such?[3] With Shakespeare as with Hawthorne, the presence of English departments cannot fully explain the longstanding canonical status of a writer who was canonized long before English departments existed. An approach that identifies "literary institutions" with "the academy" helps explain how a canon is maintained, but not how it originated or evolved. Even such a committed institutional theorist as Kermode admits that "as for the *academic* canon of literature, it has certainly been protected in the academy, but it was not formed there" (*Appetite* 17). An institutional model centered, as most are, on the academy works best for canons shaped during this century. This makes it appropriate for American poetry, however, given that any sense of a formal "canon" in that poetry precedes the foundation of university English departments by only a few decades; given poetry's historical centrality to those departments' professional self-definition; and given that the literary academy has itself largely erased the canons of American poetry that preceded its own establishment.

Although Smith holds only to a modified form of the institutional approach, she offers a representative argument against traditional aesthetically based accounts of literary value, finding them circular and essentialist: *The Waste Land* is a great poem because it possesses those ineffable qualities that all great poems possess, qualities illustrated by poems like *The Waste Land.* Such reasoning "effaces both the historicity and cultural specificity of the term 'art' and also the institutionally and otherwise contingent variability of the honorific labeling of cultural productions" (35). For Smith, as for Tompkins, aesthetic value is, at least in part, institutionally determined and maintained: one function of the academy, historically, has been to perpetuate the aesthetic point of view. "The literary and aesthetic academy" seeks to keep those generally unstable labels "art" and "literature" as stable as possible, and to maintain a subpopulation that appreciates them. This is how an institution maintains a canon:

> The academy produces generation after generation of subjects for whom the objects and texts thus labeled do indeed perform the functions thus privileged, thereby ensuring the continuity of mutually defining canonical works, canonical functions, and canonical audiences. (44)

The point is not so much that this institutional view is somehow in conflict with the aesthetic; it is rather that it actually creates the aesthetic, so that the aesthetic point of view itself has, especially for most poetry readers today, an institutional origin.

What are the limits of an institutional model? One can be the kind of ahistoricity that I have noted in Eagleton. (For institutional theorists to stress the distinction between creating and maintaining canons, and to attend more to literary institutions beyond the academy, would be one way around this limitation).[4] A second limitation is that, in its extreme form, such a model has no place or explanation for the efficacy of individual agency. Yet individuals do contribute to the formation of canons, in historically verifiable ways. Lawrence Buell argues for just this combination of institutional and economic interest and individual agency in discussing the canonization of Thoreau. A key date in this process, Buell argues, is 1906, which saw the publication of the twenty-volume Houghton Mifflin edition of Thoreau's *Complete Writings*. He uses archival evidence to suggest both that the publishers' decision to adopt Thoreau rested on economics rather than on any considered effort to "revise" the canon, and that, nevertheless, it was the firm's literary adviser, Bliss Perry, who persuaded them to publish Thoreau. Buell concludes, then, that "enthusiastic intervention on behalf of artistic greatness by the forward-looking intellectual broke down the cautious, pragmatic resistance of the boss and his senior staff," that "at the heart of the Houghton Mifflin institutional juggernaut, the discretionary role of the (well-placed) individual actor was crucial" (28, 37–38). Such an example shows that the canonization process is not solely explainable as a function of generalized "institutions," with individuals acting merely as anonymous functionaries or extensions of those institutions.

A third risk of the institutional approach to canons (at least of the academy-as-institution version of the model) is that it downplays the effect on canon formation of individuals and groups acting outside the boundaries and assumptions of the academy—groups such as the writers associated with *Origin* to be discussed in chapter four. Although Fish's valuable concept of interpretive communities can in theory be extended to all readers, in practice (including Fish's own) it is confined to academic readers.[5] To put it another way, a theorist like Fish can explain convincingly how and why readers within the academy (teacher-critics, students, even academically based poets) read and value poems as they do. But he can explain much less effectively how and why nonacademic readers, especially other poets, read poems as *they* do.

In contrast to these institutional theories, a second school of thought holds that poets themselves have a significant effect, through their own work, on the canonization of other poets. While G. Robert Stange acknowledges that "the making of a literary reputation requires outside agencies" (162) such as journals, sympathetic publishers, anthologies, and academic literary histories, he argues that the principal agents of canon formation are the poets themselves who alter the poetic tradition by disvaluing some accepted "classics," giving authority to certain earlier art that has special meaning for them, or redefining in the interests of their own practice . . . the nature and responsibilities of poetic language. (159)

Over the past decade this has been a minority position in the profession, but still a highly visible one, represented in the pages of some influential journals (various articles in *Critical Inquiry*'s 1983 special issue on canons), in the work of some influential poetry critics of otherwise different persuasions (Harold Bloom, Helen Vendler, Hugh Kenner), and in essays and books by, among others, Christopher Ricks, William Phillips, Henry Louis Gates, and Charles Altieri.[6] A number of essays in the "canons" issue of *Critical Inquiry* take the view, in the words of the issue's editor, Robert von Hallberg, that "artists determine canons by selecting certain styles and masters to emulate" (1–2). Meanwhile, Hugh Kenner has argued that the modern American poetry canon was shaped "chiefly . . . by the canonized themselves, who were apt to be aware of a collective enterprise, and repeatedly acknowledged each other" ("Making of the Modernist Canon" 374). Helen Vendler, agreeing with Kenner, proposes that poetic "canons are not made by governments, anthologists, publishers, editors, or professors, but by writers. The canon, in any language, is composed of the writers that other writers admire, and have admired for generations"; "the evolving canon is not the creation of critics, but of poets" (*Music* 37–38). This model, however, both oversimplifies the process of canon formation and involves a certain circularity of argument. Vendler phrases the argument thus: "It is because Virgil admired Homer, and Milton Virgil, and Keats Milton, and Stevens Keats, that those writers turn up in classrooms and anthologies" (37). This view seems to explain how a major poet can preserve or revive an earlier one, and so to explain how a tradition or canon develops. But actually it begs the question of how the later poet comes to be designated "major" and acquires the power or authority to canonize others. Nor, in its straightforward linearity, can it explain how very different poets turn to the same precursor and use him or her in different ways; after all, many of Stevens' contemporaries, including Williams and later Olson, admired Keats. I have already suggested some limits to the institutional view of canons. In the next few pages, I will take issue also with this poet-centered view of canon formation, and argue that the shaping of canons involves something beyond Milton admiring Virgil, Keats Milton, and so on.

I take Vendler's position to be not so much wrong as partial, only half right. Certainly I would not deny that poets often emulate and extend the style of others, or that their work can confer authority on an earlier writer's practice or derive authority from it. In large part these dynamics are what constitute the idea of "tradition" (even while cultural and intellectual institutions such as the academy make up another large part). The poet-centered approach to canon formation is important for restoring some sense of individual agency to the canonizing process, and it can remind academic critics to take poets' views on these matters as seriously as their own. It is also suggestive in describing relationships among poets widely separated in time and place, and thus in describing one way in which a canon or tradition has been preserved long-term, before the intervention of the academy or even the formulation of the idea of "literature."[7] It emphasizes only one aspect of canon formation, however. Further, as I have said, it offers a largely circular explanation for the questions of who canonizes the canonizers (how did Stevens get the authority to have his opinion of Keats matter?) and of whose construction of "tradition" gets to count most. Thus it is limited as an account of how tastemaking functions as a total process, especially in the present. In other words, Vendler's model describes what has happened more effectively than it describes what is happening. (And as historical scholarship continues to uncover the canonizing role of past institutions, the poet-centered model may lose some of its effectiveness even for describing the relationship between earlier and later periods and poets.) My doubts about the viability of this model, then, involve not so much the model per se as the use of it to the exclusion of other instructive approaches. That is, my differences with Vendler (and with Hugh Kenner and Harold Bloom) stem from their underplaying of institutional factors in canon formation as much as from their proposal of an aesthetic model that indeed has some value. My objections are matters more of degree than of kind.

In Vendler's view, writers respond mainly to others' styles: "writers admire writers not because of their topics (Blake and Keats thought Milton quite mistaken in his attitudes) but because of their writing" (*Music* 37). This is often, but by no means always, the case, so that on this point the aesthetic model of canon formation proves only partially convincing. Indeed, later in this chapter I will examine the case of a writer (Berryman) who explicitly responds *not* to another's (Bradstreet's) "writing" but to what he imaginatively reconstructs as her "attitudes." For Vendler, when a later writer claims value for an earlier,

especially in the form of allusion or imitation, he or she claims a spe-
cifically aesthetic value, and Vendler sees this as the fundamental value
underlying canons: "I myself think aesthetic value, properly under-
stood, quite enough to claim for a poem" (39). When poetry lasts, in
Vendler's view, it does so for aesthetic or stylistic reasons, an idea that
she stresses at some of the most prominent points in her essays. In the
second sentence of an essay on Adrienne Rich, she writes, "issues wax
and lapse, and poetry, if it is good poetry, remains interesting after the
topical issues it has engaged are dead letters" (368). A review of Amy
Clampitt's *The Kingfisher* ends with this sentence: "And . . . when (if
man still exists) its cultural terminology is obsolescent and its social
patterns extinct, it will, I think, still be read for its triumph over the
resistance of language, the reason why poetry lasts" (412).

Vendler first articulated this position explicitly in the introduction to
her *Harvard Book of Contemporary Poetry*. There we find the argument
that poets make canons; that they do so on an aesthetic basis, respond-
ing to style and a distinctive voice; and that a canon consists of a hier-
archy of distinctive styles and voices:

Though it is easy to find a feeling to express or a cause to espouse, it is next
to impossible to find a stylization that succeeds: only a few poets in each cen-
tury have done it. These are the poets who are elevated to canonical status by
the envy and admiration of their fellow poets. As Hugh Kenner reminds us,
it is poets—and not anthologists or professors—who eventually decide which
poets are read after their own generation has disappeared. All poets envy that
authority of style on the page which says, even in a few lines, "Milton" or
"Tennyson". . . . (7)

Vendler gives precedence to the canonizing power of poets, then, over
that of "anthologists or professors"—her own roles in compiling this
collection. Rhetorically this stance serves to downplay the exclusive-
ness of the view of American poetry that the anthology represents, an
exclusiveness constructed not at all by poets with Vendler as innocent
bystander and reporter, but by Vendler herself. It also serves as a ratio-
nale for beginning an anthology of *contemporary* poetry with a poem
published in 1915, "Sunday Morning," by a poet born in 1879. Stevens,
implicitly, is the modernist poet whom our contemporaries should
canonize as America's "central" twentieth-century poet—although
Vendler offers only a one-sentence explanation for beginning with
Stevens, a sentence that oddly lifts him out of his own generation and
makes him "the chief link between the earlier high modernists (Eliot,
Pound, Williams, Crane, Moore) and the later poets" (16). Many review-

ers of the volume wondered, justifiably, where this revisionary liter-
ary history (not to mention revisionary chronology) leaves Pound and
Williams especially; and in doing so, many of them noted the egregious,
even polemical, narrowness of the canon that Vendler's anthology rep-
resents.[8] Without denying these objections, my point here is to stress
that—despite her own stated views on canonization—that canon is Vend-
ler's, not the poets' own, construction. As often happens, an anthol-
ogist's publicly stated principles and her canonizing practice conflict.

Vendler brings her poet-centered model of canonization into the
undergraduate classroom in her co-editing of a 1987 textbook anthol-
ogy, the *Harper American Literature*. In her prefatory essay to the anthol-
ogy's section on American poetry 1940–1973, Vendler remarks how
"history winnows literature to the few poets of each century that sub-
sequent poets can admire for their language and form" ("Literature of
Postwar America" 2253). Later in the anthology, she observes that "the
canon of American poetry . . . is decided upon chiefly by subsequent
poets, who find only some of their predecessors worthy of admiration,
imitation, and homage" ("Literature of Contemporary America"
2737).[9] To compare the *Harper* anthology with the 1985 *Harvard Book*,
however, only confirms the institutional aspects of canon formation that
Vendler tends to deny. That is, it confirms how different branches of
the publishing industry mutually reinforce each other in the creation
of a public canon that Vendler would have us believe is the creation of
poets. The *Harvard Book* includes thirty-five poets, beginning with
Stevens and Langston Hughes. Not only do all thirty-five reappear in
the *Harper American Literature*; but the thirty-three poets beginning with
Roethke who make up the *Harvard* selections are transported almost
wholesale to make up the two sections on "postwar" and "contempo-
rary" poetry in the *Harper* textbook. The *Harper* adds only one poet,
Gwendolyn Brooks, to the *Harvard* selection. Meanwhile, a remarkable
fifty-one of the essays and reviews that Vendler collected in the eighties
as *Part of Nature, Part of Us* (1980) and *The Music of What Happens* (1988)
concern these same thirty-three poets. Certainly one can attribute the
massive degree of overlap among the classroom textbook, the anthol-
ogy from a highly prestigious university press, and the two volumes
of criticism from that same press to the coherence and consistency of
Vendler's taste. And one can praise and envy her ability to write well
on so many poets. Nevertheless, this overlap also shows three thor-
oughly institutionalized means of shaping taste and critical opinion
coming together to create *a* (but not the only possible) postwar canon.
Again, this is hardly a canon created by poets.

Try as she may to dispute the pervasive presence of various institutions in shaping canons, then, Vendler's poet-centered or aesthetic model of canon formation ends up being less pure than she suggests. She denies that "the acclamations of governments" and "the civic pieties of anthologists" have any effect on a writer's survival (*Music* 37). Yet she also admits that European cultures derive their national canons as a result of institutional forces: "Each European nation cherishes its poetry . . . as part of the deposit of patriotism, and therefore institutionalizes it in the schools." A comparable American canon will not come into being, and poetry will not occupy a comparably central place in literary culture, "if a large social commitment to it as a patriotic value does not exist" (35). But what could be a more direct result of "the acclamations of governments" and "civic pieties" than a canon based on these principles?

Further, even the poets seem to be letting her down. Vendler admits that the canons of many contemporary American poets—those who, in her view, should currently be shaping or preserving the canon of poetry written in English—extend geographically rather than chronologically:

The contemporary American poet-critic is far more likely to read across—in world poetry of the nineteenth and twentieth centuries—than to read back in English verse. (A well-known poet and teacher of creative writing remarked to me, unashamed, that he had never read George Herbert.) . . . It looks as if the classical and English canon may be slipping out of our grasp, to be replaced by a modern canon of unrhymed and translated pieces. (*Music* 38)

Vendler maintains here her premise that poets shape canons. At the same time, she takes Robert Hass to task, for instance, for praising Milosz and Tranströmer when he is unable to read their original Polish and Swedish. But if canons are made by poets, apparently today's American poets are shaping a very different canon from those of the past. More to the point, they are doing so out of something other than aesthetic pleasure, appreciation of style, for they often turn to languages that they do not know.

Since I depend on a synthetic model of canon formation throughout much of this book, using elements of both the institutional and the aesthetic approaches, I should discuss further what value the latter approach does have in considering how later poets can affect the canonical status of earlier poets. Paradoxically, a case for the explanatory power of Vendler's model could rest on the very tradition that she has excluded from her own critical work and anthologies, the Pound/

Williams–Objectivist–New American Poetry line that extends up to Language poetry in the present. As I shall argue in Chapter 4, it was mostly the poets associated with Cid Corman's countercanonical little magazine *Origin* (Creeley, Olson, Duncan, Levertov) who initiated renewed interest in Pound and (especially) Williams. At around the same time, as I show in Chapter 3, poets helped significantly in maintaining Whitman's reputation against New Critical efforts to dismiss or diminish him. A few years later, the poet-editor Corman centered *Origin*'s second series on the Objectivist unknowns Zukofsky and Niedecker. And closer to the present, the turn among many Language writers to the Objectivists, to Stein, and to Laura Riding preceded or helped resuscitate academic interest in the earlier writers' work. The aesthetic or poet-centered model of canonicity can indeed explain the internal workings of this tradition, and explain how later writers preserve, promote, and seek to canonize earlier ones. In fact, the aesthetic model may be *especially* useful for understanding the survival and development of a countercanon during those periods of its growth when it is receiving no institutional attention.

However, while the canonization of writers in the Pound tradition can show how the aesthetic model works, it also reveals that model's limits. For only an institutional model can explain the suppression of this particular poet-derived canon—the suppression that is so acute in Vendler's own work. That is, in her position as an institutionally well-placed critic Vendler promotes *one* poet-derived canon (centered on Stevens) over another, exercising her canonizing power without acknowledging it. Further, in considering the revival or emergence of the Objectivists, Stein, Riding, or even Frank O'Hara, or the continuities from Milton to Keats to Stevens, as examples of a poet-created canon, one has to ask: a canon for whom? [10] At this point one is forced to return to the institution of the academy, the site of most debates about canonicity, of the main (though not the only) audience for poetry, and—most crucially—the site where poets' canonizing efforts and judgments, whether explicitly stated or implicit in their own practice, get preserved, perpetuated, and disseminated (or, alternatively, suppressed) by nonpoets.

Since Vendler consistently cites Hugh Kenner as one who shares her poet-centered view of canonization, it is appropriate to turn to Kenner next. Kenner gives more weight than Vendler to the role of critics in canonizing. He recalls how, in mid-century, New Critical principles marginalized Pound and wholly excluded Williams from "a canon pedagogues were defining"; he acknowledges that "part of a canon is the state and history of the relevant criticism"; he allows that "the Modernist canon has been made in part by [academic] readers like me" ("Making of the Modernist Canon" 371–74). Like Vendler, however, Kenner finally emphasizes the role of writers themselves. Hence this canon partly defined by professors has mainly been made "by later writers choosing and inventing ancestors" and "*chiefly* [my emphasis] . . . by the canonized themselves, who were apt to be aware of a collective enterprise and repeatedly acknowledged one another" (374). This view comes close to that which Vendler takes in the foreword to *Part of Nature, Part of Us*: "the best expositors of [a new poetic style] will be the poets themselves, who, when they write criticism, create a prose so pressing in its self-justification that it lasts, with their poems, forever" (x–xi). It also anticipates the efforts at self-canonization of John Berryman that I shall discuss later in this chapter. But such self-canonization or self-promotion does not occur in a vacuum. If, as Kenner says, "how canons are determined is in general unwritten history" ("Making of the Modernist Canon" 365), central to that history are the forces that mediate poets' canonization of themselves and others. Kenner limits the usefulness of his nascently synthetic model by compartmentalizing in his discussion the roles of "pedagogues," "criticism," and "poets." He does not fully acknowledge how the self-promotion that Vendler points to so approvingly gets carried out—how the "canonized" cannot shape a canon that will include them *without* a mediating network of magazines, presses, anthologies, and so forth.

The third major critic of American poetry to adopt a poet-centered model of canonization is Harold Bloom. Bloom's version of the model appears in its most sustained form in his influence studies of the nineteen seventies. The premise that poets can and do canonize themselves is central to Bloom's work, underlying such characteristic assertions as the claim that "Wordsworth imposed himself upon the canon" or that Blake "intended us to canonize" "London" and "The Tyger" (*Poetry and Repression* 31, 34). (This position also points to a difference in emphasis between Bloom, who tends to focus on how poets canonize themselves, and Vendler, who tends to focus on how later poets canonize earlier ones.) The premise also informs his subsequent work, however, as a 1984 essay makes clear: "As critics we can only confirm the self-canonization of the truly strong prophets and poets. What we cannot do is invent their canonization for them" ("Criticism" 17). Like Vendler's, however, Bloom's model turns out to be less genuinely poet-centered than it first appears. Here is Bloom commenting on the importance of Stevens for his work:

To a considerable extent, the way in which I read all of the Romantic poets, all of the nineteenth-century poets, the way I read Whitman is all powerfully conditioned by my reading of Stevens and by what I would say is Stevens's implicit reading of romantic tradition, of Whitman in particular. ("Interview" 15)

Again, the critic sneaks in as a crucial link in the chain of poets canonizing each other. For Stevens to canonize Whitman (whatever that might mean) is one thing; for Stevens to affect how an institutionally powerful and well-placed critic reads Whitman and then passes on those readings is quite another. Like Vendler, Bloom downplays or suppresses his own crucial role as an institutionally based interpreter of how one poet reads another.[11]

Agon (1982) contains a useful summary of Bloom's ideas on poetic self-canonization:

But the Greek poets themselves, at least from Hesiod on, invented poetic self-canonization, or self-election. I am going to suggest the antithetical formula that a contemporary American poem, to have any hope of permanence, necessarily builds the canonical ambition, process and agon directly into its own text, as Hesiod, Pindar, Milton, Pope, Wordsworth and Whitman did also, as indeed all the poetic survivors have done. (284)

Bloom continues:

Milton . . . assured not only his own place in the canon, but taught his poetic successors how to make themselves canonical by way of their transumptive imagery. This remains the canonical use of strong poetry: it goes on electing its successors, and these Scenes of Instruction become identical with the continuity of poetic tradition. (286)

What Bloom offers here is less an explanation than a description of "the continuity of poetic tradition." In Bloom's view, and in the aestheticist view of canon formation generally, the canon being discussed is self-authenticating and always already in place.

Bloom takes this position most explicitly in *The Breaking of the Vessels*:

Great poets directly related by a tradition share qualities we recognize yet find difficulty in describing; indeed we have trouble now recollecting that a criticism adequate to such poetry must be able to convey what greatness is. Touchstones Arnoldian or Blackmurian are a start, but do not take us far. Perhaps my revisionary ratios are in some sense only more developed touchstones, but the development is of the essence. (13)

This passage raises one of the central contradictions in Bloom's view of canon formation: he acknowledges the possibility of "strong" criticism (and openly credits Samuel Johnson as his own critical father), but finally sees the tradition as the creation more of poets than of critics. "We" merely describe the characteristics of a tradition that is already in place, by appealing in circular fashion to the touchstones or revisionary ratios that constitute the object of description. And this position rests on "an aestheticism, which is the only justification for our readings and unreadings, of the poets and of ourselves" (*Vessels* 40).

Such aesthetic theories of canon formation do not explain so much as simply invite assent to the claims to canonical status of a text, a writer, or a poetic mode such as the Sublime with which much of Bloom's work has been preoccupied. Arguing for a revisionary reading of Stevens as a poet of the "modern Sublime," Bloom writes, "the Stevens I am sketching can be conveyed in a rapid and arbitrary cento of a few Arnoldian or Blackmurian touchstones." In this set of "touchstones," five passages from Stevens' own canon, the modern Sublime is self-evidently present and self-evidently compelling: "you need but hear it to recognize its giant authority" (*Poetry and Repression* 282). Even at those few points where he seems to express some ambivalence about the use of "touchstones," Bloom disingenuously reinscribes them. He compares A. R. Ammons' "Saliences" with Wordsworth, Browning, Whitman, and Stevens, and then continues: "This is not to play at touchstones, in the manner of Arnold or of Blackmur, but only to record my experience as a reader, which is that *Saliences* suggests and is worthy of such company" (*Ringers* 280). Further, for all his self-conscious prophecies, and his playfully extreme and outrageous judgments, Bloom has rarely written on a canonically marginal poet.[12] Despite all his efforts, he finally never shows *how* a poet becomes canonical, or why one self-canonization gets accepted, by poets and other readers alike, over another.

If Bloom sees the poetic canon as a linked chain of self-canonizations, a succinct statement of the opposing view can be found in a critic such as Kermode who holds to an institutional model of canons. Generally, Kermode defines a canon not simply as a body of texts, but as the texts *plus* the history of commentary upon them (*Forms* 75).[13] He will argue, directly contradicting Bloom, that "since we have no experience of a venerable text that ensures its own perpetuity, we may reasonably say that the medium in which it survives is commentary" (36). "Only interpretation," for Kermode, can "maintain the life of a work of art from one generation to another" (30). In principle this is adaptable to Bloom's position, according to which poems are interpretations of earlier poems, but clearly Kermode has critical, not poetic, interpretations in mind. Sometimes Kermode can seem, surprisingly, in accord with Bloom. He shows, for instance, how Botticelli, rescued from oblivion in the nineteenth century, "owed his promotion not to scholars but to artists and other persons of modern sensibility, whose ideas of history were more passionate than accurate, and whose connoisseurship was, as I have said, far from exact" (6). Bloom would call this process an example of strong misreading (or, perhaps, strong mis-seeing) by Pre-Raphaelite artists and writers (Burne-Jones, Swinburne, Ruskin, Rossetti). Still, it remains the case that poets and artists are not nearly as central to Kermode's view of canonization as they are to Bloom's. As Kermode puts it in *An Appetite for Poetry*, "it is by no means the case that canon-formation is invariably the project of a privileged class of priests or academics; the preferences and vogues of lay persons, the force of relatively uninstructed opinion, are often decisive" (17). And if an artist can initially be rescued by the force of opinion largely divorced from knowledge, as was Botticelli, his or her canonical status is nevertheless maintained by knowledgeable institutionalized commentary and because his or her work invites "continued *institutional* inquiry" (my emphasis; *Appetite* 18).

Up to a point, as I have said, Bloom does acknowledge the influence of strong readers who are not poets. In fact, from one point of view, Bloom's definition of the "strong" or canonical poem is surprisingly conventional: "a strong poem, which alone can become canonical for more than a single generation, can be defined as a text that must engender strong misreadings, both as other poems and as literary criticism" (*Agon* 285). This restates the traditional view—of which Kermode's institutional theory is a refinement—that the "classic" or canonical status of a text is reflected in its ability to yield different readings by different generations of reader. To notice how Bloom describes these readers helps us see another unacknowledged institutional element to canonization creeping into his poet-centered theory. Bloom's comments on poetry readers show a consistent set of qualifiers: "the strength of trope can be recognized by skilled readers in a way that anticipates the temporal progression of generations" (*Agon* 285); "the revisionist work, through canonization, is misread by being overfigured by the canonically informed reader" (*Poetry and Repression* 34); "the accomplished reader responds to [Geoffrey] Hill's work as to any really strong poetry, for the reader too needs to put off his own belatedness, which is surely why we go on searching for strong poetry" (*Figures* 242). "Skilled," "canonically informed," "accomplished"—the only word that rarely occurs in Bloom's work, but that underlies all these others, is "professional," and here lies the circularity of any poet-centered view of canon formation. For most of these readers became "canonically informed" and "accomplished" in the academy, the primary medium for at least the last fifty years for the canonization of poetry. Outside of poets themselves, this is the readership most likely to respond to the trope of transumption: a professional readership interested in and concerned with ideas of tradition and continuity, and trained to recognize the presence of Keats in Stevens, of Stevens in Ashbery, and so on.[14] "But why should the order of institutions be more valid for poetry than the order of a gifted individual?" Bloom asked in 1971 (*Ringers* 197). As Jonathan Arac points out, Bloom has never answered this rhetorical question, so "the question remains how institutions operate in the canon formation at which [Bloom's] theory increasingly aims" (16). The answer is that "institutions," broadly defined, mediate and even determine the nature of the individual's "gifts."

I have mentioned *Critical Inquiry*'s special issue on canons as another highly visible place where an artist-centered model of canonization gets proposed. Introducing the book version of that issue, Robert von Hallberg offers a brief but persuasive summary of this model's possible usefulness. In the face of "academic critics overestimating their own importance and autonomy in the process of canon-formation," an explanatory model for that process that is "attuned to the way in which artists, in choosing their models, set the terms for disputes among academic canonizers . . . is important as a corrective." This model helps us to "test not only the limits of institutionalized literary and artistic study—that is, our own limits as students and professors—but those of the interest model of canon-formation as well," the model that sees canons as the result of various, usually unacknowledged, ideological and institutional interests. For as von Hallberg rightly says, artists often resist efforts to explain their relationships to their important precursors and contemporaries as "politically motivated or even importantly freighted with ideological significance" ("Introduction" 2–3).

I am arguing that, as von Hallberg suggests, a poet-centered model of canon formation should supplement an interest or institutional model. But I would argue further that the two models cannot, and should not, be separated. The first model seeks to explain how it is that "poets and painters, by emulation, sometimes produce art (critical polemics aside) that institutes the authority of certain earlier art" (von Hallberg, "Introduction" 2). But there are two problems with this model as von Hallberg summarizes it. First, the earlier art does not always maintain the authority that the later artist ascribes to it. To use one example from the *Canons* collection itself, Winthrop Wetherbee's "*Poeta che mi guidi*: Dante, Lucan, and Virgil," if Virgil, Lucan, and Statius constitute Dante's classical canon, who, outside of classics scholars, now cares about Lucan, or Statius? Dante has not turned Lucan into a "classic." Second, von Hallberg suggests that this phenomenon of "emulation" is, at least in some cases, somehow immune to social analysis. But to emulate is, in part, to accept a set of established conventions; and conventions are always social as much as they are aesthetic and generic. That is, to some extent, the apparently freely chosen emulation of an earlier artist by a later is in many cases a "choice" dictated by period or genre conventions. What James E. G. Zetzel calls "the Augustan poets' seemingly conscious emulation of the canonical works of early Greek literature" (109), for instance, is a matter of convention. In this view, "the truly successful poet was one who imitated his *exemplar* so faithfully that he became an *exemplar* himself." The later poet derives authority from successful imitation of a canonical earlier poet—but only within a historically specific set of conventions, enforced by the cultural institutions of the period and not constructed by poets, that held that "the goal of poetry is not to be original but to follow a model so closely that the new work might be taken for the old" (109).

In practice, most arguments for a poet-centered model of canon formation boil down either to standard linear narratives of literary history or to Bloomian accounts of poets' struggles with their precursors. Nor do they question from where the later poet derives his or her putative power to canonize. My point is not that poets lack that power. It is that they exercise it, and it has its effects, through institutions. The mutual promotion of the modernists that Kenner notes did not occur in their poetry, so it is not (or is not only) a matter of the aesthetic power of their work. The modernist situation is closer to that of the *Origin* writers discussed in Chapter 4, who used a journal, essays, and correspondence to promote each other. Poets may seek to canonize themselves and their contemporaries in various ways, but to do so successfully in their *poems* still requires institutional mediation.

John Berryman's "Homage to Mistress Bradstreet"

Seeking to examine these issues more concretely as I developed this chapter, I turned to the example of John Berryman's "Homage to Mistress Bradstreet": a work that openly concentrates on the later poet's response to the earlier, the breakthrough poem of a poet preoccupied with his own and others' reputations, a poem that alludes in its title to an earlier twentieth-century effort at revival, Pound's "Homage to Sextus Propertius." I posed myself this question: could "Homage to Mistress Bradstreet" be read, along the lines of "Sextus Propertius" (which Berryman himself praised as "fresh delicate firm" [*Freedom* 289]), as an example of a poet seeking to canonize, or invite reevaluation of, an earlier one? I found I could answer that question fairly simply and quickly, and the answer was "no," for two reasons. First, even though Berryman quotes from and alludes to Bradstreet's work, he did not care for Bradstreet's poetry, and so did not seek to emulate, preserve, respond to, extend, or revive it. On this point he is quite clear. In the poem itself, Berryman writes of her "bald / abstract didactic rime" (*Collected Poems* 135), her "proportioned, spiritless poems" (143). In a 1965 essay he describes Bradstreet as a "boring high-minded Puritan woman who may have been our first American poet but is not a good one"; he claims to be interested in her "as a woman, not much as a poetess" (*Freedom* 328). He repeats this claim in 1968—"I don't like her work" ("Interview" 10)—and in 1970: "The idea was not to take Anne Bradstreet as a poetess—I was not interested in that" ("Art of Poetry" 33).

Second, when we move from intention to result, again we find that by most conventional measures Berryman's poem seems to have done little to convert readers to Bradstreet. *Homage to Mistress Bradstreet* won its author a high reputation when it appeared in book form in 1956 in the United States and in 1959 in England after its initial 1953 publication in *Partisan Review*. Subsequently it was reprinted seven times, in various formats, on both sides of the Atlantic, between 1964 and 1973. But generally Berryman's reviewers and critics—many of them poets themselves—concurred in his low estimate of Bradstreet's poetry. Stanley Kunitz writes of Bradstreet that "the mediocrity of her performance is too blatant" for anyone to take her seriously "as the symbolic mother-muse of American poetry" (244). John Ciardi dismisses her as an "amateur poetess" who has been preserved mainly for historical reasons, "despite the general insipidity and awkwardness of all but a few passages of her work" (36). For Philip Toynbee, "Mr. Berryman demonstrates in the course of the poem that Anne Bradstreet was herself a very bad poet" (136). (Actually Berryman *demonstrates* nothing of the sort, although he does *assert* it.) Among later commentators on "Homage," Carol Johnson describes Bradstreet as "an undistinguished versifier" characterized by "endearing incompetence" (42); Joel Conarroe writes of her "derivative blandness," and calls her work "tedious," "extraordinarily dull" (58); Gary Arpin asserts that "Anne Bradstreet is hardly a major poet; indeed, she is seldom even a good one" (59); William Martz feels that, "despite her prolific output, Anne was not much of a poet at all" (28). In the face of this consensus, there seems little basis to Alvin Rosenfeld's lonely claim that Berryman "brought many contemporary readers to rediscover her and evaluate her writings anew" (124), especially when Berryman does not invite a positive reevaluation. Even Hyatt Waggoner's view that "the best way to become interested in her poetry today is to start by reading John Berryman's *Homage to Mistress Bradstreet*" (8) appears in the general context of an argument that Bradstreet's poetry does not compel interest on its own merits.

I have argued that poetic canons are not only the matter of texts and of writers that Vendler, Bloom, and to some extent Kenner would have us believe they are. Any given period has its canonical genres; its canonical critical paradigms, or ways of seeing and reading; its canonical critical languages; its canonical definitions of "the poet," and of "poetry," and of the poet's place in his or her culture; its own media for reinforcing and disseminating judgments. Hence one poet's reading of another, especially in the twentieth century, does not take place in isolation. It cannot be separated, and our understanding of it cannot be separated, from these surrounding conditions. While Berryman did not set out to revive Bradstreet's poetry in "Homage to Mistress Bradstreet," he did set out to canonize her position as, in his view, a poet—and the first American poet—in conflict with her culture. Further, in doing so he sought to define his own poetics, to justify what he considered his own marginal cultural position as an American poet, and to perpetuate an already established version of American literary history into which he might fit himself. It might be argued that if Berryman did not respond to Bradstreet's poetry, then "Homage" is not an appropriate test case for the poet-centered model of canon formation. But "Homage" is appropriate precisely *because* it shows, contrary to Vendler's view in particular, that poets do *not* always respond to other poets chiefly on the basis of style. Berryman responds to Bradstreet's social and historical situation; apparently, in their turns to other writers, poets are not always the aesthetes that Vendler claims.

For Berryman, as for most literary historians, Bradstreet's "firstness" was particularly important.[15] In fact, Berryman suggests, her firstness partly explains why he chose her as a subject: "she was the first poet of this country and . . . her great effort to create, to exercise her intellect is to be greatly admired. She lived in a society which frowned on a woman's interest going beyond the home, where harsh circumstances made survival of prime importance" (quoted in Conarroe 81). Self-irony cannot conceal the nature of his interest: "I was interested in her as a pioneer heroine, a sort of mother to the artists and intellectuals who would follow her and play a large role in the development of the nation. People like Jefferson, Poe, and me" ("Art of Poetry" 33). Berryman has this mother of artists give birth to her son Simon in the central sections of his poem, and from reading Bradstreet, he would know her use of the traditional metaphorical identification of children and poems, in "The Author to Her Book," "Before the Birth of One of Her Children," and "In Reference to Her Children." Bradstreet organizes the first of these poems around the controlling metaphor of the book as child; annoyed and embarrassed at the poor production quality of her volume *The Tenth Muse Lately Sprung Up in America*, she addresses her book as an "ill-formed offspring," a "rambling brat" (221). Fearing death in childbirth in "Before the Birth . . . ," she asks her husband, if she should die, to "look to my little babes, my dear remains"—her children and her poems (224). In these examples, Bradstreet bears poems that are children, children that are poems; in "Homage," Berryman has her give birth not only to her literal son Simon but also to her literary son, Berryman himself, and thus to the very poem, the "Homage," in which she finds herself. [16]

In the last line of "Homage," Berryman addresses Bradstreet explicitly as "a sourcing" (*Collected Poems* 147). He finds in her a particular kind of source for American, and hence for his own, poetry. As a way to validate his own poetics, his own sense of self, he has Bradstreet act out a longstanding American literary-historical drama: the lone artist struggling to write in a hostile environment. Thus Berryman finds himself a tradition, a usable past. He participates in an already familiar version of American literary history by placing himself in a line of outsiders, of *poètes maudits*, stretching back to Bradstreet, whom he establishes as the source for this line of poets. Berryman often complained that "few critics have seen that ['Homage'] *is* a historical poem" (*Freedom* 329), and he insisted on that aspect of it: "There is a lot of history in the poem. It is a historical poem." He adds, "A lot of it is invented too" ("Art of Poetry" 33). What Berryman invents or exaggerates are those features of the poem's "history" that most effectively support his view of the poet's place in American culture, his view of the history of American poetry, and his attempt to carve himself a place in that history—Bradstreet's dissatisfaction with her marriage, her resistance to dogma, her close friendship with the antinomian Anne Hutchinson (to whom she cries out "Bitter sister, victim! I miss you" [*Collected Poems* 139]), the intensity of her yearning for children.

As one step toward canonizing a particular view of Bradstreet, Berryman (in common with most readers, it must be said) denigrates her public, historical poetry. He has Bradstreet comment as follows on her long poems:

> Versing, I shroud among the dynasties;
> quaternion on quaternion, tireless I phrase
> anything past, dead, far,
> sacred, for a barbarous place.

His own response to these poems? "All this bald / abstract didactic rime I read appalled" (*Collected Poems* 135). It is Bradstreet's private, personal lyrics and the prose meditations expressing her spiritual doubts and struggles that Berryman incorporates, both by direct quotation and by allusion, into his own text. These are the Bradstreet poems that have subsequently come to be most valued. This valuation does not clearly result from Berryman's efforts, however. Rather, his and other readers' preference for Bradstreet's lyrics can more readily be explained as a matter of *generational* taste and, more generally, as part of the post-Romantic habit of equating poetry with the lyric. (Gender, of course, is also a relevant factor here. In reassessing women poets, and in redeeming the private, domestic sphere and women's personal experience as subjects for poetry, feminist criticism has tended to privilege the same poems, though for different reasons.) He uses phrases from the prose "Meditations Divine and Moral" in stanza 8; from "Another Letter to Her Husband" in stanza 9; from the late semiconfessional prose meditation "To My Dear Children" in stanzas 13, 14, and 51; and he alludes to "Upon the Burning of Our House" in stanza 49. Thus "Homage" becomes historical in another sense—a direct reflection of its own literary-historical moment in privileging the voice and mode of lyric, and the rhetorical stance of the cultural outsider, suggesting this voice, mode, and stance as defining characteristics of American poetry, with a longstanding history behind them.

In the spirit, if not the letter, of his inventions about Bradstreet's personal life, Berryman actually anticipates a later influential critical view of Bradstreet as a poet whose work illustrates Puritan conflicts between dogma and rebellion.[17] At the same time, it is not clear that Berryman actually *led* later readers to such a view. That argument has ample precedent in a view of Puritanism as inimical to poetry running through much of the background material that Berryman read while working

on "Homage." For however much Berryman adapted or improvised
upon the history of Bradstreet's life, work, and times, still he researched
that history exhaustively. A review of this background reading is rele-
vant for my argument because Berryman's research almost certainly
helped shape or confirm his view of Bradstreet as, at least in spirit, a
rebel poet—and he described "Homage" as organized around "a series
of rebellions" (*Freedom* 328).

In researching his poem, Berryman gathered twenty-eight pages of
notes from Helen Stuart Campbell's 1891 biography of Bradstreet alone;
by June 1952 he had accumulated " 'more than 125 draft lines of
poetry' " (Mariani, *Dream Song* 247) and eighty pages of notes from
other reading that included Perry Miller's *The New England Mind*, John
Winthrop's *Journals*, and, in his own words, "narratives, town histories"
(*Collected Poems* 147). When Berryman was reading for "Homage" in
1950–52, and working on it in early 1953, there was little readily avail-
able criticism on Bradstreet, and even less that was reliable. The only
biography, beyond sketches, was Campbell's. (In fact, reviewing *Hom-
age* in 1956, Bradstreet's biographer-to-be, Elizabeth Wade White, called
the poem "the first twentieth-century biography" of the poet [545].)
The field of Puritan studies was building on the early work of Samuel
Eliot Morison, Perry Miller, and Kenneth Murdock, but essentially was
still getting off the ground and seeking respectability. More important,
most of what Berryman might have read offered what Robert Daly con-
vincingly argues is a systematic misconception of Puritan poetry—the
belief that the Puritans considered poetry trivial and fanciful and that
their theology limited them and allowed them to produce only rhymed
religious abstractions. In *The New England Mind*, for instance, Perry
Miller summarizes his version of the Puritan view of poetry thus:
"Poetry existed primarily for its utility, it was foredoomed to didac-
ticism. . . . Poetry in Puritan eyes, therefore, was a species of rhetoric,
a dress for great truths, a sugar for the pill" (360–61). If Berryman did
not get this view from critics and social historians of Puritanism, he
could have got it from Lawrence's *Studies in Classic American Literature*
or Williams' *In the American Grain*. He would also have found it reflected
in the literary histories of his time, first in Samuel Marion Tucker's essay
"The Beginnings of Verse, 1610–1808" in the *Cambridge History of Amer-
ican Literature* (1917–21) and then later, as he began the poem, in the
Literary History of the United States (1948). He would have found it even
in the introduction to the edition of Bradstreet he presumably used—
"presumably" because it was the only one available outside a literary
archive—the 1932 Peter Smith reprint of John Harvard Ellis' 1867 edi-

tion of her *Works*. Ellis explains his view of Bradstreet's work as lacking "much poetic genius" and as "quaint and curious" by claiming that "the people among whom she dwelt were the last in the world to stimulate or appreciate a poet" (xlii). In fact—though typically for a nineteenth-century reader of Bradstreet—Ellis ranks her prose far above her poetry. Almost any critical and historical material that Berryman turned to, then, would have reinforced his sense of Bradstreet as a poet-rebel in conflict with her culture's dogma.

By adopting the role of cultural outsider for himself and Bradstreet, Berryman inserts himself into one of the canonical narratives of American literary history. By his use of Bradstreet as muse, he also aligns himself with the longstanding phallocentricity of that narrative—a narrative in which the individualists who constituted the American literary canon at mid-century were nearly all men. Berryman is unusual among male American poets of his generation in turning to a woman writer to define his poetics.[18] Nevertheless, his appropriation of Bradstreet remains open to the kind of feminist critique that Ivy Schweitzer offers:

The male poet's voice begins and ends the poem, framing and containing the speech of the woman he imagines. He resurrects Bradstreet, confines her to her body and the traditional feminine role of reproduction, narrows and distorts her, dismisses her poetry, and buries her. (145)

Nor does Schweitzer spare those many critics of "Homage," mentioned earlier in this chapter, who are swayed by Berryman's view of Bradstreet to the point where, in their readings, "a woman mistaken for a poet is rescued from misprision by a male poet who accurately repositioned her as his source of inspiration" (132). Bradstreet serves for Berryman that most canonical, even stereotyped, of functions, that of the woman as muse and lover, a function that involves dismissing her poetry so that, if Berryman's Bradstreet is not entirely a passive object, neither is she seriously accorded the status of a writing subject. As Alicia Ostriker puts it, "Berryman created, out of his own yearning, a lover-anima-muse figure who would never be seen as a colleague, collaborator, or equal" (27).[19]

Berryman does not find in Bradstreet a Bloomian strong poet with whom he has to engage in an oedipal struggle before he can write his own poetry. In turning to her as a rebellious precursor, however, he does find a stance with which to identify; and further, Bradstreet is the figure who empowers him to struggle with a strong poet whom he did feel compelled to exorcise—T. S. Eliot.[20] For, as Berryman wrote in 1949, if his main precursor, Yeats, was "the major poet," *The Waste Land* was "the major poem . . . of the century so far" (*Freedom* 254). If Eliot's poetry did not dominate each member of the middle generation of Schwartz, Jarrell, Lowell, and Berryman equally, his *ideas about* poetry did. In the pages of the magazine with which Berryman most identified, *Partisan Review,* his friend Schwartz (engaged in his own struggle with Eliot) termed Eliot an "international hero" and a "literary dictator." There is only slight exaggeration in Bruce Bawer's claim that "virtually every line of poetry that they wrote during their early years was brought into being by a poetic faculty that had been shaped by Eliot's doctrines. . . . to the Middle Generation poets such expressions as impersonality, the objective correlative, and the dissociation of sensibility were not merely useful locutions but dogma, even revelation. They were the rules by which the Middle Generation, in their early period, conducted their careers" (60–65).[21]

In the memory of his friend and student W. S. Merwin, Berryman even adopted Eliot's personal mannerisms. Berryman was in his early thirties when Merwin first met him; nevertheless, Merwin recalls his "cadaverous features and vaulted intonation," and how "he enacted an imperious need to be one of his elders. He talked as though he were a contemporary of Allen Tate's, at least" (188). (Berryman said of himself that "I always wanted to be much older than I was, and from an early age I took to advising my seniors" [Kostelanetz, "Conversation" 342].) Merwin goes on to relate this "false-ripe manner" (typical, he admits, of many aspiring poets of the period) partly to the example of Eliot, who himself had been "at forty, and perhaps long before that, the aged eagle" (189). Berryman's charmingly candid admission that he began his career as "a burning, trivial disciple of the great Irish poet William Butler Yeats, . . . whom [he] didn't so much wish to resemble as to *be*" (*Freedom* 323) is well known. His manner suggests, however, that he felt an equally strong desire, less candidly admitted, to "be" Eliot.

Equally revealing, I think, is one of the functions that Berryman saw his discipleship as having served: "Yeats somehow saved me from the then-crushing influences of Ezra Pound and T. S. Eliot—luckily, as I now feel" (*Freedom* 324). He often linked Yeats and Eliot as the dominant poets of the modern period: "the grand cases—as in our century, Yeats and Eliot," as he puts it (*Freedom* 163). Addressing in an interview what he calls "the issue of our common human life," he says that "one way in which we can approach it, by means of art, coming out of Homer and Virgil and down through Yeats and Eliot, is by investigating the

individual human soul" (Kostelanetz, "Conversation" 345). Further,
at least some of his readers found Eliot and Yeats cohabiting Berryman's
early work. When Malcolm Cowley rejected four Berryman poems for
the *New Republic* in 1938, he wrote to the poet, "these . . . poems strike
me as very skillful exercises, based on the very best models—Yeats,
Eliot, with a touch of Allen Tate" (quoted in Thornbury 144).

Berryman's engagement with Eliot began inauspiciously when Eliot
rejected five of Berryman's poems for the *Criterion* in 1936, and when,
that same year, Berryman found himself singularly unimpressed by
the older poet's lecture "The Idiom of Modern Verse." He wrote to
his mother that "the Eliot lecture was interesting for I expected
nothing. . . . monotonous and humorless delivery . . . ; insulted
Hopkins and Housman gratuitously; slow mind apparently; his dis-
cussion afterward was unsatisfactory." In a letter to Mark Van Doren,
he described Eliot as possessing "competence, but not genius" (Thorn-
bury 128). Later, however, Berryman engaged himself more positively
with Eliot at a number of points during his career. He included Eliot's
work in his poetry readings.[22] The day after meeting Eliot for tea in
1947, he wrote a sonnet about the experience—a poem in which he
shows himself more than a little concerned with poetic reputations. In
the poem's ambivalent first line, Eliot is "the poet hunched, so, whom
the worlds admire." Later in the poem, Berryman shows the same pre-
occupation with fame when he recalls a similar meeting with Yeats at
"the great man's club" (*Collected Poems* 73). He taught Eliot's poetry for
many years: from a three-week course on contemporary poetry at
Briarcliff Junior College in 1944, to a 1952 lecture at the University of
Cincinnati so successful that he was asked to give an additional one,
to a 1956 public lecture in Minneapolis on Eliot as poet and critic, to
a 1962 course at Bread Loaf on "deep form" that concentrated on "Song
of Myself" and *The Waste Land*. In 1960 he contributed an essay on
"Prufrock" to a textbook on critical reading. By the time of the Cincin-
nati lecture, given while he was working on "Homage," Berryman con-
sidered Eliot "the 'greatest living poet' in the language" (Mariani, *Dream
Song* 244). And by 1970, "secure in [his] own style," he could call Eliot
"one of the greatest poets who ever lived" (with the sly addition that
Eliot was "only sporadically good" ['Art of Poetry" 25]).

Amid this longstanding involvement with Eliot's work, Berryman
steadfastly resisted the older poet's impersonal theory of poetry. When
Berryman remarks that Yeats saved him from Eliot, it may be this aspect
of Eliot's work and thought that Yeats saved him from. Charles Thorn-
bury, for one, strongly suggests that Berryman derived from Yeats his

conviction that poetry came from personality—a conviction that flew in the face of contemporary critical orthodoxy, and of Eliot's then widely accepted theory of impersonality. Accepting the National Book Award in 1969 for *His Toy, His Dream, His Rest*, Berryman called "Homage" "an attack on *The Waste Land*: personality, and plot—no anthropology, no Tarot pack, no Wagner" (quoted in Haffenden 352). These remarks reiterate a 1965 comment in which Berryman had noted how, in writing "Homage," he saw himself as consciously producing an anti-*Waste Land*:

> When I finally woke up to the fact that I was involved in a long poem, one of my first thoughts was: Narrative! let's have narrative, and at least one dominant personality, and no fragmentation! In short, let us have something spectacularly NOT The Waste Land, the best long poem of the age. So maybe hostility keeps on going. (*Freedom* 327)

In 1970 he was equally explicit: "In *Homage to Mistress Bradstreet* my model was *The Waste Land*, and *Homage to Mistress Bradstreet* is as unlike *The Waste Land* as it is possible for me to be" ("Art of Poetry" 29). Given these feelings, it is ironic that Edmund Wilson, who had written an early major critical essay on *The Waste Land* and who hosted a private reading of "Homage" in his home when Berryman finished the poem, should in a jacket blurb call "Homage" "the most distinguished long poem by an American since *The Waste Land*."

Berryman objected, as I have said, to Eliot's theory of impersonality, a theory that in his view threatened to negate the expression of angst that he had used the voice of Bradstreet, rather transparently, to achieve. He tended not merely to suspect but directly to invert arguments about impersonality. In his biography of Stephen Crane, the book for which he suspended his work on "Homage," he writes: "The new *Literary History* [*of the United States*] describes the hero of *The Red Badge* as 'impersonal and typical,' for which read: intensely personal and individual" (290). This issue became such a bête noire for Berryman that even in so obscure a place as his introduction to a paperback edition of Thomas Nashe's *The Unfortunate Traveller*, he refers to Eliot's "intolerable and perverse theory of the impersonality of the artist" (*Freedom* 12). Yet he could also, in the course of contrasting Eliot and Whitman, describe the theory less vehemently as "amusing," while opting himself for a different (and Whitmanesque) theory:

> The poet . . . fills with experiences, a valve opens; he speaks them. I am obliged to remark that I prefer this theory of poetry to those that have ruled the critical quarterlies since I was an undergraduate twenty-five years ago. (*Freedom* 230, 232)

Berryman returns consistently, almost obsessively, to this point. In a 1968 interview he comments on his "strong disagreement with Eliot's line—the impersonality of poetry . . . ; it seems to me on the contrary that poetry comes out of personality" ("Interview" 5). In the year that he began "Homage," he reviewed a collection of critical essays on Eliot, and used the occasion to question again Eliot's critical theories: "Perhaps in the end this poetry which the commentators are so eager to prove impersonal will prove to be personal, and will also appear the more terrible and more pitiful even than it does now" ("A Peine Ma Piste" 828)—a prophetic insight. One year later, in an essay originally intended as the introduction to a New Directions selection of Pound's poetry, he traces this "perverse and valuable doctrine" back to Goethe and Keats.[23] What it obscures in Keats, he argues revealingly, is what we might now call the anxiety of influence: "It hides motive, which persists. It fails to enable us to see, for instance, that the dominant source of inspiration in Keats's sonnet on Chapman's Homer is *antagonism*, his contempt for Pope and Pope's Homer" (*Freedom* 264–65). To espouse such a "personal" theory of poetry was to deny and seek to displace the most widely held aesthetic tenet of his age. In 1970, when Berryman recalls that as a younger poet "I had to fight shy of Eliot," he adds, "there was a certain amount of hostility in it, too" ("Art of Poetry" 24), echoing the comment on Eliot quoted earlier: "Maybe hostility keeps on going."

I have mentioned earlier the conjunction of Berryman's identification with *Partisan Review* and that journal's promotion of Eliot. The extent to which *Partisan* was a Middle Generation organ can be measured in a number of different ways. Berryman published more poems (thirteen) in *Partisan* than in any other periodical except *Poetry*; he appeared in more issues of *Partisan* than any other magazine, including six out of seven issues between February and August 1948 (the year in which he began "Homage"). Berryman published his thirteen *Partisan* poems between 1939 and 1962. Over that same approximate period, the magazine showed remarkable consistency in its commitment to the poetry of Berryman's group. Schwartz published sixteen poems in *Partisan* between 1938 and 1976; Jarrell published twenty-two from 1939 to 1963; Lowell published thirty-eight (excluding his Baudelaire "imitations," which also appeared there) from 1943 to 1966. The record of poets peripherally associated with this group is similar: *Partisan* carried seventeen Bishop poems from 1938 to 1961, eleven Roethke poems from 1939 to 1963. During the early years of Berryman's career—the forties and early fifties—*Partisan* served equally as an organ for Middle Generation criticism. Jarrell published nine essays there between 1940 and

1952, and Schwartz, the poetry editor, ten essays between 1939 and
1953. (It was Schwartz who requested "Homage" for *Partisan* when he
first heard Berryman read the poem.) In an intense burst of involve-
ment and activity, Berryman published six essays and reviews between
1947 and 1949, and overall he published more critical prose there than
anywhere else.

While Berryman and the others were trying to establish themselves
as the poets of the coming age in *Partisan*, the magazine celebrated Eliot
as the Poet of the current Age. That is, Eliot's reputation, clearly estab-
lished well before Berryman began his own poetic career, was debated,
perpetuated, and celebrated in the magazine with which Berryman and
his closest contemporaries most fully identified. It was in *Partisan* that
Delmore Schwartz published his well-known essays on Eliot as "inter-
national hero" (1945) and as "literary dictator" (1949)—essays that stress
Eliot's representativeness, the dominance of his reputation, and, not
least important, his successful shaping and reshaping of the Anglo-
American poetic canon. Eliot himself published both "East Coker"
(1940) and "The Dry Salvages" (1941) there, as well as the essays "The
Music of Poetry" (1942) and "Notes toward a Definition of Culture"
(1944), and a 1942 letter to the editors.

The particular forum in which "Homage" first appeared is just one
of many factors suggesting that the can of canonization has more in it
than a few worms reading each other's poems. Canons are more than
a series of triple plays, Milton to Keats to Stevens. Berryman's use of
Bradstreet must be looked at from a more multifaceted perspective. He
finds in her a female precursor who enables him to sidestep issues of
literary paternity, specifically his relationship with Eliot. He turns to
her as an inspirational example (not only for himself but implicitly for
his contemporaries too) for dealing with the poet's situation in a cul-
ture seen as inimical to poetry. Berryman mythologizes Bradstreet,
turning her into a figure in the psychic melodrama of his whole "tragic"
generation, the generation also of Jarrell, Schwartz, and Lowell. We
have, then, a case of one poet canonizing not another's actual work,
but her poetic stance, in his poetry. To the extent that Berryman writes
his own self-canonizing ambitions into "Homage," the poem seems to
confirm Bloom's view of how poets canonize themselves and others.
Berryman's response to Bradstreet, however, is not aesthetic. He does
not incorporate her work into his own through the metalepsis or
transumption that Bloom sees as the defining trope shaping poetic
traditions; and he writes in full awareness of the institutional factors
affecting his own canonical status.

Berryman's putative power to revive interest in Bradstreet through his own poetry cannot in practice be separated from the institutional conditions of his poetry's creation and reception or from his own self-interest and needs as a poet. Though Berryman sometimes complained about the initial lack of attention paid to *Homage*, the reviews that helped secure the book's and the poet's reputations appeared in highly influential outlets: the *New Yorker, Poetry, Partisan Review, Saturday Review, Hudson Review, Yale Review, New Republic*, the *New York Times Book Review, Prairie Schooner*. Further, these institutional conditions, and the view of American literary history that they sustained, were especially receptive to Berryman's particular version of Bradstreet's career, a version that presented her as a pre-Romantic *poète maudit* in conflict with her culture. By celebrating the margin, Berryman inserts himself at the center. Compared with a contemporary like Olson—who, ironically, published an essay in the voice of Berryman's hero Yeats in *Partisan Review*—Berryman can hardly be described as a marginal poet in critical and institutional terms after the first ten years of his career. In fact he inserts himself into the most established narrative in American literary history, that of the major writer in conflict with his or her culture. In this story, "major" literary status is almost synonymous with social marginality: the latter does not guarantee the former, but the former is rarely conferred without the latter.

It has not been my intention in this chapter to refute the aesthetic model of canon formation directly, but rather to offer a counterexample that can illustrate what that model leaves out. My point in discussing Berryman and "Homage," then, is threefold. First, poets' interest in or canonization of others does not always rest on matters of style or language, and indeed sometimes involves specifically dismissing style as a factor—contrary to Vendler and Bloom, who make style central to their poet-centered theories of canonicity. Second, contrary to Bloom, ambitious self-canonization and the (apparent) canonization of others are intertwined in ways that also do not involve style. And third, especially from the mid-twentieth century on, questions of canonicity cannot be adequately understood without reference to the institutional contexts of poetry's circulation and reception. Such questions can be *partly* understood through an aesthetic model of canon formation, I agree. But they cannot be wholly understood in this way, despite what Vendler and Bloom's rhetoric often suggests. Some of the institutional forces that the aesthetic model overlooks, then, form the subject of my next chapter.

3

The New Criticism and American Poetry in the Academy

As my preceding discussion of institutional theorists suggests, much recent work on canons holds the academy to be a crucial force in canon formation in this century. This is especially so in poetry, given the fact that the academy is the main (though not the only) site for the consumption and production of poetry, given the dominance of poetry publishing by university presses, and given the small amount of serious attention paid to poetry outside of scholarly and university-affiliated literary publications.[1] This situation has its roots in the moment of the New Criticism, which, with the decline of literary journalism, successfully moved poetry criticism into the university in the thirties and forties. To reconstruct some features of this historical moment illuminates the process by which the academy became a central canonizing force in American poetry. As it becomes increasingly clear that the traditional high modernist canon is only one possible canon among many, there is a special historical lesson in seeing how that canon, dominant for decades and even now recontextualized rather than superseded, was constructed. The fact that the New Criticism made questions of value, of canonicity, explicit in a way that they had not been before makes the movement additionally important for any historical understanding of canons in American poetry.

I will begin this chapter, then, by examining the institutional politics of the New Criticism, to show how the movement placed evaluation—acts of canonizing—at the heart of its defense of English studies. I will go on to discuss who exactly was doing the evaluating. Criticism moved into the academy—to the point, as William Cain argues, where "English studies" and "criticism" became virtually synonymous—largely under the auspices of people who were poets first, professors second: men (for they were all men) who could be termed poet-professors. Yet few historians of the profession have asked why this matters, or treated the figure of the New Critical poet-professor as significantly different from that of the nonacademic poet-critic like Pound or Eliot. I propose to do so, and to examine how the interests of the poet-professors, as a distinctive kind of literary professional, shaped their thinking about poetic canons.

Then, since to talk about *American* poetry, not just poetry, is to raise questions about literary nationalism and an indigenous poetry, I will review the particular version of American literary history that the New Critics proposed—including their suppression of the very category "American"—by analyzing their treatment of Whitman. Whitman is an especially useful figure for this discussion because a number of factors relevant to understanding the creation of the modernist canon converge in the New Critics' treatment of him: their resistance to nationalism and to Romanticism, their generally conservative politics (and their related opposition to Whitman's widespread adoption by the American left), their hidden homophobia, their not so hidden masculinist biases (occasionally, though not consistently, expressed as overt misogyny). Finally, I will address one particular means through which New Critical judgments and methods were spread through all levels of the academy and to a next generation of teachers and readers: the influential textbook *Understanding Poetry*.

Evaluation and the Institutional Politics of New Criticism

We actually have a good deal for which to thank the New Critics. For decades, it has been critically *de rigueur* to deprecate the narrowness of New Critical paradigms for reading poetry. But before the New Criticism, nobody in the academy had any paradigms to offer at all. These critics were "New" not so much in contrast to an earlier group of "Old" critics, but rather by virtue of simply being *critics*. In the institutional history of English departments, the New Critics are important not only for the nature of their definition of poetry, but also for the simple fact that they had a definition—one that provided a set of interpretive principles for a discipline that hitherto had lacked them, and that provided a basis for subsequent debate, disagreement, and divergence. In gaining acceptance for these principles, the New Critics changed the very definition of English studies. They proposed both a critical method, to counter the profession's almost exclusively historical emphasis, and a canon, that of modernist poetry, which seemed to prove not merely the method's usefulness but its necessity to the profession's survival.

An academic field of study defines itself and justifies its existence by foregrounding and laying special claim to a certain area of knowledge. Thus English, like all other academic departments, "emphasize[s] the unique identity of its subject, its special qualities and language, its special distinction as an activity of research and investigation" (Bledstein 327). Historically the canon—the *idea* of a canon as much as a specific group of texts, authors, and reading practices—has demarcated the boundaries of English studies and acted as a form of quality control; it has helped English departments present themselves as having a specific body of knowledge to impart. As Richard Ohmann bluntly remarks, from its beginnings "English had to look like a subject" (*English in America* 243), and the canon was its subject. Similarly, the New Criticism had to look like a valid method, and (along with metaphysical poetry) the canon of modernist poetry was a crucial part of the "subject" that it promoted to validate itself.

The institutional beginnings of the New Criticism are familiar enough to most readers, and laid out thoroughly in books like William Cain's *The Crisis in Criticism* and Gerald Graff's *Professing Literature*. The New Critics sought not merely to read poems closely but, in doing so, to reconstitute the field of English studies. This ambition emerges clearly from John Crowe Ransom's often-cited 1938 essay "Criticism, Inc.," one of the first calls for a professional literary criticism, and a response to historical scholars who claimed that criticism was not intellectually rigorous enough to qualify as a professional activity (*World's Body* 335). Ransom reports the case of the head of a major graduate English program telling an uppity graduate student that "we don't allow criticism here, because that is something which anybody can do" (335). Similarly, Allen Tate's 1940 essay "Miss Emily and the Bibliographer" begins with a story about a professor "whose special field is English bibliography of the decade 1840–1850" and who warns his graduate students that in their papers "there must be no impressionism. There must be no literary criticism. Anybody can write that" (*Essays* 141). Whether such anecdotes are apocryphal or true does not matter; they attest clearly to the sense of mutual antagonism that critics and historical scholars felt in the late 1930s.

Against the charges of amateurism, Ransom argues that criticism should be "professional," and "must be developed by the collective and sustained effort of learned persons—which means that its proper seat is in the universities." One job for such professionals will be "the erection of intelligent standards of criticism" (*World's Body* 328-29) for making the evaluative judgments that shape and reshape canons, and Ransom contrasts the new critic with the old historical scholar on precisely this basis: the historian can "spend a lifetime in compiling the data of literature and yet rarely or never commit himself to a literary judgment" (328). No more equipped to make such canon-forming judgments, in Ransom's view, are those who, lacking independent principles of taste, teach subjective "appreciation" of a canon already established for them: "The professors so engaged are properly curators, and the museum of which they have the care is furnished with the cherished literary masterpieces, just as another museum might be filled with paintings" (339). The contemporary canon in particular will be shaped not by historical methods but by the criticism that Ransom proposes: "Contemporary literature . . . is almost obliged to receive critical study if it receives any at all, since it is hardly capable of the usual historical scholarship" (336).

The New Critics were actually entering an already strongly contested domain, following through on (rather than originating) a methodological debate that went back at least to Irving Babbitt's *Literature and the American College* (1908) and Joel Spingarn's 1910 essay "The New Criticism," with its proposal of criticism rather than scholarship as the profession's proper focus. In 1928 Henry Seidel Canby argued that it was "time to turn some portion of our great energy away from the accurate recording of literary history to the study of literature itself" ("American Scholar" 3). Two decades of such arguments, then, paved the way for the New Critics' efforts to displace the historical method from its professional dominance.

Why, in the moment of transition, did the New Criticism win out over a number of other methodological options—Marxist criticism, the neo-humanism of Paul Elmer More, Babbitt, and Norman Foerster (the two schools that Allen Tate complained in 1937 "have dominated recent criticism" [*Reason* 160]), the "transactional" theory of reading espoused in Louise Rosenblatt's *Literature as Exploration*? Why, indeed, did the critics think that "history," historical scholarship, needed replacing? First, Marxism was not a viable alternative for a discipline both pretending to ideological neutrality and seeking to establish its own distinctive method, and thus its separateness from other humanistic fields. Marxist critics probably went too far in collapsing disciplinary boundaries through their use of political and sociological analysis, while "English" sought to bolster its disciplinary identity precisely by differentiating its concerns from those of ethics and politics (Cain, *Crisis of Criticism* 98). It had not yet acquired the solidity that more recently has allowed it to assimilate Marxist criticism as another field under the umbrella term "theory." Moreover, a young discipline undergoing a crisis of confidence will almost inevitably exclude a critical ideology that implicitly undermines the institution (the academy) in which the discipline is seeking a stable position. In addition, the Hitler-Stalin Pact left many literary intellectuals disillusioned with leftist politics, further reducing the viability of a leftist criticism in the academy.[2]

Turning to the other available alternatives to historical scholarship: neohumanism, as Gerald Graff has argued, came with too much ethical and moral baggage attached, and with too ill-defined a method, to answer the profession's needs to prove its intellectual rigor and unique disciplinary identity. Moreover, neohumanism shared the historicists' distaste for contemporary literature. Its demise was effectively announced by C. Hartley Grattan's 1930 essay collection *The Critique of Humanism*, which included work by Tate, R. P. Blackmur, and Yvor Winters. Meanwhile, Rosenblatt's early form of reader-response theory, focusing as it did far more on the reader than on the author or text, must have appeared to the old guard even more impressionistic than "criticism." Moreover, like Marxists and humanists, Rosenblatt "mixed" aesthetic with other concerns. As Temma Berg puts it, "Rosenblatt's pedagogy is deeply ethical. For Rosenblatt, the aesthetic and the social are not divorced from one another; they are, in fact, the same" (253). Given too the difficulties faced by a lone female critic writing in a time dominated by groups of men, it is hardly surprising that Rosenblatt's theories made little initial headway.

While the historical scholars thought that all of these alternatives had their weaknesses, their own method was hoist on the petard of its limited self-definition. Norman Foerster made the classic argument against the old historicists in *The American Scholar* (1929). He argued that they were preoccupied with description at the expense of analysis, and so were just as interested in bad books as in good ones; they had given literary study over to the scientific method and so betrayed it. Despite spirited and convincing theoretical defenses of the kind offered by Edwin Greenlaw in *The Province of Literary History* (1931), the discrepancy between emerging theory and the old trivia-grubbing practice made historical scholarship increasingly hard to justify to students.[3] Further, canon formation was not a project, but a precondition, for the historicists' practice. Hence they could not accommodate a lively contemporary literature that, despite academic hostility to it, insistently demanded attention and that modified radically the sense of "tradition" within which the historicists worked. In contrast, the emerging New Critical view of criticism as evaluation and of modernist poetry as a body of work ripe for evaluation dovetailed conveniently. The poetry also gave the critics a subject with which not only many general readers but even plenty of academics could make no headway. Confronting its complexities, the New Critics would seek to assess, explain, and canonize the "difficult."

One key document for understanding the New Critics' campaign to change the nature of English studies is Ransom's 1940 essay "Strategy for English Studies," the title itself a clue to his concerns. Ransom's topic is quite explicitly the survival of the profession. Historical scholarship has done all that it can, he argues, and has outlived not only its scholarly but its institutional usefulness. If the professors don't look around for something else to do, they'll be out of work. English departments need "a new order of studies: the speculative or critical ones" (227).

Ransom reviews a familiar body of differences between the old historical scholars and the new critics: while literary history is too general, criticism will be more specific; while literary history avoids value judgments, criticism actively pursues them. The emphasis on judgment, here as elsewhere in Ransom's writing, is especially strong.[4] Consistently Ransom links evaluation, seen as central to the critical act, and the ambition to change the nature of the discipline, to change English teachers' own definition of their profession. For the New Critics, making informed aesthetic judgments will be what defines English studies as a distinctive professional enterprise. To see this explicit conjunction of evaluation and professionalism in the New Critics' thinking gives some historical perspective to contemporary views of the academy's central role in canon formation.

To the extent that it stresses evaluation and judgment, criticism creates or preserves canons, and canons preserve the institution of "English" by providing its subject matter. The New Critics were quite aware that the institution of English studies had to do something to survive in an increasingly scientific and technocratic culture; the canon and critical method that they carved out mutually reinforced each other and helped preserve the institution.[5] In this way, new as their critical methods and the particular canon that they promoted were, the New Critics continued to do what the earliest professors of English had done: they privileged a canon as a way to define and justify their work, to demonstrate their standards, and to perpetuate a particular version of "culture."

In much the same terms as Ransom, other New Critics similarly link evaluation with the future of the profession. Cleanth Brooks presents the evaluative dimension of criticism as essential to the survival of the humanities; in *The Well-Wrought Urn*, he argues that "the Humanities are in their present plight largely because their teachers have more and more ceased to raise normative questions, have refrained from evaluation." Hence "the proponents of the Humanities have tended to give up any claim to making a peculiar and special contribution." Criticism, however, will save the day; or at least it will save literature teachers from being "quietly relegated to a comparatively obscure corner of the history division" or "treated as sociologists, though perhaps not as a very important kind of sociologist" (235). For Tate, evaluation is a moral responsibility; "the literary source-hunter" who evades judgment cheapens literature and is no more than a mere sociologist (*Essays* 202). Yvor Winters, who shared a number of New Critical principles, states that "the primary function of criticism is evaluation, and . . . unless criticism succeeds in providing a usable system of evaluation it is worth very little" (*Function* 17). In *Theory of Literature*, René Wellek and Austin Warren link evaluation with the "intrinsic" study of literature, a form of study that carves out a special niche for literary professionals by separating literature from—to use their chapter titles—biography, psychology, society, ideas, and the other arts. W. K. Wimsatt and Monroe Beardsley assume, throughout "The Intentional Fallacy," that poetry criticism means "the public art of evaluating poems" and therefore requires formulating "precise terms of evaluation" (*Verbal Icon* 9).

Changes in the literary profession's self-definition, in what its members think they are doing, affect, of course, the view of what constitute canonical texts within the profession. Equally, changes in the canon will affect the profession's sense of identity and purpose. Given this close relationship between canonical texts and professional identity, changes in the literary academy that stress the act of evaluating or reevaluating texts, authors, and basic principles are likely to have an especially powerful impact. Canons are most likely to be explicitly at issue when the field is undergoing a paradigm shift, as it was in the late thirties and as it has in the last two decades. (This is one reason why the contemporary debate on canonicity, because it is deeply linked to issues of professional self-definition, is likely to have a lasting effect.)

It is well known that the advent of the New Criticism affected profoundly the shaping of the modern American poetry canon, that New

Criticism and modernist poetry were, almost literally, made for each other. The difficulties of modern poetry required both a defense and a trained audience that did not yet exist for these "poets without laurels," as Ransom called them. The New Criticism was designed both to defend and to explicate this poetry, and to reconstitute the English and American poetry canons in accord with a revised "tradition" that led directly to Eliot. It was to this end that the work of the New Critics constituted the first systematic attempt within the academy to establish an American poetry canon. Brooks articulates the conjunction between New Critical method and modernist texts in one of the movement's central (and more polemical) texts, *Modern Poetry and the Tradition* (1939): "Most of the modern poets treated herein are regarded as being excessively difficult. This study provides, I hope, some sort of explanation for that 'difficulty.' But the best defense against the charge of unintelligibility is to submit detailed interpretations." Modern poetry needs a new kind of reading:

From time to time, poets appear, who, if they are accepted at all, demand a radical revision of the existing conception of poetry. Of this sort are our modern poets, and herein lies the difficulty of accepting them, or, if they are accepted, the difficulty of accommodating them in the traditionally accepted pattern. (xxxi)[6]

In his 1940 essay "Understanding Modern Poetry," Allen Tate echoes Brooks by arguing that current academic reading habits are inapplicable to that poetry, and, like Ransom, mocks his colleagues' dependence on historical materials and received opinion. Discussing the negative view of modern poetry represented in Max Eastman's *The Literary Mind*, Tate comments that "Mr. Eastman has been widely read by professors of English, who are really rather glad to hear this sort of thing, since it spares them the trouble of reading a body of poetry for which there are no historical documents and of which generations of other professors have not told them what to think" (*Essays* 158).

By 1951, the year of his *Autobiography*, William Carlos Williams had substantial basis for his well-known complaint that *The Waste Land* "gave the poem back to the academics" (*Autobiography* 146). Brooks's *Modern Poetry and the Tradition* contained a pivotal essay on Eliot, "*The Waste Land*: Critique of the Myth." Brooks begins his comments on Eliot by claiming that "there has been little or no attempt to deal with [*The Waste Land*] as a unified whole" (136), and as Peter Middleton argues, in 1939 *The Waste Land* represented the ultimate test of a critic's ability to find unity in disparateness ("Academic Development" 154).[7] It was also the ideal ground on which to respond to contemporary historical scholars and to prove the validity of New Critical method. A large percentage of people might be able to read, or write criticism on, Carl Sandburg, Vachel Lindsay, Edgar Lee Masters, Edna St. Vincent Millay, Sara Teasdale, or even Whitman or Frost—a number of whom Brooks dismisses in his Eliot essay and elsewhere in the book. Far fewer could deal with *The Waste Land, The Cantos,* or a Dickinson lyric. A critical method that could unlock the mysteries of the more arcane modernist texts, that could create unity and coherence out of discontinuity and fragments, could instantly prove its value and necessity to the profession. Thus it served the interests of up-and-coming academics in the 1930s and 1940s to canonize "difficult" work, work not readily accessible to the unaided general reader, and that justified the existence of "specialists." A New Critical reading of *The Waste Land* showed that in fact not just anyone could do criticism—only the pros could.

Amateurism, Professionalism, and the Poet-Professor

I have shown how criticism as the New Critics conceived it would be centrally concerned with evaluation. I now want to address the fact that this professional academic criticism was started by critics who were poets first, professors second. I am thinking especially of Ransom, Winters, Tate, Blackmur, and Warren, all of whom published between one (in Blackmur's case) and six (in Winters' case) books of poetry before publishing a book of criticism or theory. This has a number of implications. First, as practicing writers, they saw evaluation as one defining feature of criticism. Second, their concept of criticism was, at root, an amateur or nonacademic one. And third, they therefore felt a certain conflict over the project of professionalizing criticism, even as they saw the necessity of that project. In what follows, I'll explore the implications of these implications. In the previous chapter, I proposed a model of canonicity that could account for the influence in twentieth-century canon formation both of poets and of institutions. Looking at the New Critics in these terms allows us to understand more deeply the dynamics of poetic canon formation at one of its central defining moments. The New Critics were poets who sought to shape canons; but they did so in their roles as professor-critics, from positions of institutional authority.

How does the figure of the New Critical poet-professor relate to those of the poet-critic and the man of letters—the public critic or literary journalist? In *The Function of Criticism,* Terry Eagleton suggests that the role of the "man of letters" evolved as an attempt to reconcile quasi-professional critical expertise with the amateur's appeal to an educated lay audience. That is, it became the site where conceptions of the amateur and professional critic met. As Robert von Hallberg and Herbert Lindenberger, among others, have observed, such critics—frequently, though not always, poets—have traditionally felt themselves responsible for evaluation, especially of contemporary literature. Public critics have typically sought to instruct readers on the best and worst and train them to make these distinctions for themselves—the activity that the New Critics tried to transfer to the classroom. In 1928, for instance, Edmund Wilson wrote to Maxwell Perkins on his plans for *Axel's Castle*: "I want to give popular accounts of [modernist writers] which will convince people of their importance and persuade people to read them" (150). The significance of the New Critics' status as poet-professors, then, lies in their effort to import the role of the evaluative poet-critic into the academy. They wanted both to maintain evaluation as the central critical function of the amateur, nonacademic man of letters and also to give that function a professional power base. The New Critics realized that, with the demise of literary journalism (outside of leftist publications to which they were unsympathetic), it was through the academy that they could most effectively institutionalize and gain an audience for the acts of evaluation that had historically been the preserve of public criticism. As Blackmur put it in 1939, "I do not see how aside from journalism serious and technical literary criticism can command more than an audience of a few thousand, *unless it is taken up in the colleges*" ("Situation in American Writing" 118; my emphasis).

The New Critics' concept of professional criticism involved maintaining a close connection between the functions of poet and critic—a connection embodied in the poet-professor. If Ransom wanted the poetry critic to be a professional, the professional critic who was also a poet knew best what he or she was talking about. One of Robert Penn Warren's qualifications for editing *Understanding Poetry* is that he is a poet, Ransom notes in a review, and "an understanding of poetry must be considered as beyond dispute only when it is referred to the possession of the poet himself." Ransom goes on to argue that the graduate training of poetry professors should include "courses in the actual operation of the art, as composition" ("Teaching of Poetry" 82). Likewise, Ransom writes elsewhere, "Mr. Tate is not the ordinary university professor. He has generally had his own vocation as an actual creative writer and critic" ("Mr. Tate and the Professors" 348). The role of the poet-professor, for Tate, was to make a "contribution to the education of new artists," and "Mr. Tate defines the project of creative writing indifferently under three heads: as fiction, as verse, and as literary criticism" (349).[8] The New Critics had little problem with the notion that poets could influence criticism and that criticism could, and should, influence poetry.

Some of the most vigorous defenses of the poet-professor's function come from Yvor Winters, beginning with the "Post Scripta" to *The Anatomy of Nonsense* (1943). Winters shares the skepticism of Ransom and others about the average English professor's ability to "judge a new poem accurately," but finds one important exception among the professors: that of "a few relatively young men who are also poets" (*Defense* 557). For Winters, the best critic combines the talents and discipline of poet and scholar, and this poet-professor-critic "offers more hope for the invigoration of American literature than does anything else in sight" and "the only hope for American criticism" (574).

Winters' key exception—the young poet-professor-critics—was sometimes overlooked by his readers. Reviewing *In Defense of Reason* in 1947, William Barrett writes, "the university life that Winters lauds is, after all, the one that has produced and permits" this alleged professorial inability to judge contemporary writing. Barrett continues, "How is it he does not see that this is an appalling indictment of the institution he expects will foster the production of new literature?" ("Temptations" 549). Appalling indictment, perhaps—but Barrett glosses over Winters' hope (frustrated in his own lifetime, one has to feel) that poets in the institution might change it.[9] Barrett's own agenda, which also drove much of his work as a central contributor to *Partisan Review*, becomes clear later in his review: "The sociological fact is that academies in the past have maintained their vitality . . . through the existence of a vigorous intellectual elite outside the university," he argues, but unhappily "this extra-university elite has been rapidly disappearing from the general scene, as it is devoured by one or another corporate form of culture" (550)—including, Barrett would presumably claim, the university. By the mid–late 1940s, *Partisan* saw its role as that of preserving this elite.[10]

Winters, however, maintained his view of the poet-professor throughout his career. Against Hayden Carruth's claim that the academic life forced the poet out of "real" life and into an ivory tower, Winters asserted that university teaching had saved his poetry:

It was the necessities of teaching which forced me to clarify my ideas about literature, and it was this clarification of ideas which enabled me to write the only poems which I am interested in preserving. Had it not been for my academic career, it is quite possible that I should still be a minor disciple of W. C. Williams, doing little impressionistic notes on landscapes. ("Poet and the University" 308)

Winters was not alone in his view of the relations between teaching and writing. Robert Penn Warren similarly thought teaching of great value to a writer: "a teacher is forced to clarify—or try to clarify—his own mind on certain questions which are necessarily involved in the business of writing" (*Wilson Library Bulletin* 652). In a 1942 review of Allen Tate's anthology *Princeton Verse between Two Wars*, Warren devotes his central paragraph to the "tendency to bring the arts, as practiced, and not merely as a subject for scholarship, into closer contact with the academic world." He argues that the "potential gains" far outweigh the "dangers":

The teaching of literature . . . could well profit by a fuller understanding of the nature and vital processes of literature. And contemporary writing could well profit, in intellectual depth and technical range, by a more intimate contact with the literature of the past. It is possible that such a tendency may help to raise both artistic and academic standards. ("Poets and Scholars" 137)

Reviewing his own career in a 1956 essay, Winters recalls how Irving Babbitt had been considered "a dangerous innovator" at Harvard for defending criticism as a valid academic discipline. Yet many of Winters' generation considered Babbitt the quintessential Professor. Why? Because "he was quite obviously imperceptive in writing about poetry" (*Function* 11). Winters turned to Pound, who "for about fifteen years . . . was the most influential critic in American letters" until replaced by "his disciple Eliot" (12). Aspiring poet-critics in Winters' youth learned from poets, not professors; but still he came to feel that the best way to combat professors' obtuseness about poetry was to have poets as professors.

What allowed critics like Ransom and Winters to think they could professionalize criticism without turning it into a mechanical routine? In the late 1930s, the idea of the disinterested professional still carried a moral and ethical weight that fit closely with the New Criticism's claim to perform disinterested criticism. Thomas Haskell glosses this belief as the idea that people in professions characteristically subordinate self-interest to higher ends—the truth, the public interest, the welfare of individual clients, the quality of the work itself—and thereby stand on a higher moral plane than those who merely truck and trade in the marketplace. (181)

In this context, "professionalism appeared to be a promising corrective, or even antithesis, to capitalism" (186)—a notion especially appealing, I suspect, to those New Critics who had only recently abandoned the agrarian agenda of *I'll Take My Stand*. Among academics generally, and even among sociologists, those most likely to be occupied with the nature and functions of professions, this idea of professional disinterestedness was not seriously challenged until 1939 (in an early essay by Talcott Parsons). Rather, Haskell argues,

professions and professionalization were not subjects of great interest to sociologists before the late 1930s. What sociologists did have to say on the subject in these years presupposed both a strong kinship between university professors and non-academic professionals, and the moral superiority of all professionals to businessmen. (220)

This opposition of professionalism and capitalism has been untenable for a long time now. It was still thought tenable, however, when most of the New Critics were starting their careers, and it helps explain why Ransom might seek to professionalize criticism.[11]

At the same time, in the first generation of New Critics we find, along with the push toward professionalization, a deep self-division over that issue. Ransom was always reluctant to explain why he stopped writing poetry in his major years as a critic, but Robert Penn Warren suggests that Ransom did so because "he did not want to be a 'professional' and merely build a reputation. He wanted to be an 'amateur' " and not have poetry become a job (*New and Selected Essays* 326). Apparently Ransom associated the amateur with poetry, the professional with criticism, and held "amateur" as something of an honorific term.

Meanwhile, although the criticism that Ransom proposed would reside in universities, he also stressed that it had its roots outside them. In 1940 he defines criticism as "a kind of discourse I have come to know from the writings of such critics as Richards, Eliot, Empson and Winters, none of whom so far as I know is a professor of literature or a contributor to PMLA" ("Strategy" 230). Well, three out of four isn't bad. Winters, of course, *was* "a professor of literature" at this time, though he felt himself outside the professional mainstream and was also a well-published poet.[12] The point is that Ransom wants to establish a professional criticism while maintaining a sense of its nonacademic, amateur, or maverick origins. His view recalls Blackmur's well-known definition of criticism as "the formal discourse of an amateur" (*Language* 372).

Blackmur himself records a wariness, characteristic among first-generation New Critics, as to the consequences of the very professionalism they sought—Blackmur, of whom Russell Fraser writes, "He had wanted to be a great poet, and became in his own view a mere professor" (540). By 1950, Blackmur feels, New Criticism is already sterile; means have become confused with ends, "a skill [has] become a method and a method become a methodology" (*Lion* 190–91). In response, Blackmur imagines a new rapprochement between criticism and scholarship, and his terms are revealing:

> the complete scholar-critic . . . must be the master-layman of as many modes of human understanding as possible. . . . I do not say a master but a master-layman . . . he will conceive of himself, as a lover ought, as only a layman with respect to his beloved, and at best a master-layman. (183)

Notice this professional critic's ambivalent rhetoric of amateurism and professionalism: "master" on the one hand, "lover" (or amateur) and "layman" on the other. For Blackmur, the routinizing (to borrow Gerald Graff's term) of New Criticism involves too much professionalism, and a corrective dose of amateurism is needed. Along similar lines, five years later Allen Tate complained that "our critics . . . have been perfecting an apparatus for 'explicating' poems . . . , *innocent of the permanently larger ends of criticism*" (*Essays* 212; my emphasis).

Complaints about this critical routinization from other quarters similarly associated it with an excess of professionalism. (These complaints, it is worth adding, make clear that the New Critical hegemony of the fifties, often presented in histories of criticism as all-pervasive and relatively uncontested, was in fact strongly contested even at its peak.) Leslie Fiedler called for an "amateur criticism" "wary of bureaucratization," arguing that "the ideal form for critical discourse is the irresponsible, non-commercial book-review" ("Toward an Amateur Criticism" 562, 571). This is one of many arguments in the 1950s for what W. K. Wimsatt terms "a sort of emancipation from criticism, a New Amateurism." Wimsatt cites, as one instance among many, James Sutherland's 1952 opposition between English and American criticism, the clinching virtue of the English tradition being that it is "'amateur' rather than 'professional'" (*Hateful Contraries* xiv).

In particular, as I have already argued, postwar commentators in *Partisan Review* consistently portrayed the literary academy as just another bureaucratic corporate structure, with the professor as manager, the work environment "resembling the assembly line," the MLA as "one of the large holding-companies of the profession," and its annual convention as "a version of the businessman's club" that "takes on the character of the market-place" (Wolpert 473; Arvin, "Report" 277; Wolpert 475). The skepticism about professionalism that informs William Barrett's comments on Winters and the poet-professor surfaces vividly in one of his *Partisan* essays, "The Resistance" (1946). In terms whose currency has recently been renewed, Barrett bemoans what he calls the institutionalization of the avant-garde and the bureaucratization of the writer, seeing the development of New Criticism as an example of an avant-garde's assimilation into the academy. The New Critics have become too much like other academics who

> have stakes in preserving their own form of bureaucratic specialization expressed by PMLA. Much of the critical writing by the academic avant-garde in recent years has tended to differ from the PMLA contributions of their colleagues, not so much in fundamental interest or temper, as in mere choice of subject—Eliot and the late Yeats instead of, say, Shelley and Browning. (486)

This diagnosis reads like a direct response to an essay such as Ransom's "The Bases of Criticism" (1944), in which Ransom aligns New Criticism with poetic avant-gardism. Both Barrett and Ransom grant first-generation New Criticism the status of a critical avant-garde; Ransom argues that "the professional critic is always *avant-garde*, occupying himself with poetic effects that are strange, and eventful for the development of poetic practice. Consequently he occupies himself preferably with recent and contemporary poetry." However, Ransom also characterizes "the best of the professional critics," synonymous for him with "the 'new' critics," as "writing for the bright general reader, and distancing themselves so decidedly from the all-round or academic performance" (570). He finds in these critics an ambivalence that Barrett does not acknowledge about their own academic status: "Those who have had academic titles have worn them a little cynically, and been on guard against the occupational hazard of their employment" (571).

Along with their hopes for a kind of professional amateurism, the original New Critics' commitment to evaluation was also lost in the routinization process; as Blackmur noted, the criticism designed to cope with Eliot and Yeats now refused to offer judgments on them. This commitment stayed lost. By 1952 it seemed that the association of criticism and evaluation had been institutionalized at the profession's highest levels. In that year the MLA Committee on Research Activities announced that "the essential nature of literary criticism turns on value judgments. In all of its forms, literary criticism has evaluation or judgment as its purpose. It is this characteristic which distinguishes criticism from other forms of scholarship" (29). But by this time evaluation had actually started to drop *out* of criticism, as part of the routinization that I have described. It had become an empty rhetorical convention confined to the last sentence or paragraph of an otherwise descriptive or analytic academic essay (Parrinder 269). As a number of commentators have pointed out, most recently and visibly Barbara Herrnstein Smith, for much of the post-World War II period "the entire problematic of value and evaluation has been evaded and explicitly exiled by the literary academy" (17).[13]

With the sustained attention in recent years to questions of canonicity, evaluation, both as a critical act and as a subject for theorizing, has surely returned—though not, given the intellectual climate, as pervasively as one might expect. (What has happened, rather, is that evaluation has been historicized, its contingency made clear, but it has not returned to a central place in critical practice.) One could argue that evaluation had never gone (because it *can* never go) away, that it had merely gone underground, but had continued to work implicitly all along through anthology selections, publishers' and magazines' editorial policies, teaching practices, unspoken ideological biases, and so on. Indeed, that is one of this book's central assumptions: that evaluation never disappears; it just hides out for a while. It is not, in Henry Louis Gates's formulation, "that anybody actually stopped judging. Literary evaluation merely ceased to be a professionally accredited act" ("Good-bye, Columbus?" 715). In the postwar period to which Herrnstein Smith refers, then, evaluation may have been "evaded" as an explicit topic, but it has still been *performed* in various *implicit* ways. The first New Critics were at least more open, making explicit evaluation—which means explicit canonizing—central to their notions of criticism and teaching.

Sharing the view that criticism and theory have tended away from evaluation, Bernard Bergonzi sees the history of English departments as organized around a split between competing notions of the place of evaluation in literary study: a split, that is, "between those who saw it as inevitably involved with making judgments and those who did not" (143). Bergonzi argues, as I have here, that

evaluative criticism enters institutional literary study under the influence of practising writers, or of critics who have a close discipular relation to them, but that in time it is rejected, like an alien organ. Writers, whose criticism arises directly from the problems and possibilities of their art, are inevitably evaluative. (146)

This "split" is finally more complicated than Bergonzi's general overview suggests, however, for it involves two stages. The first stage pitted critics against historical scholars in a struggle for control of English departments, and the critics (the "evaluators") won. But in the second stage, it was critics themselves who rejected from literary studies the evaluation that their predecessors had embraced.

The early New Critic had hoped to be a man (and they were all men) of letters in the university, a kind of amateur professional; Tate, for one, always described himself as such. But in the course of the New Criticism's institutionalization, the split between poet and critic that its first practitioners hoped to avoid did indeed occur. Symbolically, the University of Iowa writer's workshop, one of the earliest, was founded the same year as the publication of Brooks and Warren's landmark textbook *Understanding Poetry*. Many later creative programs have their origins in poets' desire to preserve poetry from an increasingly arid and routine criticism. Ron Silliman has argued, rightly, that the effect of the institutional split between criticism and the writing workshop "was to cleave critical thinking about the poem, particularly among academics, from the writing of the poem itself," and that if the original goal of writing programs was to keep theory from overwhelming practice, that goal has been achieved only by isolating and impoverishing poetry ("Canons and Institutions" 158, 167). The opposition between poetry and "theory" in the contemporary academy is only the latest manifestation of a split that began to be built into the structure of English departments forty years ago, counter to the original impulses of those critics who, as poet-theorists, were shaping a modernist canon.

The New Criticism, Whitman, and the Idea of a National Poetry

As the New Critics realized, one way that criticism could influence poetry was by proposing (and suppressing) possible models and particular versions of literary history. While we know how selective their approach to English literary history is, it is worth stressing how that selectivity extends to or affects their reading of American poetry. In fact, the New Critics rarely look at American poetry per se, because they do not, finally, see it as having its own history separable from the

English tradition. Since these critics were generally skeptical of the idea of a national poetry, it is especially revealing to examine their reading of that self-consciously national poet, Whitman, and how that reading relates in turn to their judgments on some of their contemporaries. The New Critics' Anglocentrism, and their active resistance to Whitman and the idea of an indigenous poetry, went a long way toward shaping what was for some decades an influential view of the American poetry canon.

Susan Stanford Friedman effectively collapses the binary opposition between an indigenous and an international modernism in her account of how H.D.'s expatriatism allowed her to occupy a "dynamic middle position between the internationalism of Pound and the nationalism of Williams" (96). In *A Mirror for Americanists*, William Spengemann examines it from a different angle in questioning the very category of "American literature." But the instability of this opposition does not lessen its importance in modernist critical debates. Along with the professional conflicts described earlier in this chapter, debates about literary nationalism were lively and widespread in the 1920s and 1930s (as they had always been in American literary history). During this period the Marxist Granville Hicks proclaimed the great tradition in American writing an anticapitalist one; Norman Foerster called for the reinterpretation of American literature from the humanist perspective; Van Wyck Brooks continued to argue for a democratic, progressivist reading of American literature; Parrington sought the main currents of American thought, describing his point of view as "liberal" and "Jeffersonian" (i); Perry Miller essentially founded Puritan studies. All these different endeavors shared two common features. One was a willingness to look for "extraliterary" historical continuities and large-scale sociohistorical narratives of the kind that the New Critics disavowed. The other was an interest in defining the essential "Americanness" of American thought and literature.[14] One widely read text that had helped define and formalize this approach to American literary history was the *Cambridge History of American Literature* (1917–21). Here, Norman Foerster concentrated his chapter on "Later [by which he meant 'modern'] Poets" heavily on poets in the Whitman tradition. The New Critics polemically rejected this "nationalist" interest, and their refusal had significant consequences for their evaluation of American poetry, fueling both the fierce anti-Whitmanism that pervades their work and their construction of a metaphysical Dickinson as America's key nineteenth-century poet. At stake in the New Critical rejection of

Whitman, then, were much larger questions of tradition and of American literary history, questions involving not just one poet but the whole American poetry canon.

The New Critical emphasis on the text made it inevitable that their versions of literary history would be more partial and fragmentary than most. For most of these critics, literary history is the history of a particular *kind* of text: the lyric poem to which can be attributed the characteristics of seventeenth-century English metaphysical verse. To put this slightly differently, their notion of "tradition" is a transhistorical narrative of the writing of metaphysical poems—a tradition of texts taken out of time, their historical specificity erased. This explains why Allen Tate can insist, in an essay on Dickinson, that she is like Donne; it explains why Cleanth Brooks can assert so baldly, "Blake is a metaphysical poet" (*Modern Poetry* 235).

Brooks's influential *Modern Poetry and the Tradition* exemplifies the New Critical view both of tradition and of the idea of an American poetry. Its final chapter, "Notes for a Revised History of English Poetry," is one of the few New Critical works that explicitly presents a historical argument. As the title suggests, Brooks sees his tradition as indeed an *English* one, and in defending it he shows himself actively suspicious of claims about American literary nationalism. Although he wants to rewrite the history of poetry in English to lead up to his own particular modernist canon, and although his modernists are mostly American, he shows himself largely indifferent to questions of nationality—which means that he is, in a sense, indifferent to difference, both within and between cultures. It is unnecessary here to review the stages of Brooks's revised history. Of special interest to the historian of *American* poetry, however, is the set of charges leveled against the Romantic poet-seer, explicitly against Shelley but implicitly against Whitman too: "charges of sentimentality, lack of proportion, confusion of abstract generalization with symbol, and confusion of propaganda with imaginative insight" (*Modern Poetry* 237). In contrast to Whitman, meanwhile, and in company with Hopkins, Emily Dickinson "transcended Victorianism" in her "use of vigorous metaphor, the incorporation of the difficult and unpoetic, and the use of dramatic shifts of tone" (241).[15] What Brooks calls "metaphysical structure" thus becomes a way for both critic and poet to ignore the contingencies of time and place.

When Brooks writes of the "modern poet" in his title chapter, he means, in practice (and despite his interest in Auden, Hardy, and Yeats), the modern *American* poet. Thus the burden of his argument is to suggest how the modern American poet might develop a fruitful relationship to the English poetic tradition. He divides his modern poets into those who simultaneously align their poetry with and modify this longstanding English tradition, and those who reject it "to write of American scenes, American things, and the American people" (69). This "self-conscious nationalism" Brooks finds one unhealthy result of "a violent repudiation of the poetic tradition" (73–74). It risks a contrived husk of originality surrounding a soft Whitmanesque core; it can "make the poet content merely with the presentation of a surface. Sandburg, for example, often displays a crust of modern American materials thrown over statements which are as vague, and sometimes as sentimental, as those of Whitman" (71).

As the focus for this resistance to literary nationalism, Whitman is almost inevitably excluded from the New Critical poetry canon and from any New Critical version of the history of American poetry. Whitman is to blame for the rejection of the English tradition that Brooks finds so problematic in his own contemporaries Sandburg, Lindsay, and Edgar Lee Masters, whose alleged weaknesses Brooks traces to "Whitman's appeal to the Muse to migrate from the European scene to the poetic exploitation of a virgin continent" (71). (Paradoxically, despite the possibility of other approaches to Whitman, Brooks *accepts* the nationalistic reading of Whitman that comes through the very poets whom he dismisses.)[16] To give any weight to such originating gestures in Whitman, gestures that assert discontinuity with the English tradition, would clearly jeopardize Brooks's revised history of English poetry. Meanwhile, the terms that Brooks uses to criticize Sandburg, H.D., and Masters, for instance, terms that also govern his and Warren's *Understanding Poetry*, are surely those that he would use to criticize Whitman's longer poems:

With the rejection of formal verse systems there is a reversion to loose chant lines and repetition (Sandburg's "Chicago"); complex structure, logical or symbolic, gives way to the simple method of development by cumulative accretion—poems develop by the poet's piling up detail on detail (H.D.'s "Sea Gods"); raw "content" overrides and determines form (Masters' *Spoon River Anthology*). (74)

Brooks's title, then, with its use of the definite article, is no accident. It allows for no alternative traditions, just one Tradition. Yet one goal of Sandburg's and Whitman's work, and of work like Williams' *In the American Grain*, is to uncover or create a distinctively American tradition, not to dismiss the notion of tradition entirely. Through Whitman's addresses to "recorders ages hence," "poets to come," he proclaims himself the poet who will become the past, or one source of tradition, for future American writers.[17] In reading the Whitmanian tradition as offering a choice "between the raw, unqualified present, and the dead past" (75), Brooks denies any weight to this rhetorical strategy.

Brooks's modern poet must attempt to hold on to the English metaphysical Tradition, and to forge a formal unity in poetry between past and present, between local or national and universal. As successful examples of this effort, Brooks discusses Ransom, Warren, and Tate. Whitman, on the other hand, tried to achieve a new kind of "unity," but failed: "the diverse elements in all but his best poetry tend to stay apart: there is, on the one hand, the particularity of the long 'catalogue' passages, and on the other, the too frequent, vague, and windy generality about democracy and progress" (76). Predictably, Brooks's counterexample is Dickinson, who "does achieve very often a unity which is thoroughly faithful to her New England environment and yet is not limited to local color. Her best poetry obviously manifests a structure of inclusion, and significantly enough, displays the vigorous, sometimes audacious metaphor" of the metaphysical tradition into which Brooks wants to assimilate American poetry (76). In this reading, Dickinson becomes what a number of the New Critics aspired to be, a poet rooted in but not confined to a region, empowered by her American place but still identifying with the English tradition.

Representative, like Brooks, of New Critical attitudes toward Whitman and the idea of a national poetry, Allen Tate formulates a succinct political version of these issues in his contribution to the Agrarian manifesto *I'll Take My Stand*: "Where can an American take hold of Tradition?" ("Remarks" 166). (Here Tate has in mind "tradition" in the sense of a stable, continuous culture rather than a line of literary texts.) He offers a later, literary variation of the question in a 1936 MLA talk, "Modern Poets and Convention"—a variation possibly influenced by his reading the first version of Brooks's "Modern Poetry and the Tradition" chapter, published the previous year in *Virginia Quarterly Review*. In this talk Tate wonders how the poet may become what he calls "a modern traditional poet." In the phrase of that progressivist, nationalist archenemy of the New Criticism, Van Wyck Brooks, Tate's poet seeks a usable past: "Where shall the modern poet . . . learn anything that he can use?" (*Forlorn Demon* 166–67); "Where, in Shakespeare or some other giant of the past, can he find something useful? Something that he can carry on?" (168). In developing his answers to these questions, Tate echoes Brooks's judgment on some of their contemporaries: "Much of our best second-rate poetry today repeats the language of another age," and is thus conventional rather than traditional. Like Brooks's, Tate's examples are Whitman's descendants, "Mr. Masters and the late Vachel Lindsay, who give us the romantic sensibility disguised, and a little debased" (169).

Aside from well-known essays like "Three Types of Poetry" (1934) and his essays on Poe and Crane, Tate also develops his characteristic New Critical skepticism about the American romantic sensibility, and explicitly connects that sensibility to a nationalist poetics, in the reviews that he published so prolifically in the 1920s and 1930s. Almost from the first, these reviews promote the ideal of the modern traditional poet. The type of this poet, of course, is Eliot, as Tate asserts in a 1926 review of Eliot's *Poems: 1909-1925*: "He is traditional, but in defining tradition as life, as a living cultural memory, instead of a classical dictionary stocked with literary dei ex machina, he is also the type of [the] contemporary poet" (*Poetry Reviews* 51). The reviews also consistently exhibit the more general New Critical suspicion of programmatically American subject matter, of what Tate calls in a 1929 overview, "American Poetry since 1920," "the aggressive Americanism of Sandburg, Lindsay, Masters" (80). (Years later Tate would refer to Sandburg's "aggressive provincialism, which he calls American nationalism" [*Essays* 219], in a characteristically New Critical conflation of the two terms.) He describes his own Fugitive group, in contrast to these poets, as "indifferent to the Middle Western procedure of rendering an American as distinguished from any other scene"; the Fugitives stay "far from booming the conspicuous properties, physical and social, of their native scene" (*Poetry Reviews* 81). It is partly on this basis that Tate praises Ransom's poetry collection *Chills and Fever* in 1924. Ransom "evinces a mind detached from the American scene and mostly nurtured from England, indifferent to the current mania of critics for writers who 'express America' " (25). Tate finds in Ransom a healthy anti-Whitmanian classicism, "the repudiation of a rhetorical Infinite in which the megalomania of man rhetorically participates" (23).

Violating the first New Critical commandment by rarely writing about Whitman's actual poetry, Tate nevertheless finds his insidious presence everywhere. That presence lurks behind "the vaguely evolutionary, progressive view of American poetry" that Tate finds in reviewing Alfred Kreymborg's historical survey of the subject, *Our Singing Strength*. The last paragraph of Tate's review is revealing for its generally negative stance toward Whitman's influence on the "progressive view":

Yet Walt was the prophet and Mr. Kreymborg cannot repudiate the prophecy. He is not wholly at his ease, however, since he cannot understand why there is a *malaise* in the modern mind called "pessimism," the prophet having foretold the perfect brotherhood, the perfect society, and the "new brood." There is something disconcertingly wrong, from the Whitman viewpoint, with the new brood that has arrived, and our author does not like it; yet his "faith" in progress tells him that he ought to like it, though all the while he casts an apprehensive glance at the perfection and the liberties foretold, now grown somewhat fatuous in their realization. (*Poetry Reviews* 98)

Whitman's prophecy (a term Tate trivializes by making it synonymous with "predictions") for America turned out to be wrong, so his poetry must be dismissed. Tate does not admit of the possibility that, despite the datedness of his prophetic stance, Whitman might remain useful formally—although, as I shall show later, for Tate himself and for other poet–New Critics, Whitman seemed an actively negative influence.[18] Generally, the New Critics' anti-Whitmanism rested on narrow conceptions of what his work made possible formally, since that work was appropriated more variously than they admit; witness, for instance, Kenneth Fearing's use of Whitman's line in the service of political satire. For while Whitman was commonly faulted in the 1920s and 1930s for writing prose and calling it poetry, his destabilizing of genre boundaries could be seen as providing a model for writers from Williams (in *Kora in Hell* and *Spring and All*) and Stein to Ron Silliman and Lyn Hejinian in the 1970s and 1980s.[19]

As a figure central to the development of American literature, Whitman was by no means completely neglected during the period of the New Criticism's emergence, and students could discover him easily enough in any standard anthology. James E. Miller, Jr., later a leading Whitman scholar, recalls how for him that discovery came through Howard Mumford Jones and Ernest Leisy's *Major American Writers* in 1939 or 1940—a time when Brooks and Warren's *Understanding Poetry* carried only one minor Whitman poem. But if Whitman was not neglected, especially by Americanists, he was also not faring universally well in academic quarters. In particular, as students young American poets were being taught to dismiss Whitman. Galway Kinnell writes, "When I was in college I was taught that Whitman was just a compulsive blabber and a nut"; Kinnell was presented with "lesser poets, including . . . Ezra Pound and T. S. Eliot, whose work is so much better suited to classrooms" (134). Robert Duncan: "Everybody in college considered Whitman's poetry very poor stuff. People would be embarrassed about it all. Of course, it was poor poetry to them because they were embarrassed by the content" (Faas 67). Robert Creeley: "In the forties, when I was in college, it was considered literally bad taste to have an active interest in [Whitman's] writing" (*Collected Essays* 3). That writing was seen as "naively affirmative," and lacking the " 'structure' " necessary to sustain a New Critical reading (4). Nor, incidentally, did Whitman's literary descendants fare much better in the academy. Creeley had to ask F. O. Matthiessen's permission to write a paper on Crane, whom Matthiessen had excluded from his modern poetry course. Certainly Creeley, like Duncan, found that his fellow students responded negatively to Crane's and Whitman's homosexuality. In response to the "Indiana" section of *The Bridge* (about which Tate also privately expressed discomfort), "if they did not laugh outright at what must have seemed to them the awkwardly stressed rhymes and sentimental camaraderie, then they tittered at Crane's will to be one with his fellow *homosexual*" (5).

Kinnell, Duncan, and Creeley were not going to "get" Whitman in the college classroom. They would have to come to him through other means. The same seems to have been true for Allen Ginsberg at Columbia, where, according to Ginsberg, his favorite teacher, Lionel Trilling, had "a tin ear" and was "absolutely lost in poetry" ("From an Early Letter" 85). Although his high school English teacher had introduced him to Whitman, Ginsberg's college professors found Whitman a "provincial bumpkin" (Miles 79). To an older poet, equally, Whitman represented an alternative to New Critical values, one that saved his own poetry. In a 1987 interview, David Ignatow says, "Whitman . . . literally saved me from despair during the thirties, forties, and fifties when the metaphysicals were in ascendance: Ransom, Tate, and Eliot, the symbolist" (144).

So far I have suggested some reasons why Brooks and Tate, as representative New Critics, found it, in Randall Jarrell's words, "necessary to forget" Whitman, and how they justified their willed amnesia.[20] Whitman's nationalism, which they saw as parochialism, ran counter to the particular history of English poetry that they wanted to construct; it bolstered their new definition of English studies and their efforts to institutionalize their own brand of criticism to reject a poet who was warmly embraced by other competing critical schools. Thus the New Critical treatment of Whitman offers a specific example of what many theorists today see as the always politicized nature of allegedly disinterested aesthetic judgment. Furthermore, Whitman's suppression at the developing moment of New Critical consensus looks even less disinterested when we consider his status among leftist writers and intellectuals. Whitman is discussed and invoked throughout the thirties in such magazines as *New Masses, Rebel Poet, International Literature, Dynamo,* and *Dialectics* (all Communist Party-sponsored publications), and in books by leftist critics.[21] In 1931 Leonard Spier takes him as "the mouthpiece of the dimly dawning consciousness of the masses," a poet whose "significance . . . to the working class will increase proportionately as our own critics scan the works of the past" ("What We Need"). The central question in Newton Arvin's 1938 book *Whitman* is the extent to which Whitman can be read as a socialist poet, the ways in which he may "seem to have taken a long step toward the literature of socialism" and may be "claimed . . . for socialist culture" (4). It seems extremely likely, then, that Whitman's importance to the literary ethos surrounding the Communist Party and the Popular Front—the importance both of his poetry and of the *idea* of Whitman, what he represented—also contributed to his exclusion from a poetry canon being shaped by cultural conservatives. I want to spend the next few pages exploring the breadth of Whitman's adoption by the left, to show just how pervasively those propounding an ideology that was anathema to the New Critics embraced a poet who was equally anathema to them.

The left's embrace of Whitman was not unique to the thirties; it had begun early in the century. In 1901 the editorial announcing the first issue of *Comrade* (an "Illustrated Socialist Monthly") begins with the first two stanzas of "For You, O Democracy" to represent the journal's aims, with the comment that "the literature of the world might be searched in vain for anything more beautiful, or simple, or direct, than this Psalm of Comradeship" ([Spargo?] 12). Writers in this journal referred frequently to Whitman between 1901 and 1905; indeed, Daniel Aaron describes it as "closer to Whitman and Edward Bellamy than to Karl Marx" (36). Whitman was the subject of a short but sympathetic 1909 essay in *Socialist Woman.* Among leading socialists of the time, Floyd Dell could begin a 1915 essay with the assumption that "Walt Whitman seems to have been accepted by Socialists as peculiarly their poet." Dell found what he saw as Whitman's elevation of instinct over intelligence as threatening to the left's cause (a conclusion that he reached "on reading *Leaves of Grass* lately for the five hundredth time" [85]), but still recommended reading him. Emma Goldman similarly read Whitman avidly. Eugene Debs saw Horace Traubel's socialism as deriving from Whitman's view of democracy, and Whitman's presence was indeed central to the project of his friend Traubel's socialist *Conservator.* Some years later, in 1919, Dell noted in the *Liberator* Whitman's popularity among political prisoners. And in three novels that Dell published between 1920 and 1923, he measures characters' development by their ability to appreciate Whitman.

Daniel Aaron has documented the affinities between the highly politicized young American artists and cultural critics of the nineteen teens and the Transcendentalists—affinities acknowledged by, among others, Floyd Dell, writing in *The Liberator* in 1921, by Orrick Johns, Max Eastman, and Louis Untermeyer, by James Oppenheim in a 1917 anthology, and by Van Wyck Brooks in *America's Coming-of-Age*. In a related note, Aaron summarizes what he sees as the curve of Whitman's fortunes during the first half of this century:

Socialists and Communists claimed Whitman without being precisely sure what he really thought of capitalism and trade unions. It was enough that he believed in the future and "affirmed." . . . Coincidentally with the decline of the revolutionary spirit in the 1920's, Whitman's reputation sank. For Paul Elmer More, T. S. Eliot, Ezra Pound, Yvor Winters, and others, he was or became the poet of disorder. Revived as a socialist master in the thirties (see Newton Arvin's *Whitman*, N.Y., 1938), he tumbled again after 1946. . . . (410)

Note in Aaron's commentary the rather specific, selective group for whom Whitman's reputation sank in the 1920s—Pound, Eliot, Winters—for despite the turn of many young intellectuals toward Eliot after the publication of *The Waste Land*, this "sinking" was by no means universal. Mike Gold, for whom Whitman was both hero and role model, invoked him as early as his 1921 essay for the *Liberator*, "Towards Proletarian Art," and continued to do so; in addition, Aaron reads Gold's "America Needs a Critic," published in *New Masses* in 1926, as "an idealized self-portrait like Whitman's Poet in the 1855 Preface to *Leaves of Grass*" (234). The 1925 prospectus for *Dynamo* magazine invokes a Whitmanian spirit of cultural nationalism (Aaron 118). And Cary Nelson notes the reprinting of "Song of the Open Road" in Marcus Graham's 1929 *An Anthology of Revolutionary Poetry*, in a "Forerunners" section that also included Blake, Shelley, and William Morris (*Repression* 149). Even if Whitman was mentioned somewhat less frequently in 1920s left literary circles than he had been before, his reputation still remained fairly stable, and by the early 1930s, his general adoption by the international left, even with some demurrers, was so widespread as to be acknowledged by critics of all ideological persuasions.[22]

The left's use of Whitman also took poetic form throughout the 1930s, although again this trend had started earlier, and was not confined to the more obvious examples such as Sandburg and Masters. In her second volume of poems, *Sun-Up*, published in 1920, Lola Ridge addresses a wake-up call to industrial workers (the poem is called "Reveille") in the rhythms, imagery, and diction of "Out of the Cradle Endlessly Rocking":

> You have turned deaf ears to others—
> Me you shall hear.
> Out of the mouths of turbines,
> Out of the turgid throats of engines,
> Over the whistling steam,
> You shall hear me shrilly piping.
> Your mills I shall enter like the wind,
> And blow upon your hearts,
> Kindling the slow fire.
>
> (86–87)

As Cary Nelson rightly argues, "Whitman's enactment of a broadly democratic literature was . . . celebrated by most of the political poets of the period" (*Repression* 134). In 1935, for instance, Mike Gold, whose poetry was heavily influenced by Whitman, published his "Ode to Walt Whitman" simultaneously in *New Masses* and the *Daily Worker*. Here the speaker starts in anger at being conned by Whitman's idealism ("Doped by a priest named Walt Whitman— / Why did I mistake you for the sun?"). He goes on to reject first Whitman specifically ("Lies, lies, a lazy poet's lies on a printed page / Meant for rich college boys") and then, in a hybrid aphorism drawing equally on Henry Ford and on Eliot, poetry generally: "Poetry is the cruelest bunk, / A trade union is better than all your dreams." As the poem progresses, however, the speaker joins a strike, and, in the last line, Whitman's dream and the speaker's identification with it are revived: "Son of Walt Whitman, to strike is to dream!" (21).

One year later, Stephen Vincent Benét addressed Whitman in an elegy with the same title as Gold's: "You're still the giant lode we quarry / For gold, fools' gold and all the earthly metals, / The matchless mine. / Still the trail-breaker, still the rolling river" (38). Why an elegy for Whitman in 1936? We can answer that by looking at the context surrounding the poem. In Benét's *Burning City*, his "Ode to Walt Whitman" follows "Ode to the Austrian Socialists," which memorializes the martyrdom of an Austrian community that tried to call a general strike and was destroyed by the Nazis, and "Do You Remember, Springfield?" an elegy to Vachel Lindsay that criticizes the town for failing to appreciate its native son. Whitman, then, appears in the context of leftist populism and is called up to remind readers of an idealism that Benét sees as unfulfilled or actively negated.

Other left-leaning poets similarly turned to Whitman. Before Muriel Rukeyser's *Theory of Flight* won the Yale Younger Poets Prize in 1935, a section of the title poem appeared in *Dynamo*; here Whitman is one of the "sweet generous rebels" whom Rukeyser imagines being sentenced by bureaucratic authorities, "the voting men" of "The Committee-Room" (25–27). Putting Whitman to the political use to which, in New Critical eyes, he must have looked all too susceptible, poets often invoked his example ironically to point up the betrayal of his vision for America that the Depression represented. His style provided Carl Edwin Burklund with the basis for a parodic "celebration" of capitalism and the Depression in "A Chant for America." In 1936 *New Frontier* carried Genevieve Taggard's "Night Letter to Walt Whitman." And in 1938, the year before Archibald MacLeish was praised by Brooks in *Modern Poetry and the Tradition*, he published *Land of the Free*, a book-length poem interwoven with Farm Security Administration photos that quotes "Pioneers! O Pioneers!" to address Depression-era loss of civil liberties.

Turning to the critics associated with *Partisan Review* after its break with the Communist Party complicates this view of the left's adoption of Whitman.[23] It does so, however, in revealing ways, for the distance that developed between *Partisan* and some of its leftist contemporaries can be measured partly in terms of how *Partisan* writers treat Whitman. In his famous 1939 essay "Paleface and Redskin," Philip Rahv takes Whitman as a symbolic figurehead for the redskins whom he sees dominating the literature of the 1930s in a spirit of anti-intellectualism, "relaxation of standards," and pandering to "semiliterate audiences" (5). In 1940, in the equally well known "Reality in America," Lionel Trilling argues in the pages of *Partisan* with Parrington's expression of "the chronic American belief that there exists an opposition between reality and mind and that one must enlist oneself in the party of reality." Developing this theme six years later in what became part 2 of the essay, Trilling adopted Rahv's paleface-redskin distinction, with Dreiser standing in for Whitman; for Trilling as for Rahv, however, this distinction still represents "the dark and bloody crossroads where literature and politics meet" (*Liberal Imagination* 8). The same contrast had also helped shape a 1939 *Partisan* symposium, "The Situation of American Writing," which among other questions asked a number of contemporary writers, "Would you say . . . that Henry James's work is more relevant to the present and future of American writing than Walt Whitman's?" In its attempted Marxist defense of high modernism, then, *Partisan* ends up constructing a Whitman very close to that of the more politically conservative New Critics.

The Whitman-James contrast that Rahv codified so influentially had been in the air for some time—at least since Ezra Pound's 1913 essay "Patria Mia," one of the many places where Pound criticizes Whitman's aesthetic failures and one important source of the very opposition noted by Rahv that came to structure much literary debate of the thirties.[24] The responses to Whitman of the two most influential modernist poet-critics, Eliot and Pound, are well enough known that they do not need detailed reiteration. It is useful to review, however, those points that came to persuade the New Critics against Whitman, and the key issue is that of poetic craft. Pound consistently admitted Whitman's significance, but, in a paradoxical affinity with Marxist critics, located that significance in his "message" (" 'his message is my message,' " Pound added [Selected Prose 146]). Otherwise he saw Whitman as both a flawed artist ("not an artist, but a reflex") and a bad technical influence: "his 'followers' go no further than to copy the defects of his style" (110). In 1911 Pound had written to Floyd Dell that Whitman "was too lazy to learn his trade i.e. the arranging of his rhytmic [sic] interpretations into harmony. he was no artist, or a bad one" (Tanselle 115–16). Whitman was no artist, Pound argued in "Patria Mia," because he lacked the Jamesian and high modernist virtues "of reticence and of restraint" (Selected Prose 114). By 1934, Pound could no longer find the "thirty well-written pages of Whitman" that he claimed to have found twelve years previously (ABC 192) and insisted again that Whitman's value lay in his "fundamental meaning." After describing Whitman's failures of prosody, diction, and syntax, he concludes with a telling comment for poet-professors hoping to bring modern poetry into the curriculum: "Certainly the last author to be tried in a classroom" (ABC 192).

Like Pound, other proponents of a high modernist aesthetic predictably focused on the issue of craft. Amy Lowell echoes Pound's distinction between the importance of Whitman's message ("we needed Whitman's message; we need it today") and his failure of craft: "Whitman never had the slightest sense of what cadence is . . . he had very little rhythmical sense" and wrote "a highly emotional prose" (511, 508). Eliot—at least in 1928—saw Whitman as "a great prose writer" who spuriously "asserted that his great prose was a new form of verse." For Eliot, not even Whitman's content, which featured "a large part of clap-trap," redeemed him ("Introduction" 10).[25] Even a fairly sympathetic commentator like H. S. Canby, for whom Whitman "must be reckoned a major poet," asserts that Whitman wrote in "what is essentially a rhythmic prose that slides into poetry and out of it with equal ease" and, recalling Pound's phrasing, demands that "there must be restraint as well as release" (Classic Americans 335–37).

If Pound anticipated the Whitman-James opposition, Eliot contrasted Whitman with himself and Pound, writing of "my own type of verse, that of Pound, and that of the disciples of Whitman" ("Introduction" 8). Since the New Critics were largely persuaded by this opposition, not just a local argument but the modernist canon and competing views of American poetry are at stake in the distinction. In the 1930s, to dismiss Whitman meant dismissing not just an individual poet but a politics and a whole potential audience for poetry. Eliot may have seen in Whitman "a large part of clap-trap," and perhaps by 1934 Pound *could* no longer find "thirty well-written pages of Whitman." On the other hand, in 1936, when Joseph Freeman looked back on literary lectures that he had given to members of the Amalgamated Clothing Workers Union, he offered a rather different perspective, changing the terms of the opposition: "When I recited Walt Whitman, the workers always applauded his chants to liberty; when I read aloud Ezra Pound or T. S. Eliot, they fidgeted in their seats and looked out the windows of the Rand School lecture hall" 239–40).

It comes as no surprise to hear some of the New Critics repeat Pound's and Eliot's sentiments, in ways consistent with their general skepticism about the idea of an American poetry. In the symposium mentioned above, "The Situation in American Writing," Allen Tate observes that "until the time of Pound and Eliot, there are no American poets whose styles have been any use to me" ("Situation" 28); Robert Penn Warren agrees that "American poetry has very little to offer the modern writer—except some of Emily Dickinson and a very little of Emerson" ("Situation" 112). Both repeat Pound's and Eliot's objections to Whitman's failures of craft. For Tate, the "national" writer, one in a line "which stems from Whitman," suffers "the vice of 'imitative form' on a large scale; that is, if he assumes the national essence is unique and crude, he must develop a style that is unique and crude" (28). Warren argues that "on the technical side, the work of Whitman has, it seems to me, been exercising a very destructive influence" (112). Elsewhere he suggests that the "example and encouragement" that "American poets of the Left" derived from Whitman resulted in work "crude in technique and unconcerned with making nice poetic discriminations," "little more than a kind of journalism" ("Present State of Poetry" 386). Tate, the most energetically antinationalist of the group, exhibits the familiar New Critical (and Arnoldian) equation of the national with the parochial, and constructs the self-consciously national poet as rejecting the very tradition that he and other New Critics sought to preserve: "there is, in this school . . . , the disadvantage that every writer must begin his career as if no literature had ever been written before" (28).

Other participants in the symposium, both poets and prose writers, share these views. Katherine Anne Porter similarly objects to Whitman on aesthetic grounds: "the influence of Whitman on certain American writers has been disastrous" because he encourages "romantic superiority to the limitations of craftsmanship, inflated feeling and slovenly expression" (36). Meanwhile, both Louise Bogan and James T. Farrell uncannily echo Brooks's view from *Modern Poetry and the Tradition* of Whitman as sentimental. Bogan sees "naive vigor and sentimental 'thinking' " as the prime features of Whitman's work; "I do not return to [him], and I never drew any refreshment from his 'thought'" (105). Like Tate, Farrell finds Whitman-influenced poets of the thirties parochial, sentimental, and undisciplined.

In 1927 Amy Lowell defined the modern spirit through a contrast between "the sentimentality which underlay Whitman's coarseness" and "the complete absence of it in Sandburg" (517)—a surprising distinction, perhaps, but a common enough view of Whitman. The recurrence throughout this chapter of the term "sentimental" in the comments on Whitman that I have cited shows how both male and female modernist readers could apply a gender-inflected evaluative criterion to exclude a male poet by coding him as "female." To describe Whitman as sentimental, as the New Critics frequently did, associated him with a feminized nineteenth-century Romanticism and formed another basis for his neglect. Recent feminist scholarship has clarified the engendering of modernism by focusing on the often masculinist rhetoric of modernist poets and critics, and on their association (not one original to the modernist period, of course) of the female and the sentimental.[26] The example most often cited to represent New Critical views of women writers is Ransom's essay on Millay, "The Poet as Woman," where a male wariness of the female has a frankly material and sexual basis. Millay

fascinates the male reviewer but at the same time horrifies him a little too. He will probably swing between attachment and antipathy, which may be the very attitudes provoked in him by generic woman in the flesh. (*World's Body* 77)

In "the age . . . which has recovered the admirable John Donne," "the poet of intellectualized persons" (78), Millay suffers from "her lack of intellectual interest," synonymous for Ransom with "deficiency in masculinity." A poet who suffers this deficiency will "conceive poetry as a sentimental or feminine exercise" (98).[27]

In 1914, T. E. Hulme anticipates Ransom's discussion of Millay by associating "imitative poetry" with women, characterizing it as "the expression of sentimentality rather than of virile thought" (quoted in Gilbert and Gubar 154)—a view consistent with his and Pound's notorious distinction between the (masculine) hard and dry and the (feminine) soft and damp in poetry. Critics such as Sandra Gilbert and Susan Gubar, Alicia Ostriker, Suzanne Clark, and Andreas Huyssen cite numerous examples of this rhetoric, which consistently conflated the female, the unintellectual, mass culture, "popular" writing. (Tate criticized Millay's "Justice Denied in Massachusetts" for its use of "mass language" in the service of "sentimentality" [*Essays* 58].) Thus, as Clark puts it, "the term *sentimental* makes a shorthand for everything modernism would exclude, the other of its literary/nonliterary dualism" (9). It also became an aesthetically evaluative term, one to be used in constructing canons: "The modernist new critics used aesthetic anti-sentimentality to make distinctions, to establish a position of authority against mass culture. Mass culture was a feminized enemy they saw as powerful and dangerous" (Clark 5). And the New Critics tarred Whitman with the same brush. It is significant that one of the few women to call Whitman sentimental was Bogan, who steadfastly refused to identify herself as a woman writer and typically refused inclusion in anthologies of women poets.

Given Duncan's and Creeley's experience of their peers' negative response to Whitman's homosexuality, it may not be too far-fetched to suggest that unspoken homophobia also contributed to New Critical responses. Mark Van Doren felt that Whitman's homosexuality invalidated his "democratic dogmas" (283). Van Doren's comment shows vividly what Thomas Yingling calls "the structural necessity of the separation of the homosexual and the national" in American criticism (11). It does seem likely that, for the New Critics, Whitman's homosexuality would have further vitiated his already dubious claims to the status of national bard. At the same time, it is not entirely clear how far they allowed themselves to recognize Whitman's homosexuality, and to some extent they displace their suspicion of him onto Hart Crane—or at least use Crane as a stick with which to beat Whitman. In doing so, modernist critics not only dismiss Whitman from the American poetry canon that they are in the process of shaping but also build their anti-Whitmanism into it. That is, they canonize Crane as a moral and aesthetic exemplar to underscore the futility of the Whitman tradition and to "prove" that Romanticism is dead. Thus for Yvor Winters, *The Bridge* shows "the impossibility of getting anywhere with the Whitman inspiration" (*Uncollected Essays* 82), and for Tate it shows "the end of the romantic movement" (*Poetry Reviews* 104). The critics'

views of Crane and Whitman shape each other, in mutually reinforc-
ing fashion: if you follow Whitman, you end up like Crane, and if you
end up like Crane, then Whitman must have been a bad place to start.
Given the power of a cultural code that linked the homosexual with
the "effeminate" or feminine, and the feminine with the sentimental,
it is hardly surprising to find Tate and Winters calling Crane's attitude
toward Whitman "sentimental." As Yingling argues, "Crane's status
in the canon seems to be in spite of himself—he is the very sign of
excess for American letters, and this was his original function for New
Critics"; his status represents American criticism's "insistent need
to reproduce the 'lesson' of homosexuality's failure" (8–9). Brooks
and Warren finesse the Whitman-Crane connection by using nothing
from Crane's most Whitmanian poem, *The Bridge*, in *Understanding
Poetry*, while reprinting his elegy for the recently revived premodernist
Melville; they even confirm Crane's manliness by comparing his con-
struction of metaphors to the unconscious but well-honed skills of a
pole-vaulter or boxer. It is to the canonizing effects of *Understanding
Poetry* that I will turn next.

Understanding Poetry and the American Poetry Canon

I have already discussed the place of anthologies, including teaching
anthologies, in any history of canons in American poetry. I want to
examine now a closely related kind of teaching tool, the textbook, and
in particular the single most influential poetry textbook published in
this century, Brooks and Warren's *Understanding Poetry*, and its role in
disseminating (the phallocentric metaphor is appropriate) New Criti-
cal judgments and methodology. In these pages I first want to chart
more specifically than has been done before the range of this textbook's
influence, to ask what effects *Understanding Poetry* did have, and on
whom; second, given its influence, I want to review the perspective on
American poetry, especially modern poetry, that the book promoted;
third, I will contrast the poetry canons of *Understanding Poetry* and other
anthologies of the time, to highlight how those canons were contested
and to assess the Brooks-Warren influence from a different angle; and
fourth, in the face of claims that *Understanding Poetry* dealt more with
how to read than *what* to read, I'll suggest how critical and pedagogical
method shapes content in the construction of canons.

All the instruments agree that *Understanding Poetry* is one of the
most influential college textbooks of this century—hence one of the
most influential organs in shaping poetic canons. The text is typically

described as "primarily effective, if not ultimately causative, in bringing about a revolution in the teaching of poetry in the American college classroom," "the single most important influence upon a whole generation of teachers in college English departments," an influence that "changed the teaching of literature in American colleges" (Cutrer 183, 186). Jonathan Arac calls it "the most intellectually distinguished poetry textbook since [T. H.] Ward's" four-volume *English Poets*, with its preface by Matthew Arnold (118). Similar comments come from, among others, Richard Ohmann (New Criticism "made its greatest impression on our day-to-day lives and work . . . through the style and method of close reading displayed in a relatively small number of essays . . . and in the sacred textbook, *Understanding Poetry*" [*English* 70]); Robert Scholes ("try to imagine the New Critical revolution in literary study without *Understanding Poetry*" [18]); Grant Webster ("Explication . . . gained its widest influence via one of the few important textbooks in literary history, *Understanding Poetry*" [112]); Leslie Fiedler, who calls the text "quasi-scriptural" ("Literature" 89–90); and John Fekete: "New Criticism succeeded in effecting an educational transformation, and became established as the dominant pedagogic tradition. It is generally accepted that the vastly influential textbooks published by the New Critics (widely welcomed, used, and imitated) deserve credit for this, especially Cleanth Brooks' successful anthologies" (88).

The success of *Understanding Poetry* in both the university and the marketplace may partially explain the view that professors make canons—what I have called in Chapter 2 the institutional model of canon formation. Clearly, one means by which the academy shapes and mediates canons is through teaching, and Hugh Kenner has written of the modernist canon specifically as one that, in mid-century, "pedagogues were defining" ("Making of the Modernist Canon" 371). Robert Hemenway offers a straightforward restatement of this view: "English professors largely define the literary canon by choosing to teach certain works"; "no writer, no book, is likely to be accepted into the canon without the sanction of the university curriculum" (63). Actually canons are not defined solely by their contents; they are more than a matter of "writers" and "books." Further, I am wary of Hemenway's rather tidy equation of canon and curriculum (as if there were no nonacademic canons, or canons that might be put to nonacademic use). But Hemenway summarizes a familiar position here, one that has some weight to it—a weight assumed, in fact, by anyone who has revised his or her syllabi in the interests of broader race, class, and gender representation in recent years.

A textbook like *Understanding Poetry* anticipates this contemporary emphasis on the canon-making power of teachers. Unlike subsequent new paradigms in American literary theory, the New Criticism had its roots in the classroom and justified itself in pedagogical terms. As Michael Fischer argues, the New Criticism's basis in pedagogy is what explains its preoccupation with method (100)—an issue to which I shall return later. Brooks and Warren found their students at Louisiana State University unable to read poems competently, and the available textbooks offered only historical source material or "impressionistic criticism," "vague, flowery, and emotive" (Brooks, "New Criticism," 593). More specifically, the students were incapable of *judgment*, Brooks writes; when he began teaching, "many [students] could not distinguish between a good book and a bad. What to do?" ("Changing Culture" 392). ("Write *Understanding Poetry*" became one answer to that question.) Ransom similarly presents New Critical method as a practical solution to a pedagogical problem: the problem that "the majority of the freshmen who come to us from the schools are unable to read a page of poetry or a serious play with any comprehension, I will not say of the subtleties of its form, but even of its plainest literal sense" (21). In the thirties as now, then, the classroom was a crucial site of canonical and methodological debate; issues of pedagogy and canonicity were closely intertwined, and one justification proposed for canonical revisionism was pedagogical.

The influence of *Understanding Poetry*, constantly asserted and assumed, has rarely been measured in any detailed way. To do that, we can start by asking how many students and professors *Understanding Poetry* reached.[28] Records of printings date back only to 1949, by which point the first (1938) edition had been in circulation for eleven years. The text was apparently already well established by then, to judge from the fact that it went through 14,000 copies and three printings between February 1949 and April 1950. Between 1949 and 1976, total distribution of *Understanding Poetry* in its various forms and editions—cloth and paper, complete and shorter editions—ran to forty printings and 294,700 copies. Over this twenty-seven-year period, then, average sales remain stable at close to 11,000 a year. During the peak of the New Criticism's influence, the fifties and early sixties, the second (1950) edition went through thirteen cloth printings and 73,000 copies in ten years, while the shorter version of this edition went through nine paper printings and 24,700 copies in eight years. The third (1960) edition sold thirteen cloth printings and 153,000 copies in fifteen years, including 35,000 within a year of its publication.

The figures are comparable for another influential Brooks and Warren text, *An Approach to Literature* (1936). As with *Understanding Poetry*, data on the book's early years are spotty, although it went into a second printing in 1938, and, much more quickly than *Understanding Poetry*, into a second edition (1939). The third edition (1952) went through 184,360 copies and seventeen printings in twelve years, outselling the first and second editions combined (107,580 copies). The fourth edition (1964) performed even more strongly: 209,500 copies and ten printings in seven years, along with 76,500 copies of an alternate fourth edition. The fifth edition (1975) saw an initial printing of 20,000. All this adds up to a total of 597,940 copies and twenty-nine printings between 1936 and 1975, an average of over 15,000 a year for this period. The New Critical canon found its way, especially at the level of method, into a lot of classrooms.

Understanding Poetry achieved its impact most forcefully through the first two editions, so I will focus mainly on them. What view of American poetry do they offer? Much of it is familiar, so I will not devote a great deal of space to repeating it. The textbook's canon is predominantly and notoriously a white male one (though on this point it is hardly unique for its time).[29] Until the fourth edition (1976), by which time the New Criticism had effectively lost its power to promulgate a canon, *Understanding Poetry* contained only a tiny percentage of women writers and absolutely no minorities. Familiar too is the extent to which the American nineteenth century suffers at the editors' hands. J. R. Lowell's "After the Burial," Poe's "Ulalume," Holmes's "The Chambered Nautilus," Lanier's "My Springs," and Bryant's "Thanatopsis" are all included as examples of various kinds of badness. This abuse extends to the treatment of Whitman, for the reasons discussed earlier in this chapter. Remarkably, the second edition contains not a single Whitman poem (the first contained "Pioneers! O Pioneers!"): in 1950 Whitman was as dispensable as Howard Baker and Mark Van Doren, the only other American poets dropped from the first edition. The third edition contains two Whitman selections, the same number as John Peale Bishop.

All this is pretty much common, if distressing, knowledge. Less common knowledge, given the influence usually attributed to New Criticism in the shaping of the modernist canon, is the surprisingly low proportion of modern American work that the first edition of *Understanding Poetry* contains, even though English and Irish modernists like Housman (five poems), Hardy (four), and Yeats (four) are fairly well represented. While we are now likely to feel that American poets dominated the modern scene, they by no means dominate *Understanding Poetry,* despite substantial analyses of poems by Eliot, cummings, Crane, and Frost. Frost is the most fully represented American with five poems—level, admittedly, with Donne and Marvell, but trailing Shakespeare, Keats, Wordsworth, Tennyson, Milton, Shelley, Blake, Browning, and Herrick. In subsequent editions Frost remains by far the most fully represented American poet. He gets eleven selections in the second edition, nine in the third (which is otherwise significantly scaled back), and eight in the fourth. Meanwhile, the text contains nothing by Stevens, Moore, or Williams (never a New Critical favorite), two lines by Pound, and, as I have said, one Whitman poem. The conventional view of *Understanding Poetry* as a pedagogical extension of Eliot's canon and of the New Critical defense of high modernism, then, needs some refining. The contents of the book's first edition suggest that, if their method was in place for Brooks and Warren in 1938, the American modernist canon itself was not, given some of the exclusions that I have mentioned and the inclusion of work by Mark Van Doren, Donald Davidson, Howard Baker, and Archibald MacLeish.

Frost's simultaneous presence in American literature anthologies of the time suggests that the New Critics were, in his case, riding the coattails of an already established reputation. But it remains tempting to speculate how Frost's representation in *Understanding Poetry* increased or reinforced his importance for younger American poets in the late forties and early fifties, and determined the choice of him to introduce Hall, Pack, and Simpson's *New Poets of England and America,* an anthology very much shaped by New Critical criteria. It is hard to assess the extent to which *Understanding Poetry* created or simply reflected Frost's influence; certainly few New Critics, with the exception of Warren, wrote major favorable essays on Frost. Yet his coverage in *Understanding Poetry* peaks at eleven poems at a time when his influence on younger poets was also peaking.[30]

In fact, in Frost's case a discrepancy between pedagogical and critical practice and canons needs explaining. Although Brooks criticized Frost rather severely in *Modern Poetry and the Tradition,* Frost is still the most fully represented American poet in *Understanding Poetry.*[31] Why? Perhaps because, in contravention of New Critical dicta, he tells stories and provides a moral in a way appealing to students. And it may have seemed logical, not to mention marketable, to make one of the country's most popular poets central to a text that claimed to espouse a democratic pedagogy. The audiences for and functions of textbooks and critical essays were, for the New Critics as now, different. The essays sought to persuade professors, the texts to persuade students, even though, finally, what both groups were to be persuaded *of* remained the same.

Frost's presence also reveals Warren's influence on the text. Five of the poems that Warren discusses in his 1947 essay "The Themes of Robert Frost" are printed in the 1950 *Understanding Poetry*. Meanwhile, of the examples that Warren uses to support the argument of his 1942 essay "Pure and Impure Poetry" (what Jonathan Arac calls his "most programmatically New Critical essay" [92]), six reappear in the 1950 edition of *Understanding Poetry*, while none appeared in the 1938 edition. In this essay Warren argues for the importance of the "tension between the rhythm of the poem and the rhythm of speech" (*New and Selected Essays* 24)—a tension that is at its lowest in free verse. This helps explain the textbook's (and general New Critical) preference for a simultaneously metrical and colloquial poet like Frost over the free verse of Whitman and Williams. Even Brooks, amid his criticisms of Frost, praises his "idiomatic and flexible blank verse" (*Modern Poetry* 111).

Modern American poets' predilection for free verse may explain their relative absence from the early editions of *Understanding Poetry*. Both the first and second editions feature a "Metrics" section, but out of forty-one selections in the first edition and fifteen in the second, not one is American. The only American in the third edition's "Metrics" section, Williams, is used to demonstrate the "apparent arbitrariness" (175) of free verse lineation. Free verse poems are not systematically excluded from all sections of the text. At the same time, this limited view of prosody, that for over twenty years restricts it to a status synonymous with metrics and excludes free verse, Moore's syllabics, and much else besides, has a powerfully narrowing effect—including, we might speculate, on younger poets deriving their early notions of craft from the text. Warren especially seemed to think that free verse had simply gone as far as it could, arguing in 1939 that "the general effects of free verse on American poetry have already been achieved" ("Present State of Poetry" 394).

What about the treatment of Eliot, who conventional wisdom would lead us to believe is highly favored in *Understanding Poetry*? He receives two poems in the first edition, four in the second, third, and fourth—quantitatively solid but not dominating representation. At the same time, "Prufrock" receives the longest single analysis of any poem in the first edition. The second edition not only adds "Journey of the Magi" and *The Waste Land* but provides a twenty-two-page reading of

the latter to supplement the analysis of "Prufrock." As I observed ear-
lier in this chapter, *The Waste Land* offers an ideal test of the methods
taught in *Understanding Poetry*, for, in Brooks and Warren's opening
gambit, it "has the reputation of being a most difficult poem" (2d ed.
645). (Wright Thomas and Stuart Gerry Brown's *Understanding Poetry*
clone, *Reading Poems*, "concludes with *The Waste Land*, mastery of which
we regard as ample test of the reader's ability and maturity in the skills
of reading poems" [v].)

It is actually the 1950 edition of *Understanding Poetry*, the largest of
the four at 727 pages, that brings the New Critics' defense of high mod-
ernism more forcibly into the classroom. and by this point their essays
had successfully prepared teachers for it.[32] By adding a section of 41
"Poems for Study" that contains 26 from this century, Brooks and
Warren expand their text's agenda: "We have undertaken in particular
to strengthen the representation of poetry from the present century"
(xxvi). The first edition included 40 selections from 21 twentieth-
century poets, the second 94 selections from 36 poets. Of the 15 modern
poets added, 10 are Americans: John Peale Bishop, Eberhart, Fearing,
Jarrell, Lowell, Moore, Schwartz, Shapiro, Stevens, Williams. The rep-
resentation of American poets generally increases from 24 poets and
37 poems in 1938 to 33 poets and 69 poems in 1950. What is surprising,
however, is that it took Brooks and Warren until 1950 to do this explicitly.

As part of its increased size, the 1950 *Understanding Poetry* adds more
critical essays, which also serve the function of proposing a particular
modernist canon. Beyond new mini-essays on three different Hous-
man poems and Karl Shapiro's "The Minute," the additional material
includes an extended reading of "After Apple-Picking" (based on
Warren's "The Themes of Robert Frost") and the long essay on *The Waste
Land* mentioned above. The latter is perhaps the most significant critical
addition, another step in the poem's already well advanced canoniza-
tion. Based on how much critical attention the poets are seen to deserve,
then, the first tier of Brooks and Warren's modernist canon in 1950
consists of Housman, Yeats, and, among Americans, Eliot and Frost.
(Similarly, Ransom, at mid-century, finds Robinson, Eliot, Frost, and
Hardy "major" poets—with Hardy topping the lot—and places Hous-
man only slightly behind them ["Poetry of 1900-1950"].)

Understanding Poetry is often described as canonizing a method more
than a content, despite Ransom's rather disingenuous claim in a 1939
review that it "assumes no particular theoretical apparatus" ("Teach-
ing" 83). Richard Ohmann describes the lessons learned from New
Criticism in just this way: "how to write papers as students, how to

write articles later on, and what to say about a poem to our students in a 50-minute hour" (*English* 70). In other words, "the issues for teachers of literature were once again primarily those of method" (82–83). New Critical method extended beyond college classrooms to reach the secondary school student and teacher. That the impact on such teachers *was* one of method is confirmed by John Myers, who writes, "the most significant aspect of the critical revolution has been not so much the shift in our thinking about *what* to teach but the *knowledge* it has given us of *how* to teach *a poem*" (60). This revolution was heralded by *Understanding Poetry*, and Myers stresses the book's pedagogical, rather than critical, importance: "for many of us who were preparing ourselves to *teach* English (and I must insist upon a distinction between those who were preparing to teach English and those who were preparing to perpetuate a system of scholarship) this book . . . came as a kind of revelation" (60). A text like *Understanding Poetry* shifted teachers' attention from sociological to formal categories: "we should be and, in fact, have been getting away from the study of *American* poetry *as such* and are focusing our attention more and more on *poetry* as language and as art—as *poetry*" (58). And Myers adds how this revelation, and revolution, in method resulted in more anthologies like *Understanding Poetry*, in "the appearance of a number of excellent critical anthologies designed to be used as textbooks" (58).

Reviewing the text's second edition, Hugh Kenner attests to the impact of *Understanding Poetry* on pedagogical method:

The revolution was touched off, if not exactly masterminded, by Messrs. Brooks and Warren in 1938. Today the market for "How to Read Poetry" books seems inexhaustible; the revised Brooks and Warren (1950) is now used, according to its publishers, by over 250 institutions; and at least five new publishers have clambered aboard the bandwagon in the past three years. Disseminating poetic taste among college freshmen has become a big business. ("Subways" 44)[33]

This is a significant measure of *Understanding Poetry*'s influence: the number of similar texts that were modeled on it. (One still used in college and high school classrooms is Laurence Perrine's *Sound and Sense*.) Kenner bemoans this trend when he concludes his review by arguing for an approach modeled more on Pound's *ABC of Reading* or Zukofsky's *A Test of Poetry*, a canon conceived in terms of its contents: "whoever set out to nominate a list of poems, with reasons, . . . would perhaps prove to have done more for pedagogical enlightenment than the editors of a dozen text-books who at bottom don't care which poems the student has read so long as he has learned how" (53).

To the extent that method shapes content, however, the method-content distinction itself needs complicating. The examples used in critical essays, the poems chosen for inclusion and exegesis in textbooks, blur the lines between method and content. Brooks and Warren raise the issue of both pedagogical and aesthetic method themselves throughout their introductory "Letter to the Teacher," and at one point they write: "A poem . . . is placed in any given section because it may be used to emphasize a certain aspect of poetic method and offers, it is hoped, an especially teachable example" (1st ed. xi). Questioning the distinction that many later commentators went on to employ, Brooks and Warren realize that how you teach poetry shapes what poetry you teach. Critical and pedagogical method determines the contents of the text, the examples of the particular "poetic method" that the editors favor. Consistent with this approach, "the modern poems included . . . are intended to represent some of the various lines taken in the development of poetic method in this century" (xiii). Although this sounds like a claim to eclecticism, these poems are all praised according to the same, now familiar, criteria—indirectness, irony, tonal complexity, avoidance of sentimentality, and so on. Thus the poems "represent" a very specific version of modernism, one that canonizes not just a poetics but even certain themes. Tate's "The Last Days of Alice" is chosen, for instance, because it "makes . . . implied reference to the decay of religious faith under the impact of modern science; and . . . implies that man cannot consider life merely in abstract and quantitative terms, such as pure science dictates. 'The Last Days of Alice' makes an indirect and ironical approach to the matter" (562).

Rather than being separable from the book's contents, then, the critical method of *Understanding Poetry* determines those contents. The text institutionalizes both a way of reading and a body of work that, in circular fashion, proves the efficacy of that reading. At the same time, despite the quickly achieved dominance of their *method*, the *content* of the New Critical canon did not come to dominate the textbook market—the pedagogical canon—as quickly as it dominated the critical canon. "The modern" as a period label became established more quickly than many of the particular modern American poets whom the New Critics favored. Examining American literature anthologies of the period reveals substantial differences between the modernist canons of the Americanist and New Critical communities. In five anthologies of American literature published between 1934 and 1941, ranging in their allegiances and selection criteria from the primarily aesthetic (*The Oxford Anthology of American Literature*) to the primarily political

(Bernard Smith's *The Democratic Spirit*), only three poets appear in all five: Lindsay, Sandburg, and Millay.[34] The following poets appear in only one of the group, the *Oxford*: Ransom, Tate, Crane, cummings, Stein, Stevens, Moore, Williams, H.D. For American literature anthologists of the late thirties, the contemporary poetry canon consists of Frost, Robinson, Lindsay, Masters, Sandburg, Millay, Jeffers, and, less confidently, Eliot, with Wylie, Teasdale, and Amy Lowell also getting considerable play.[35]

This picture had not changed much ten or fifteen years later, when Ben Fuson surveyed twenty-seven single- and multivolume anthologies of American literature. The only modern American poets to appear in each of the fifteen multivolume anthologies examined were Robinson, Sandburg, and Frost—not Eliot, nor any of the other high modernists whom the New Critics promoted. The only modern poet in every single-volume anthology was Frost again; the next highest level of representation went to Sandburg and Lindsay. (It should also be acknowledged, however, that *The Waste Land* was reprinted five times.) As for the nineteenth century, Dickinson is the only poet over whom the editors of mid-century American literature anthologies and the editors of *Understanding Poetry* seem to agree. Whitman is accorded a much higher place in the Americanist canon than in the *Understanding Poetry* and New Critical canon; he is consistently, along with Dickinson, the most heavily represented poet. Clearly, then, New Critical neglect of him was strongly contested. Further, among the nineteenth-century American poets whose reputations were supposedly affected most severely by modernist and New Critical views of poetry, the breadth of representation seems little short of remarkable. Among the multivolume anthologies, Longfellow averages 26 poems, Emerson 23, Whittier and Poe 16, Bryant and Lowell 15, Holmes 11. A similar balance obtains in the single-volume anthologies, where Longfellow averages 20 poems, Emerson 17, Whittier and Poe 14, Bryant 12, Holmes 11, and Lowell 8.

I do not want to make too much out of comparisons between *Understanding Poetry* and American literature anthologies of the period. They are different kinds of book, with different purposes and different markets. The New Critics were interested in canonizing on the basis of genre, not nationality, and only in 1973 did Brooks and Warren get round to editing an anthology of American literature, *American Literature: The Makers and the Making*. But for a reader interested specifically in American poetry, these comparisons do yield some insights: while the New Criticism and American studies became established in the academy more or less concurrently, they barely overlapped at all in their sense of the American poetry canon, with Americanists of necessity holding more to a historical criticism than the New Critics.

Other data support this view. An NCTE committee studying American literature in the college curriculum found that among ninety syllabi for American literature survey courses offered in 1945–46, Whitman was the second most frequently taught author, in seventy-three courses (tied with Hawthorne, and just behind Emerson at seventy-four). Dickinson, taught in twenty-four courses, occupied seventeenth place on this list, behind Longfellow, Bryant, Lowell, and Whittier, and tied with Holmes. The only modern American poets taught were Frost (appearing on ten syllabi) and Robinson (eight); in fact, in 1947–48, only around ten per cent of institutions surveyed offered a course solely in modern American poetry.

All this, however, was changing even as Fuson was conducting the survey that I have just summarized. The successful establishment of New Critical method started to produce a canonical narrowing even in these anthologies. In other words, the canons of American literary anthologies up till the late forties were fairly diverse and capacious (not in race and gender terms, but in genre terms and in terms of the writers accepted within the familiar white male limits), *until* formalist criteria started to take over the ongoing development of a national canon. As a result of the New Critical focus on close reading as a tool of evaluation, American literature anthologies around 1950 started to move toward a "depth" rather than "breadth" model of representation. Henry Pochmann and Gay Wilson Allen look back on their 1949 anthology *Masters of American Literature* as reflecting a time "when the demand for fewer authors and more complete coverage put the scatter-gun kind of anthology virtually out of business" because "the most effective teaching can be accomplished by concentrating on the 'literary masters'" (v).[36] This was the point at which, under the influence of New Critical method, the New Critical and Americanist canons started to converge more closely.

I stress the connection between evaluation and close reading in early New Critical methodology because in principle there is no reason why close reading could not be performed on the wide range of authors in an old-style anthology. In practice, however, the method became a way to weed out the aesthetically unworthy, narrowing the base of representation, and thus shaping the contents of canons not just in poetry but in all genres. Brooks and Warren announce evaluation as central to the method of *Understanding Poetry*, as it was central to the whole

New Critical enterprise from the beginning: "it is hoped that the jux-
taposition of good and bad poems . . . will serve to place emphasis
on the primary matter of critical reading and evaluation" (1st ed. xiii).
That their method would provide a basis for critical judgment and thus
for canonical inclusions and exclusions is exactly what they intended.
To argue that *Understanding Poetry* canonized mainly a method, as many
historians of the profession have done, is to miss a major point. For a
method that leads to the exclusion of Williams, of Whitman and nearly
the whole Whitman tradition in American poetry, of most free verse,
of the poetry of most women and all minorities, and of much pre-
twentieth-century American poetry is certainly legislating a content,
a canon that betokens suspicion of the very idea of an "American"
poetry. Robert Bly wasn't fooled. In 1961, when as editor of *The Sixties*
he awarded Brooks and Warren his magazine's Order of the Blue Toad
for *Understanding Poetry*, and noted Whitman's absence from the text,
he said, "Obviously, if Whitman wrote poetry, it cannot be under-
stood. . . . The book should have been called *Understanding A. E.
Housman*" (91).

4

Little Magazines and Alternative Canons

The Example of *Origin*

When the little magazine *Trace* compiled its first annual listing of magazines published in English in 1952, it rounded up 182 (Anderson and Kinzie 739). In contrast, by one 1987 estimate there were around 5,000 little magazines being published in the United States, varying widely, as such magazines always have, in size, quality, goal, editorial stance, financial stability, and regularity of appearance (Kniffel 103). The Poetry and Rare Books Collection at SUNY Buffalo alone subscribes to 1,300 of those, and has holdings in 3,600 magazines in a collection that specializes in the period from 1978 to the present (Fox 143, 152). Since this explosion of magazine publishing began in the 1960s, and since many more universities began to sponsor literary magazines, the formerly sharp lines between academic quarterlies and little magazines can no longer be clearly drawn (Anania 11, Robinson). In particular, it has become much more difficult to locate any one magazine or group of magazines at the center of American literary culture. That culture no longer has a center.

As a result, now little magazines can less easily be said to affect poetic canons as they once did, to realign the center from their marginal positions by their efforts to gain attention for neglected work. As a further result, traditional definitions of the little magazine as a publishing outlet for writers opposed to some putative center have also become less tenable.[1] When we turn to a time of greater consensus about literary values, however, which means a time when alternative voices were less audible, it becomes more relevant to talk about "centers" and "margins," and about how a little magazine can affect the formation of canons in poetry. One such time in America was the 1950s, and one such magazine was Cid Corman's *Origin*. In any period the story of canon formation is a story of conflicts, and thus the history of *Origin*, as with most little magazines, is partly the history of its conflict with the dominant poetics of its time. Felix Stefanile, editor of *Sparrow* magazine, and one who learned much from *Origin*, contrasts the 1950s with the present thus: "There was a real and powerful establishment to fight [in the 1950s]. Because it deprived us, it gave us a vision of the Enemy that the new pluralism has taken away from young poets starting out now" ("Little Magazine" 649).

Although *Origin* went into a fifth series in 1983, its greatest impact on American poetry came through its first series, twenty issues published between April 1951 and winter 1957, a period during which it had virtually no competition as a durable little magazine receptive to experimental work.[2] Reconstructing the history of that first series can show how a representative little magazine may challenge the canonical poetics of its time and, eventually, expand significantly the possibilities for the writing and reading of poetry. It can also reveal some of the contradictions involved in the process of a self-consciously "anti-academic" magazine's making its way in the face of, but sometimes in uneasy truce with, that central canon-making institution, the academy. *Origin*'s impact was not sudden or obvious. Little magazines rarely have the immediate effect on sales, critical visibility, or teaching syllabi—to mention only the more material manifestations of canonical status— that an anthology or an award-winning book might have. But in retrospect, *Origin* clearly helped shape the postwar American poetry canon in numerous indirect but traceable ways: by publishing and thus encouraging, against the current of the times, poets who went on to produce a significant and substantial body of work; by creating contacts and a sense of common endeavor among those poets that helped them continue their work; by representing a "school" or "movement" that itself influenced later poetic practice; by rereading Anglo-American modernism so as to further the Pound-Williams tradition; by acting as apologist and outlet for a poetics generally considered marginal when the magazine began; and by offering a model for later aesthetically and institutionally independent magazines seeking further to build an alternative poetics on the base that *Origin* had established. Beyond the obligatory lists of writers whom a given magazine published, the role of little magazines in shaping canons is rarely analyzed in depth. This chapter seeks to provide such an analysis.

Charles Olson and Robert Creeley will figure heavily in any discussion of *Origin*, because they figured so heavily not just in the contents but in the shaping of the magazine's stance. In almost daily letters, they cajoled, bullied, guided, criticized, and cheered Corman on; in response, he showed himself persistent, flexible, willing to learn, but always independent. Despite the personal conflicts and deep disagreements that this correspondence often reveals between Corman and his main contributors, its importance to *Origin*'s development, and to the choice of writers whom Corman promoted, cannot be overestimated. Corman organized the first two series of *Origin* around particular individuals whose work he valued and whom he thought unjustly overlooked. In the second series, which ran from April 1961 to July 1964, he promoted Gary Snyder and Lorine Niedecker, but the primary figure was Louis Zukofsky: "I wanted, at the minimum, to bring his work to the attention of his peers and other younger poets" (*Gist* xxxii). The first series centered on his two main correspondents, but more especially on Olson, whom Corman described in a contributor's note to *Origin* #4 as "the man from whom our creative impetus must spring." Corman gave Olson thirty-one pages of his first issue, a gesture that announced his position more clearly than any editorial. Later he devoted *Origin* #8 to Olson's selected poems, which eventually became the volume *In Cold Hell, in Thicket*. Something by Olson appeared in twelve of *Origin*'s twenty first-series issues, a total of fifty-eight items in six years; Creeley appeared in fifteen of these twenty issues, contributing a total of forty-six items. The frequency with which their names will appear in this discussion is one measure of the importance to *Origin* that Corman himself granted them.

In arguing for *Origin*'s effect on the developing American poetry canon—or on the diversification of that "canon" into "canons"—some background is in order. In 1950 the writing of poetry was dominated by the models of Eliot, Yeats, Frost, and Auden, of Lowell's *Lord Weary's Castle* and Wilbur's *The Beautiful Changes* and *Ceremony*; the dominant reading habits were those of New Criticism. Among magazines, the distribution of this poetry and criticism lay largely with the New Critically-oriented editors of such quarterlies as the *Kenyon*, *Sewanee*, and *Hudson Reviews*. (Nor, in fact, were little magazines uniformly resistant to these tendencies: in an issue of the English little magazine *Nine* on contemporary poetry, American poetry was represented by John Crowe Ransom and Allen Tate [Paul 50]). This situation is well-known enough, described fully in recent histories like James Breslin's *From Modern to Contemporary*, that I need not review it here. More relevant is what this context meant for the writers who were to publish in *Origin* in the 1950s. Creeley summarizes how these writers felt: "each one of us felt that the then existing critical attitudes toward verse, and that the then existing possibilities for publication for general activity in poetry particularly, were extraordinarily narrow" (quoted in Duberman 414). Elsewhere Creeley has written more specifically, that "we felt, all of us, a great distance from the more conventional magazines of that time. Either they were dominated by the New Critics, with whom we could have no relation, or else were so general in character, that no active center of coherence was possible" ("On *Black Mountain Review*" 253).

This situation also helped *Origin* define its consciously marginal identity, however. The circumstances—the felt need to create alternative possibilities for publication in resistance to a poetic and critical center perceived as moribund—replicate those faced by the avant-garde little magazines of the 1910s that played such an important role in shaping the modernist canon. Contrasting the seventies with the modernist period, H. L. Van Brunt writes, "there are so many littles today (thousands) that a new one can't hope to have the concentration of talent (Pound, Stevens, Stein, et al) the *Little Review* enjoyed" (180). True enough. But in the early fifties a new little magazine *could* hope for such a high "concentration of talent"; there was, simply, virtually nowhere else for certain kinds of writer to go. Before he began *Trace* in 1952, James Boyer May wrote a regular feature for *Matrix* during 1950–51, the years of *Origin*'s inception, that "was intended to aid new writers to find markets." He recalls of those years that "more so than today [1978], there was a dividing line between old-line literary magazines (chiefly those sponsored by schools) and independent littles. Virtually nowhere, except in the latter, could unknowns find print unless they adopted somewhat commercial patterns or imitated prominent writers in accepted modes" ("*Trace*" 376).

We can sketch the canonical poetics against which *Origin* set itself by looking at what the more influential literary quarterlies—those most often attacked in Corman, Olson, and Creeley's correspondence, and by other *Origin* contributors—were publishing when *Origin*'s first issue appeared in April 1951. The *Sewanee Review* generally carried rather undistinguished poetry, and 1951 was no exception; but those names that today's readers will recognize are the names of writers who, at the time, were working in a formally traditional vein: Richard Eberhart, James Dickey, David Wagoner, Ben Belitt. Kenneth Rexroth received a favorable review, but in the contradictory context of an omnibus discussion of J. V. Cunningham, Howard Nemerov, Delmore Schwartz,

and W. S. Graham. Critical discussion of modern poets was limited to
cummings, Eliot, and two essays on Auden, while the critics who
appeared in the journal throughout the year show an overwhelmingly
New Critical emphasis: Cleanth Brooks, Monroe K. Spears, Q. D.
Leavis (each of whom published two essays), Arnold Stein, Robert Penn
Warren, W. K. Wimsatt.

Hudson Review, less specifically literary in its concerns and modeled
more on the *Dial* of the 1920s, showed its adherence to a late modern-
ist formalism more in its reviews. Eleven books of poetry were reviewed
in its pages in 1951. Auden, Schwartz, Lowell, Wilbur, Eberhart, James
Merrill, Theodore Roethke, and Paul Engle produced eight of them,
with Wilbur described as "the strongest poetic talent . . . in America
below the generation now in their fifties" (J. Bennett 142). At the same
time, *Hudson* also promoted the canonical representatives of interna-
tional high modernism and their successors outside of its reviews. The
spring 1951 issue, for instance, carried two Stevens poems; two by Yvor
Winters' student Edgar Bowers; translations of a Valéry notebook; and
translations of two Nerval sonnets, including "El Desdichado," prob-
ably best known to mid-century readers for being quoted by Eliot at
the end of *The Waste Land.* Meanwhile the spring 1951 *Kenyon Review*
carried three Randall Jarrell poems and represented its critical position
via essays by Arnold Stein on Donne, Empson on Wordsworth, and
Blackmur on Eliot's criticism.

Corman consciously defined his magazine's purpose against this
academic publishing context. He was encouraged in this purpose by
one of Olson's first letters: "And why should I weep to see you get out
only another of such MAGS as Hudson, or PNY [*Poetry New York*], or
NINE?" (Evans 1:38).[3] Even before *Origin* saw the light of day, Corman
tried to reassure Olson, in October 1950, that his magazine would have
a distinctive identity: "How can a mag that will START with 40 pages
of madman Olson be anything like those miredin mags? . . . It's going
to be like: nothing else" (Evans 1:49). *Origin* reassured Olson enough
that, in a 1951 letter, he contrasted it with other contemporary maga-
zines that he described thus: "the tendency of all the new American
magazines is *reactionary,* is back toward tradition, and a whole series
of cliche positions" (1:175).

Corman did not articulate his goals for *Origin* in terms of "canon
formation"—terms dictated by the critical concerns of the eighties and
nineties, not the fifties. But still those terms can usefully describe
Origin's importance to recent American poetry; they can describe the
magazine's *effect,* if not Corman's stated purpose. Corman rarely stated

his goals explicitly at all, and within the magazine itself, he was reluctant to editorialize. He preferred to let *Origin*'s contents and arrangement speak for themselves: "My absence of editorial comment is radical, but I believe that ORIGIN is my comment, is its own editorial, and reflects my person as well as anything, superfluous, I could say" (Evans 1:146). On manifestoes, Corman maintained the position that he laid out to Olson in planning *Origin*: "My program, whatever, will be a positive one. Have no use for vindictive attacks (purely negative approach) since they achieve only enemies that dont deserve the recognition. The positive weight of fine new writing in bulk will outholler any of the 'opposition'" (1:82). Proposing alternative canons rather than merely attacking existent ones—that would be the goal of *Origin*.

Corman proposed his alternative canon partly through his strategy of "featuring" a new writer in almost every issue. This approach clearly implies an evaluative judgment: the featured writer deserves an attention that he or she has not yet received. Olson distinguished *Origin* from its mainstream contemporaries on precisely this basis: "you have shown already," he wrote to Corman in May 1951, "that you are willing to risk an issue of yr magazine on ONE MAN or ONE CONCEPT—a daring thing, that, a mag like NINE, or anyone of 'em, would only do if, they rested on a man whom the taste or culture generally had taken to its bosom" (1:140). Charles Molesworth points out how many poetry magazines contribute to a "cult of personality, for often they feature the work of established writers as a way to draw attention to themselves" (192). Corman states his purpose as exactly the opposite: "I have featured writers consistently on my cover whose names were unknown or practically unknown at the time, and I would not use the names of better-known writers who had work within, unless they were truly 'featured,' that is, occupied a notable part of the issue. Needless to say, this was not aimed at winning a large public, but was aimed (and I think vindicated) at giving fair attention to writers of distinctive promise and achievement" ("In the Word" 71).

To an extent, of course, Corman's statements about *Origin* represent the usual declaration of intent to promote the new that occurs in most little magazines, and that is by no means always borne out by their contents. A more reliable way to assess *Origin*'s effect on American poetry is to look not at Corman's statements of intent but at the results. To whom did he offer their first consistent outlet and audience? Whom did he successfully promote who might otherwise have been neglected? Through *Origin* Corman was the first editor who consistently published Olson, Creeley, Robert Duncan, Paul Blackburn, Denise Levertov,

Theodore Enslin, Larry Eigner, and Wiliam Bronk. Blackburn appeared in 11 first-series issues (with 37 items), Levertov in 8 (26 items), Eigner and Enslin in 7 (12 and 25 items, respectively), Bronk in 6 (30 items, all poems). Other significant contributors included the Canadian poet Irving Layton, who published 35 items and guest-edited issue #18, and Corman himself, with 31 items.

One way in which *Origin* helped shape the postwar American poetry canon, then, is by doing what little magazines have usually done—publishing and supporting writers who otherwise had no regular outlet for their work. *Origin* encouraged its writers in the same way that magazines like the *Little Review,* the *Egoist,* the *Glebe, Others, Poetry,* and the *Dial* once encouraged Pound, Williams, Eliot, Moore, Stevens, Crane, cummings. Olson, in fact, sensitive to *Origin*'s place in an alternative publishing tradition, compared the magazine to Emerson's original *Dial,* and Corman variously to Margaret Anderson and Jane Heap, editors of the *Little Review,* and Ford Madox Ford of the *English Review* (Evans 1:30, 63, 181). As a beginning poet himself, Corman knew the value of the support he was offering: "I know, as a poet, that a writer may become unusually productive once he feels secure in having a regular outlet, and one that is pressure-free, and one that maintains a level of importance to satisfy his pride" ("In the Word" 72). Regular publication, Corman realized, helped confirm the writer's sense of identity, created the opportunity for valuable feedback, and allowed the writer to view his or her work with some distance ("*Origin*" 246).

Publishing the neglected does not in itself constitute "canon formation" in any significant sense, and as Creeley saw early, " 'good new work' is the most amorphous phrase/ possible" (*Olson-Creeley Correspondence* 3:16). Significant changes in poetic canons involve changes in reading and writing practices, not merely correcting individual cases of neglect. Adding individual writers is only one stage of "opening up the canon"—though a crucial stage, especially when those figures represent groups and writing practices that have been systematically suppressed. Hence Corman's "giving adequate outlet" might seem a rather limited form of canonizing. But if we see this provision of an outlet not as an end in itself but as a stage in a process, it becomes a necessary first step in establishing alternative canons—a step analogous to the preserving in anthologies of texts that might otherwise disappear. This is particularly true when, as was the case in the early 1950s, durable and coherent publishing outlets for experimental work are limited. Sometimes Olson, in fact, needed the magazine quite literally to preserve his poems, of which he often kept only muddy carbon copies: *Origin* #1 concludes with the letter Olson wrote to Vincent Ferrini requesting return of his only copy of "I, Maximus, of Gloucester, to You," which *begins* both that first issue and the first volume of *The Maximus Poems*.

To catalogue the individuals whom *Origin* published offers only a partial account of how a little magazine can affect poetic canons. At the same time, the institutional habit of organizing literary history around particular figures may help explain the dearth of commentary on magazines in surveys of postwar American poetry. Even as they invoke group labels like "Black Mountain," "New York," and so on, historians of postwar American poetry tend to underplay the ways in which a sense of collective purpose may have empowered the poets' work. In critical overviews of the period, only Charles Molesworth, in *The Fierce Embrace*, pays more than passing attention to little magazines. Closer attention to those magazines would force us to see literary history not only as a history of individual careers, important books, and competing discourses but also as a history of writing *communities*—a possibility of which, today, the Language writers are most acutely aware and which they have embodied in their self-created network of little magazines and small presses.

Such a sense of community or collectivity was central to *Origin's* enterprise from the beginning. One commonplace about little magazines is that they exist mainly for their contributors and other writers, and thus lack a numerically significant audience. On the surface, this may seem to limit their effect on poetic canons. But that effect is not necessarily to be found in subscription statistics, in the size of an audience, and traditionally little magazines have, like Milton, sought to "fit audience find, though few."[4] If little magazines invite the same inbredness that they often criticize in their more established counterparts, still for them it is necessary for survival, as much a strength as a limitation. According to Gilbert Sorrentino, when he was starting *Neon*, a descendant of *Origin*, William Carlos Williams remarked to him that "a little magazine's only rationale is its editor's belief that the writers he prints must be presented as a group. Anything else is just a collation of pages" (314). Corman worked on exactly this principle, and defended it in closing *Origin's* first series:

Sure, I have been called the organizer of a clique, and the poets who have regularly appeared have come to be called the "ORIGIN school," but this is unimportant, apart from being inaccurate. I have not been convinced that fine new writers crop up every month and that one must not, for fear of dulness or being labeled a "closed shop," print the same writer or writers in consecutive issues. On the contrary, I have felt that the event of any new worthwhile writer was worth continuous celebration and subscribing as much space to as the writer might require. ("In the Word" 72)

The impulse behind Corman's, and indeed Olson's, networking is analyzed in an essay by Paul Goodman that Olson read enthusiastically and recommended (*Olson-Creeley Correspondence* 7: 58–59), "Advance-Guard Writing, 1900–1950," published, paradoxically, in the rival *Kenyon Review*. Writing around the same time as *Origin* started, Goodman describes one strategy of the twentieth-century poetic avant-garde as "the physical reestablishment of community," a strategy designed to combat writers' sense of alienation from an audience and from themselves. This strategy involves writing to and for "a small community of acquaintances, where everybody knows everybody and understands what is at stake" (375). Goodman argues that, in a culture lacking intimate community, "the advance-guard action helps create such community, starting with the artist's primary friends" (376). Among other things, this helps explain Olson's faith in the Black Mountain experiment; and it certainly helps explain the thinking behind *Origin*, which, in the absence of a literal, physical community, established a metaphorical one in its pages.

A little magazine editor can thus act as a significant catalyst for new developments in poetry, by using the magazine to create contacts among writers who then, with a sense of shared goals, spur each other on to important work. Ron Silliman has written persuasively on the general absence of any group strategy among "outsider" poets of the last forty years ("Canons and Institutions"); similarly, Richard Kostelanetz comments on the postwar avant-garde's failure to establish enough alternative literary institutions, observing that most writers "seem reluctant to pursue even minimal collective action in a serious way, no matter how necessary or opportune such initiative might be" (*End of Intelligent Writing* 264). But to the extent that any such initiative *has* existed, little magazines like *Origin* have provided it. Part of *Origin's* historical importance is that it helped *create* a movement or sense of community, rather than simply providing an outlet for an already constituted group. In his earliest extant letter to Olson, from 5 October 1950, Corman wrote, "I think there is a continuity of effort in what we're doing and that we can go a hell of a lot farther together (in helping others go that way, this way) than apart" (Evans 1: 28). For his part, responding to *Origin* #1, Olson wrote to Corman that the little magazine editor "is the agent of a, collective, right?" (1:138). Less than three months later, Olson received *Origin* #2, and again praised Corman specifically for his ability "to compose a collective" (1:179).

This stress on community provides a way to propose a *collective* alternative canon that stands more chance of being taken seriously than the work of isolated poets. It can offer an alternative to the traditional notion of a poetic canon as a hierarchy of ranked individuals. Robert Duncan, for one, took this view of little magazine publishing, as the poet and editor John Logan reports:

I know that fraternity is more important for instance to Duncan than hierarchy for when I wrote him in 1961 or 1962 at the time of the beginning of my poetry magazine CHOICE and asked him for poems (having stated that I did not believe in schools because schools tended to elevate lesser talents in the same swim and to ignore greater talents not in the same swim), Robert replied that he did not agree with the policy of printing the best wherever you could find it and thought it much more important to print members of a group. (240)

When poets become visible presences on the poetry scene, it is frequently through their connection with a group. Aware of this, Corman, like Pound in an earlier period, has been one of recent American poetry's great networkers. His network had its beginnings in his weekly fifteen-minute radio program "This Is Poetry," aired on a local Boston station from 1949 to 1951. He used the program, as he would *Origin*, to bring writers and readers into relationship with each other:

When comment is interesting, I have made a practice of sending the proper excerpts to the poets involved. I have many appreciative notes from such poets. And in a number of cases I have brought about direct correspondence between the poet and a previously unknown member of his audience. This relationship seems to me not only sound, but healthy, removing what is a partly self-sustained injury of poetic segregation. ("Communication" 213)

The Corman who hosted "This Is Poetry" hardly looks a likely candidate for editing such a self-consciously countercanonical magazine as *Origin*. His show featured live readings by Archibald MacLeish, John Crowe Ransom, Richard Wilbur, Theodore Roethke, Stephen Spender, Richard Eberhart, and John Ciardi, and a tape of Eliot (though also one of Olson). At the same time, however, the show brought Corman into contact with Creeley, who gave his first public reading on the program in December 1949, and with Larry Eigner, who wrote every week in response. (It also put him in touch with Evelyn Shoolman, who helped float *Origin* during its first year with a donation of $550.00.) Through Samuel French Morse, a friend in the Cambridge area, came Corman's contact with William Bronk. By July 1950 Corman knew of Olson through Creeley and Vincent Ferrini, who had also read on the show. From there, the ripples continued to spread, as through Olson and Creeley came Corman's connections with Blackburn, Levertov, Duncan, and Edward Dorn (who had studied with Olson and Creeley at Black Mountain College).

Corman describes this networking as one of his goals for the magazine: "I made a conscious effort to bring many of the writers into active relation with each other, not as a school or group, but for mutual stimulation, exchange of thoughts, community of feeling" (*Gist* xxvii). Thus *Origin* helped to make possible a coherent group challenge to the contemporary canon, rather than the relative ineffectiveness of individual, isolated practice. As he writes elsewhere, "many writers who had never been aware of each other were suddenly brought into contact" ("*Origin*" 241)—through correspondence or response to each other's work, for which Corman often acted as a mediator, or simply through being published side by side. "The 'speed' of transference of work to public," the speed with which Corman was able to accept and publish work and distribute responses and that Olson, for one, found "in itself, generative," increased the value of these contacts (*Gist* xxxvi; Evans 1:214). In less than two months in the fall of 1951, for instance, Corman passed on to Creeley and Olson Williams' response to *Origin* #2; Vincent Ferrini's responses to their work; criticism by Bronk of Olson; and Robert Duncan's more positive reactions.[5] Indeed, the magazine converted Duncan to the value of Olson's work. Duncan had thrown out Olson's first book of poetry, *Y and X*, finding it incomprehensible: "I tried to read this *Y and X* and I said 'Oh, for Christ's sake, I can't make anything out of this,' and I threw it in the waste-paper basket." But he continues: "Well, by 1951 *Origin* had arrived, and its first issue had such a blockbuster of Olson that I had to come off it. He was a poet, a poet like I had not seen in all my life" (Ginsberg, *Allen Verbatim* 134).

Duncan's initial reaction to Olson was not the only case of disagreement or conflict within the *Origin* group. Corman records how Creeley complained about Paul Carroll, how Levertov later complained about Zukofsky ("*Origin*" 245). Looking back, Corman observes that even Olson "rarely, if ever, grasped where I was at. He realized that I was not where he was at" (*Gist* xxx)—something that should be obvious to any reader of the Olson-Corman correspondence. Beyond personal differences and disagreements over matters of poetics, Olson wanted to exclude much of the foreign material that Corman actively encouraged; and Corman ignored a number of his suggestions for special features, such as one on the contemporary state of dance. One recurrent theme in Olson and Creeley's correspondence during *Origin*'s early years is Creeley's irritation with Corman. The contact that Corman created, then, even with his primary contributors, was not always harmonious. But contact there certainly was.

This contact, however contentious at times, nourished the work of the individual writers involved. How the "collective" represented in *Origin* affected Olson's work emerges clearly from a July 1951 letter to Corman: "the company you cause me to keep—the way you put all of us down together—the quality of what you put down beside me makes me drive on HU [Olson's essay 'Human Universe'] with a different drive" (Evans 1:180–81). This energy drawn from collectivity contrasts sharply with the poets' reactions to other little magazines of the time, which offered far less coherent and satisfying outlets. Here is Creeley, writing to Olson in September 1950:

The POEM FOR BOB LEED was printed in GRYPHON, badly, and they left out all my careful spacings in the opening section. Hence, rushed it, & made it weak. Also it looks as though the ink ran out on the bottom of the page. Also, I am facing some platitudes by Tu Fu, wherever he may be, etc. I feel dirtied & somewhat cheapened. Very little in the issue that is not blatant tripe. (*Olson-Creeley Correspondence* 2:125)

Years later, Creeley recalled that in "the early days of *Origin* . . . the people involved didn't really *simply* want to see their names in print"; what they sought was "first of all a meeting place" (de Loach 112). On this issue of "company," Corman had an investment interestingly parallel to Creeley's as a poet. In a 7 November 1950 letter, he asked Olson, "Must you be forever publishing in PNY's where the entire context militates against and negates your argument?" (Evans 1:56). "PNY" is *Poetry New York*, in the third issue of which (1950) Olson published "Projective Verse." In it, as Corman rightly points out, "almost all the verse is NON-projective" (1:53). Olson's essay, one of the central documents in post–World War II American poetics, is framed by a special feature, "New British Poets," and two poems in tidy quatrains by Barbara Gibbs, whose poetic stance Olson described sarcastically as " 'O, I am here, and O, I am human, and O, isn't it, weary-or-howlyrically lovely' " (1:39).

In creating the network that it did, *Origin* broke the ground for an alternative publishing system that steadily increased in influence and output throughout the 1950s and the first phase of which culminated in Donald Allen's *The New American Poetry, 1945–1960*, in terms of canon formation the single most influential anthology of American poetry in the post–World War II period. In describing the group of poets with which he begins his anthology, Allen acknowledges the importance of the little magazines: "The first group includes those poets who were originally closely identified with the two important magazines of the period, *Origin* and *Black Mountain Review*, which first published their mature work" (xii). To trace this lineage offers one way of measuring the impact of a little magazine like *Origin* on the American poetry canon. Obviously *Origin* did not shape that canon on its own; no single influence, whether it be a critic, an anthology, a magazine, or an institution, has the power to do that alone. At the same time, *Origin* does occupy a special, origin-ating place in the overall field of canonizing forces affecting postwar American poetry, as Mary Novik's review suggests:

The success of *Origin* was the wedge needed to open up the hoped-for alternative publishing system which centered from 1951 to 1954 in *Origin*, *Fragmente*, *Vou*, *Contact*, *CIV/n*, *Black Mountain Review*, Contact, Divers and Jargon Presses, and was pulled through to 1957 almost unassisted by Jargon, *Origin*, and *Black Mountain Review*. The last issue of *Black Mountain Review* in 1957 announced the San Francisco and New York Beat poetry renaissance and ushered in an expansive writing underground allied with the international avant-garde. City Lights, Grove, New Directions, and numerous small presses, along with Evergreen Review, *Yugen*, *Big Table*, *Measure*, and a flock of little magazines, advanced the new poetry to its presentation as an open alternative in Donald Allen's *The New American Poetry 1945–1960*—where it revealed itself as a poetry which defied limitation. (xi)

Less sanguine than Novik about the success of these ventures, Paul Blackburn could still look back from the vantage point of 1963 and say, "ORIGIN and the BLACK MOUNTAIN REVIEW: What other solid ground was there in the last decade?" (9). Certainly in its early years this "alternative publishing system" must have seemed fragile. *Fragmente*, published in Germany, lasted only two issues, ended by the premature death of its editor Rainer Gerhardt; in Canada, Raymond Souster's mimeographed *Contact* lasted ten issues, from 1952 to 1954, with a circulation of around 150, and Louis Dudek's *CIV/n* lasted seven issues between 1953 and 1954; *Black Mountain Review* also lasted seven issues. But despite the fragility of individual magazines, the overall network held, the continuity of the *group* of magazines rendering less serious the impact of any one magazine's demise. As Gilbert Sorrentino notes, "many if not most of those magazines were oddly interdependent; this gave them a presence and an influence far exceeding their numbers" (300).

Little magazine editors are perhaps more acutely aware than almost anyone in the system of literary production that canons are always in flux, never "made" but always in the process of *being* made. Canons are constantly being produced and maintained, that is, rather than standing as reified and stable objects, and the little magazine constitutes one kind of intervention in that process. Verbs like "establish," "form," "shape," the critical terms typically used for discussing canons, look rather inadequate at this point, implying as they do something settled and final. Little magazines, more than most forms of literary production, often acknowledge, and even make a virtue of, both their own temporariness and the volatility of evaluative standards. As David Bennett remarks, when the little magazine "affirms . . . its ephemerality, offering its fragmentary materials for selective insertion into the everyday life-contexts of its readers," it stands as "the antithesis of the cultural monument" (485). This does not mean, however, that only the *group* enterprise, little magazines as a whole, rather than a single magazine, makes a difference in the canonizing process. Rather, the individual magazine and the overall body of magazines affect the ongoing process of canonization differently. Historically the function of little magazines has remained stable, even as particular magazines come and go at an often dizzying rate.[6] Various characteristics that appear in isolation in other magazines will come together in one to make it stand out: hence the importance of the *combination* in *Origin* of longevity, regular appearance, editorial coherence, and a sense of communal creative purpose.

If writers can affect poetic canons by their work, generating complex webs of filial relationships, imitation, influence, and resistance among later writers, so can a magazine. A further measure of *Origin*'s long-term effect on recent American poetry can be found in the number of later high-quality little magazines that turned to it as a model. As early as 1954, James Boyer May could claim that "ORIGIN . . . to marked degrees inspired the Canadian magazines, CONTACT and CIV/N, and influenced the British ARTISAN" (*Twigs* 35). Developing this point, Ken Norris traces the influence of Black Mountain poetics on Canadian poets and magazines of the sixties, and comments that "Souster's *Contact* and *Combustion* (fifteen issues, 1957–1960) at times look like versions of *Origin/Black Mountain Review* in Canada" (99).[7] But he finds the Black Mountain and *Origin* influence most operative in "the most famous and controversial" and "certainly the best documented" of Canadian little magazines, *Tish* (97). Of the magazine's first series, nineteen issues printed between September 1961 and April 1963, its editor, Frank Davey, writes, "the immediate models were two US underground

magazines, Cid Corman's *Origin* and LeRoy [*sic*] Jones' and Diane Di
Prima's *The Floating Bear*" (150).

I have already mentioned Felix Stefanile's modeling *Sparrow* partly
on *Origin*. (Stefanile also praises the prescience of Corman's taste:
"History will reveal, for the past generation, that the real comers in the
land have been picked up first by *Origin* . . ." ["Little Magazine" 650].)
Marvin Malone, editor of *Wormwood*, borrowed Corman's idea of "fea-
turing" one writer per issue (though Corman himself may have found
a recent precedent in the *Quarterly Review of Literature*, which began one-
writer issues in 1948) (Malone 391). Of *Kulchur*, which ran from 1960
to the winter of 1965–66, Gilbert Sorrentino writes that it "most defi-
nitely reflected the close of a literary era that had begun in about 1950
and found its first voice in *The Black Mountain Review* and *Origin*." Writ-
ers who originally published in these journals were at least tolerated
by 1965, "no longer considered ignorant beatniks by the great majority
of critics and academics" (315–16). And describing *Caterpillar*, which
he edited from 1967 to 1973, Clayton Eshleman writes, "*Origin* is the
model on which *Caterpillar* is based" (*Caterpillar Anthology* xiii).
Eshleman claims to have learned from *Origin* that a little magazine must
appear regularly for several years to have any impact, and that it must
be of use to its contributors as well as its audience ("Doing *Caterpillar*"
458). One such use, for Eshleman as for Corman, lies in the creation
of a network: "the context of gathered work that the act of editing
creates is useful and encouraging to a poet who chiefly lives in that
invisible community of himself and his contemporaries" (*Caterpillar
Anthology* xi).

One defining characteristic of the tradition that many of these mag-
azines represent is a shared interest in Pound and Williams that first
achieved sharp focus in the pages of *Origin*. Support of their work
became one basis on which *Origin* contributors asserted their differ-
ence from mainstream poetics. In issue #14, for instance, Corman
reprints a letter from Wade Donahoe to John Crowe Ransom at *Kenyon
Review*, which politely contrasts *Origin* and *Kenyon* writers. *Kenyon*
prints too much of what Donahoe calls the "Poem About Culture"
exemplified by W. S. Merwin's "Canso" (later published as the final
poem in Merwin's 1954 volume *The Dancing Bears*)—"a verse of inven-
tion, decoration, but little or no action," which "becomes vaguely
generalized and easy to take, and which uses a vaguely motivated
description as its chief technical device." Otherwise, Donahoe writes
to Ransom, "[you] represent the new poetry well, with some lack of
the Pound and Williams factions which perhaps produce poems too
incomplete in themselves for the purposes of your review" (54–55).[8]

For what Donahoe calls "the Pound and Williams factions," we can safely read "the *Origin* faction." *Origin's* sustaining of the Pound-Williams tradition in a generally hostile environment gives the magazine particular importance for historians of the American poetry canon. Any editor grounding a magazine in these two poets' work and thought was, in Creeley's words to Olson, "riding against a tide, certainly actual, of altogether tangible dislike, of both gentlemen" (*Olson-Creeley Correspondence* 5:160). As Corman recalls, "All of us regarded ourselves as in the Pound-Williams orbit and had had direct contact (some of it increased and some diminished)" ("Note" 29). *Origin* would both honor and build on this legacy, in a way that Creeley describes in prophetically Bloomian terms. Creeley praises Corman for his intent to show in *Origin*

Olson's way as having overthrown Ez', and remember: that means, MEANS, he took, had taken, Ez' way as the alternative, the NEXT best. Phew. No eliot, moore, stevens, etc., etc. But, sons against real fathers: us against him, the old man. (*Olson-Creeley Correspondence* 3:74)

By the time *Origin* began, the New Critics had successfully rewritten Anglo-American poetic history to lead up to Eliot, and from Eliot to Lowell, Jarrell, Berryman, and Schwartz. Corman had once considered calling his magazine "re / SOURCE" (Evans 1:74), and indeed *Origin* re-sourced the New Critical version of American modernism to give much more weight to Pound and (especially) Williams. From these two sources, it helped establish an alternative tradition to the then-dominant Eliotic one, and Corman structured *Origin* to affirm this particular sense of tradition. (His championing of Louis Zukofsky in *Origin's* second series has the same effect.) In issue #12, for example, he precedes two *Maximus* poems, "Letter no. 13" and "Letter no. 17," with a note from Duncan praising Olson's work. That note ends by making a virtue out of what some *Origin* readers saw as Olson's derivativeness: "close to *Paterson*? yes—and there be a root / in the *Cantos*, in *Paterson* that is hardy stock / —a direction in poetry—" ("Note" 19).[9] Juxtaposing these materials allows Corman simultaneously to present Olson's current work, to provide a context for reading it, and to defend both the work and its "root." Like the New Critics in their quarterlies, but from a very different direction, Corman used his magazine to propose a particular reading of modern American poetry that helped to shape the developing postwar canon.

Of the two key predecessors, Williams was by far the more immediately visible in *Origin's* pages. The magazine carried two poems by Williams, including one major piece, "The Desert Music"; two letters, to Creeley and Corman; "On Measure," an essay on prosody that Williams used to conclude his *Selected Essays*; and his translation of a René Char story. It also carried a long essay on Williams, by Corman; and Creeley's poem "For W. C. W.," which Corman placed after "Another View," his own response to Williams' poem "The Problem," in issue #10, setting up a conversation among the members of this shared tradition. A similar dialogue occurs in issue #14, where Levertov's poem "A Story, A Play" responds to Creeley's "Jardou" and Williams' *A Dream of Love*. Corman had also solicited from Creeley an essay on *Paterson* for issue #4 that Creeley never completed (*Olson-Creeley Correspondence* 7:124). (Had it appeared, this essay might have offered an interesting counter to Randall Jarrell's remarks, first published in *Partisan Review* in 1951, that "*Paterson* has been getting rather steadily worse" and that "in his long one-sided war with Eliot Dr. Williams seems to me to come off badly" [237, 240].) For his part, Williams planned to use a letter from Corman in book 5 of *Paterson*; only at the last minute did he substitute the Edward Dahlberg letter that now stands in the poem (Mariani, *New World* 707).

Unlike Williams, Pound never appeared in *Origin* either as contributor or as a subject of commentary. Corman felt reluctant to have *Origin* become merely another outlet for Pound's fulminations on economics, and Olson insisted that, in honoring Pound and Williams, *Origin* not be dominated by their presence—with domination by the far crankier Pound being a real possibility. At the same time, Pound can be felt indirectly in *Origin*'s pages in many ways: through Olson's and Duncan's work, for instance, or through Paul Blackburn's continuing the Poundian tradition of Provençal translations. Corman clearly saw *Origin* as representing a poetics that both continued and deviated from Pound's. Of an Olson poem, "There Are Sounds," that he finally did not use, he wrote to Olson, "I like the independent movement away from and yet from Pound." This formulation, "away from and yet from Pound," captures well the *Origin* (or Corman's) view of Pound; for instance, Corman dismisses a poem by one potential contributor as "too Ezra derivative" but insists, two sentences later, that he is "interested in Pound material" (Evans 1:73).

Origin #4 provides a useful illustration of how the magazine offered both demonstrations of Pound's poetics and critical rereadings of it. It is *Origin*'s first fully international issue, Poundian in its juxtaposing of materials to strike off sparks among diverse cultures and periods.[10] It contains translations from German (in the voice of Orpheus) and Italian; untranslated poems in French by the Haitian Philippe Thoby-

Marcelin; two Paul Blackburn "transvisions" from the Chinese, along with comments in French on Chinese prosody from Paul Verrier's *Essai sur les principes de la métrique anglaise*; and even James Merrill's "Country of a Thousand Years of Peace," his elegy, set in Switzerland, to a Dutch friend. The overall effect is that of a *Canto*. Most relevantly, the issue is framed by a dialogue that involves competing readings of Pound's work. It begins with Rainer Maria Gerhardt's poem, translated from the German, "Letter for Creeley and Olson"; and it ends with Olson's response, "To Gerhardt, There, Among Europe's Things of Which He Has Written Us in His 'Brief an Creeley und Olson.'"

This dialogue involves literary and cultural genealogies, and the very cusp between literary generations that *Origin* itself occupies. When Creeley received Gerhardt's "Letter" in the mail, he wrote to Olson: "What I don't like—that he leans real hard on Ez, for his string. . . . He works a short line there, a 'phrase' string, somewhat too much so; again, the habit, some, from Ez. Damn well MUST be weaned" (*Olson-Creeley Correspondence* 4:125). These comments are just. Gerhardt, the young editor of the German little magazine *Fragmente*, writes his "Letter" in a Poundian collage drawn from the *Cantos* and "Hugh Selwyn Mauberley." His poem is packed with allusions to and direct quotations from Pound, its subject the ambivalence of a young writer in postwar Europe feeling at once dominated by the most immediately available traditions ("Dante will not let us live") yet not entirely satisfied with the new poetics offered him by Creeley and Olson: "somehow we remain empty / not fully bailed out by this / method." For his sources, he looks to Pound and Williams: "in old Europe / translate Pound / and Williams / attempt / these vocables in a way / still unknown here / for new attainments" (4–5).

In response, Olson acknowledges the shared influence of Pound through repeating Gerhardt's own allusion to "Mauberley":

> There are no broken stones, no statues, no images,
> phrases, composition
> otherwise than
> what Creeley and I also have.
>
> (*Poems* 218)

He rejects, however, the burden of Pound's literary paternity, speaking as one "without such fatherhood," with "no end and no beginning" (219), and claiming to write in characteristically Adamic fashion, "without reference to / what reigned in the house / and is now well dismissed" (218). More useful to Gerhardt than Pound's cultural nostalgia, he argues, will be the work of post-Poundian American poets: "come here / where we will welcome you / with nothing but what is, with / no useful allusions" (219).

Beyond reasserting the vitality of the Pound-Williams tradition, *Origin* also influenced the postwar poetry canon profoundly by revising certain of the aesthetic premises of high modernism. *Origin* represented not just poets but a whole poetics: the speech-based poetics and "composition by field" that Olson had proposed in "Projective Verse." Stress on the oral and the performative directly violates the New Critical poetics dominant during *Origin*'s first series; thus a move that constitutes one of the most widespread features of American poetry in the 1950s and 1960s was first consistently advocated in *Origin*.

Corman had pursued an interest in an oral poetics before *Origin*, in his radio show—a medium that he valued because "it puts the stress rightly on the spoken word" and "revives the need of the oral-aural commitment in verse" ("Communication" 212). He promoted *Origin* as standing for that same "oral-aural commitment." When the Canadian magazine *Contact* presented three *Origin* poets (Olson, Bronk, and Morse) in its third issue (May–July 1952), Corman introduced them through "A Note on *Origin*." He calls Olson "the key figure" behind the magazine's poetics, explaining his claim as follows: "He has recognized that poetry derives from the speech we use; that that is its norm and no other. Poetry becomes the voice's most articulate strategy" (15). In a 1950 letter to Olson, he had praised "Projective Verse" on the same basis: "it puts emphasis where it belongs: on oral tradition" (Evans 1:53).

As part of this effort to justify and gain attention for an oral poetry, Corman published a number of his own essays in *Origin*'s first series: "The Voice as the Instrument of Verse" (#9), "Notes toward an Oral Poetry" (## 15 and 16), "Oral Poetry (a summary)" (#20), and the related pieces "Notes toward a New Prosody" (#4) and "The Structure of Poetic Rhythms" (#17). So committed was Corman to this poetics that he even tried to enlist such an unlikely ally as Stevens, focusing in "The Voice as the Instrument of Verse" on Stevens' "purely oral-aural basic 5-stress line" and on the "simpler, more direct utterance" and greater "fluidity of speech" in his late work (1–3). Since the sweep of Olson's *Origin* essays makes them more cultural than literary criticism, Corman's essays on a speech-based poetics constitute the only sustained body of critical work that *Origin* carried in its first series. Corman usually ran them in a prominent position, often either opening (## 9, 15) or closing (## 16, 17, 20) an issue; the final pages of *Origin*'s first series were taken up by Corman's "Oral Poetry." Even when Corman did not run his own direct comments on the oral or the performative, he used someone else to push the same values. Hence Williams' essay "On Measure" virtually kicks off issue #12 (it starts on page 2), to be followed by his letter to Corman on the same subject. That issue concludes with Paul Blackburn's "Notes on Dylan Thomas," a short memoir recalling Thomas' public reading style. When issue #17 begins with Corman's similar recalling of a Stevens reading, it becomes clear that even *Origin*'s eulogies will be couched in the terms of an oral poetics.

This emphasis on the oral or performative appears in many forms throughout *Origin*, consistently enough to show it to be a consciously articulated editorial stance. It appears in details as small as the invitation to oral performance contained in Duncan's footnote to a line of his poem "Africa Revisited": on the line "bbbbbbbbbbbbbbbbbb" Duncan comments, "this sound is a voiced labial trill held for the duration indicated in the rhythmic structure of the poem" (16). More substantially, scattered throughout issue #s 1, 2, and 4 as commentary on the surrounding texts are excerpts from the French treatise on prosody mentioned earlier, Verrier's *Essai sur les principes de la métrique anglaise*. In issue #9, Corman follows his own "The Voice as the Instrument of Verse" with an essay by Harold Dicker on the oral reading of poetry, an essay that proposes, "the first step in analysing a poem is this: *listen to it read aloud*; performed, if you will," and the final sentence of which reads, "conclusion: instead of reading, listen" (8-13). In issue #12, Duncan praises Olson for "coming back to the core of speech" ("Note" 18). And the last poem in issue #18, before a concluding section of critical prose, comprises an anonymous compilation, presumably by Corman, of quotations on "speech" and "voice" from Christopher Smart's *Jubilate Agno*, under the title "IV. Oral Poetry." By this point in the series one is inclined to look back at the Richard Wilbur poem in issue #3, otherwise an anomaly for *Origin*, and wonder if its appeal for Corman lay in the poem's rhetorical stance as a "Speech for the Repeal of the McCarran Act."

As for Olson's "composition by field," how might *Origin* reflect this principle? Chiefly in its organization, Olson thought, through "composing, by discontinuity, non-deduction, field, fragment, grit & vulgarity"; "fragments and putsches, go by spontaneous, irregular, guerrilla forms; . . . make that the form of your MAG" (Evans 1:57, 45). This is what, "at root, can make a magazine, today, fresh," he wrote to Corman (Evans 1:57). Olson actually held this view before the idea of *Origin* was ever conceived (and thus promoted it to, rather than derived it from,

Corman), as he wrote to Creeley in May 1950: " 'the job: systematic dis-organization': which goes for a MAG and for a MAP and for MAK-a-pome: composition in field is such" (*Olson-Creeley Correspondence* 1:51). He also thought magazine publication could realize the possibilities of field composition more effectively than could a book, and hence that it reflected his poetics more accurately: "I *like* best, origin, the life & moving of it, the very going on, that a book never, for me, has—quite the openness" (Evans 1:215). Creeley agreed, commenting to Olson on "what a mag can have over a book—fragmentia—burst—plunge—spontaneous—THE WHOLE WORKS" (*Olson-Creeley Correspondence* 3:102). After these comments, it comes as no surprise to find Olson discuss-ing magazines in the language of "Projective Verse," telling Corman that "i have put a lot into (1) the kinetics of things—and so know how a magazine can be composed kinetically" (Evans 1:261). Nor is it a sur-prise to find him equating the reading of a magazine with that of a poem: "HOW MANY PEOPLE EVEN HAVE THE INTELLIGENCE TO READ THE (for MAGAZINE also read) THE POEM AS IT IS PUT TOGETHER?" (1:184).

On this point, Olson and Corman were in accord. Corman himself saw each issue of *Origin* as a kind of projective poem that he, as editor, structured, something that "ought to be read from cover to cover as a single effect . . . , not as an anthology"; "I think in terms of issues, not items" (Evans 1:79, 2:18). Through *Origin*, that is, he extended the prin-ciples of "Projective Verse" from poetry into editing, conceiving each issue as a text that worked according to "composition by field." In so doing, he presents "field composition" as a group aesthetic to which various individuals contribute, and reinforces *Origin*'s commitment to collectivity. Nevertheless, *Origin* did not monolithically propound a projective poetics. Less single-minded than Olson, more eclectic in his tastes, Corman used his magazine to set an "open" and a "closed" poet-ics in dialogue with each other (while clearly privileging the former). Thus he reenacted in *Origin* the principal poetic conflict of his time. Conflicts over matters of canonicity usually include competing views of the nature and function of poetry within a period. Those conflicts will often be enacted not just *between* but also *within* the canonizing forces of the period: within the academy, within the work of a repre-sentative influential poet (or one seen later as "representative" because of his or her embodiment of "representative" conflicts), within a mag-azine. *Origin* illustrates this principle. It is easy to reconstruct the magazine as a more unified entity than it actually was. In its internal contradictions, the magazine mirrors within its pages both its own conflict with the canonical poetics of its time and some ongoing differences within modernism, just as a representative modernist magazine like the *Dial* did in the 1920s.

How did Corman apparently manage not to see the incompatibility of Olson's poetics—the announced basis of his magazine—with those of contributors, a number of whom he solicited, such as Richard Wilbur, James Merrill, Richard Eberhart, Katherine Hoskins, Constance Hatson, and Samuel French Morse? These poets seem as out of place in the early *Origin* as Creeley does in the autumn 1953 *Kenyon Review* in the company of Lowell, Warren, Brooks, Ransom, and Merwin.[11] During the planning stages of *Origin*, Creeley had raised the issue of editorial focus in a letter to Olson, asserting that "I don't want to be involved with a hodge-podge" and wondering about a taste "so eclectic that it can condone: Barbara Howes/ Hoskins/ Wilbur/ Eberhart/ you/ Ciardi/ etc., etc. I. e., no NEED to point out, very damn big differences in the roots of each" (*Olson-Creeley Correspondence* 3:15–17). He feared that "[Corman] just can't see BALANCE or figure what goes with what—which is editing, which is the key. . . . All over the place, he is" (*Olson-Creeley Correspondence* 3:102). Corman chided Olson for publishing in *Poetry New York*, in a context that stood for a poetics deeply antithetical to his own. Why, then, did he, at least occasionally, create such a context himself in *Origin*?

The uncharitable answer to this question would be that Corman simply missed the thrust of Olson's poetics, and the nature of a magazine based on those poetics, entirely. The two men's early correspondence suggests that that was partly the case, with Corman struggling to stay afloat in the deluge of ideas that Olson poured upon him. Yet I would also contend that Corman used *Origin* to put a dominant, mainstream poetics and an emergent, marginal poetics in dialogue. In doing so, he still foregrounded the latter; but it remains true that he began *Origin* with an interest in, for instance, Stevens and Samuel French Morse that was not fully shared by Creeley and, especially, Olson. Perhaps, somewhere in their correspondence with Corman, Olson or Creeley passed on some version of an idea that they had derived from Pound: "verse consists of a constant and a variant. think from this to FORM in a mag[a]zine" (*Olson-Creeley Correspondence* 6:217). But whether they did or not, that idea usefully describes the organization of *Origin*, with its projective constant and its formalist variant reversing the traditional relationship between a basic form and deviations therefrom. At least within the space of the magazine, the emergent poetics temporarily assimilates the canonical, rather than vice versa, with Olson and Creeley making up a "center" in relation to which *Origin*'s more traditional contents appear "marginal."

For evidence that Corman reproduced the canonical and aesthetic debates of his time within *Origin*, we can turn to the organization of a sample issue. The inaugural issue itself shows a structure of systematic alternation between "opposing" poetics. While this structure may reflect nothing more than Corman's ideas of editorial balance, nevertheless the main poles represented by this distribution emerge clearly. The issue is shaped as follows: two Olson poems and a letter to Ferrini; an extract, untranslated, from Verrier's treatise on prosody; four poems by Morse; a Ferrini poem and more Verrier extracts; five more Morse poems; a long Olson poem, and two Corman translations of Catullus; Bronk's "Some Musicians Play Chamber Music for Us"; a Williams letter to Creeley and Olson's essay "The Gate and the Center"; fairly traditional poems by Katherine Hoskins and Richard Wirtz Emerson; more Verrier and more Olson ("The Moon Is the Number 18"); two formally traditional Constance Hatson poems followed by Creeley's "Hart Crane" (later the first poem in Creeley's first major book, *For Love*); and finally a Richard Eberhart poem and another Olson letter to Ferrini.

At the most general level, we can read this issue as moving between work loosely in the Williams line and what Olson called "neoclassicists," between open and closed verse: Olson, Ferrini, Creeley, and Williams on the one hand, Morse, Bronk, Hoskins, Emerson, Hatson, Eberhart on the other. If this schema does some injustice to the complexity of a poet like Bronk, still the overall point stands. Apparent confusions in Corman's early editorial policy, deriving perhaps from a conflict between his traditional education and his incipient commitment to an alternative poetics, paradoxically have the effect of enacting a coherently shaped dialogue between a central and a marginal poetics.

This dialogue also reenacts, as does *Origin* generally, buried oppositions between a Stevensian and a Poundian modernism. Critics still tend to see Stevens, on the one hand, and Pound and Williams, on the other, as representing the divergence of the Symbolist and Imagist traditions in twentieth-century American poetry. If this supposed divergence needs reassessing, still it remains widely held and forcefully argued from various positions by, for instance, Marjorie Perloff, Christopher Beach, Harold Bloom, Helen Vendler, and Albert Gelpi.[12] Despite the magazine's general devotion to the legacy of Pound and Williams, Stevens is by no means absent from *Origin*. *Origin* #4 carried

Corman's playful homage "Insurance for Wallace Stevens"; Corman devoted issue #5 entirely to Samuel French Morse's essay on Stevens, the longest and most traditionally expository critical piece the magazine ever carried (and which Corman "followed" by placing Williams' "The Desert Music" at the beginning of issue #6);[13] he kicked off issue #9 with some of his own commentary on Stevens, and issue #17 with a prose eulogy following Stevens' death; and ran in #18 an elegy to Stevens, E. W. Mandel's "Palisade of Images."

These differences within *Origin* expose the inevitable limits of a binary insider-outsider model even for describing a period where such a model seems most appropriate. They also complicate—though they do not necessarily invalidate—any view of the canonization process as a move from "outside" to "inside." On the whole Corman consciously located *Origin* in a culturally and poetically marginal, anti-academic position. By definition, an avant-garde needs an aesthetic and cultural establishment or center to react against, and by the early fifties the academy already represented that center.[14] At the same time, to put *Origin* and its writers unambiguously in the redskin camp is to oversimplify. Not only did *Origin* accommodate mainstream poetics to some extent, but interchange (both actual and attempted) also occurred in the other direction. Creeley published in *Kenyon Review,* and in previous years both Olson and Duncan had tried to do so. Jackson Mac Low and Paul Blackburn both published in *Hudson Review,* and Corman in *Sewanee; Hudson* carried Pound's translations of the Confucian *Analects* in 1950; it was in *Kenyon* that Olson found Paul Goodman's essay on avant-garde communities. Olson submitted work to, among others, *Hudson, Sewanee, Virginia Quarterly Review,* and *Partisan;* the latter rejected what became perhaps his best-known poem, "The Kingfishers," but published his essay in defense of Pound, "This Is Yeats Speaking." His submission to these journals can be explained partly by the paucity of other available outlets; but it still makes a revealing point about the perceived importance of these mainstream journals even among the most ex-centric of beginning poets.[15]

This uneasy but real relationship between the avant-garde and the quarterlies and poetics of the academic center becomes even more evident in the *Black Mountain Review,* the equally important offshoot of *Origin* edited by Creeley, that published seven issues between 1954 and 1957. Both *Origin* and *BMR* show the postwar avant-garde's typical ambivalence toward the academy's institutionalization of literature. Not only was *BMR* affiliated with a college, but, like *Kenyon,* it was created partly to promote that college (as well as out of Creeley and Olson's

increasing dissatisfaction with Corman). Black Mountain College need-
ed to increase its enrollment, and so, in Creeley's words, Olson "pro-
posed to the other faculty members that a magazine might prove a more
active advertisement for the nature and form of the college's program
than the kind of announcements they had been depending upon" ("On
Black Mountain Review" 249–50). In a December 1953 letter to Corman,
Olson announced the magazine thus:

i hope i am the first to tell you that Robt is coming here as of March 29th [1954],
not only as an addition to the faculty in writing, but as editor of a new quar-
terly, to be called "The Black Mt. Quarterly," 100 pages, big review section, and
planned to compete with Kenyon, Partisan, NMQ [*New Mexico Quarterly*]. . . .
Anyway, that sort of thing. And with a circulation of 2500 to be shot at. Also,
to carry ads. (Evans 2:103)

BMR did have all the surface features of an academic quarterly. It
carried critical essays with titles like "Eliot and the Sense of History,"
reviews, advertisements. At the same time, however, its writers (many
of whom had also written for *Origin*) criticized the professionalization
of poetry and criticism—in the same way, ironically, that a more main-
stream journal like *Partisan Review* had been doing for some years.
Martin Seymour-Smith puts the point bluntly: "literature is an indus-
try, and it must have its raw material." If poetry is that material, it must
be "in some way useable in an industrial (noncreative) sense." In this
view, the "industrial" (or academic) and the "creative" are polar oppo-
sites. Hence Seymour-Smith's complaint that, to the academy, poetry
is fuel for the explication and tastemaking factories: Dylan Thomas'
poetry, for instance, "has imposed itself on contemporary readers as
'major'—or, rather, it has been made 'major'" (58).

I do not mean to argue that the barriers that many *Origin* writers felt
to exist between their magazine and the academic quarterlies were
illusory. As is well known, the polarization of the two factions in the
subsequent anthology wars was affirmed by both sides, and it was
couched explicitly in terms of the poets' relationship to the academy.
In the second edition of *New Poets of England and America* (1962), Robert
Pack, while he questions then-current distinctions between "Academic"
and "Beat," "cooked" and "uncooked" (177), goes on to argue that in
the coming years poetry will thrive best in the university:

The problem of an audience—of a community of informed and open discus-
sion and dissent, concerned and yet free from commercial or vested interest—is
inseparable from the question of the vitality of any art. In our time, the uni-
versity, rather than the literary cliques, the poetry societies, the incestuous

pages of little magazines, is capable of nurturing and supporting such an audience. (182)

Donald Allen, in contrast, had claimed that the New American Poetry of his anthology "has shown one common characteristic: a total rejection of all those qualities typical of academic verse" (xi). But if the anthology wars began as a little magazine skirmish, pitting *Origin* against *Kenyon*, so too, in surprising ways, did the resolution of those wars have its seeds in the occasional cross-fertilization that went on between those magazines and between the poetics that each stood for. While the differences between "academic" and "outsider" publications were much greater than any similarities, those differences were not as irreconcilable as they are usually made out to be.

When Olson distinguished, in a letter to Corman, between "scholars" and those lesser beings "academics" (Evans 1:34), he defined in microcosm both the extent and the limits of the relationship *Origin*'s writers felt themselves to have with the academy. Duncan and Olson especially had genuinely scholarly minds, and were "learned" writers—but in an amateur, or nonacademic, sense. Their scholarly interests did not add up to, and should be distinguished from, an affiliation or identification with the academy (even given Olson's brief career as a college administrator or his later years at SUNY Buffalo). To put this another way, they used their learning to fuel their writing, not their careers. Olson defined "knowledge" in resolutely nonacademic terms. *Origin* #1 carried his essay on education, "The Gate and the Center," which begins: "What I am kicking around is this notion: that KNOWLEDGE either goes for the CENTER or it's inevitably a State Whore—which American and Western education generally is, has been, since its beginning" (*Human Universe* 17). It seems symbolic of *Origin*'s relation to the academy that Olson and Creeley did not complete their degrees at Harvard; that Corman was tempted by but finally turned down a sponsorship offer from Brandeis; that one branch of the *Origin* aesthetic became associated with a college, Black Mountain, but an unaccredited college on the verge of bankruptcy. Thus the association of the *Origin* avant-garde with a single, marginal corner of the academy hardly constitutes "institutionalization" in any useful sense of that term. Nor can it be said that those writers now most associated with *Origin* were first exposed to literary culture through mainstream academic institutions in a way that significantly affected their writing. Their work was not shaped by academic poet-critics as the poetry of, say, Lowell or Jarrell was. Olson and Duncan counted historians rather than poets and critics as their early academic mentors: Frederick Merk for Olson, Ernst Kantorowicz for Duncan. In the contemporary poetry course that Creeley took at Harvard, F. O. Matthiessen did not include Pound, one of the writers most important to Creeley. Indeed, one notable feature of Creeley's memories of his Harvard years is the number of young writers more or less contemporary with him in Cambridge whom he never mentions, with whom he seems to have had little or no contact: Ashbery, O'Hara, Bly, Hall, Rich.

The occasional blurring of the boundaries between margin and center is all the more surprising when we realize that essential to Corman's editorial vision, and to *Origin*'s importance as a model for later little magazines, was creative and institutional independence—an independence that meant staying outside the academy. Indeed, Corman saw such independence as the little magazine's main raison d'être (*"Origin"* 243), and came to feel that only editorial compromise could result from academic sponsorship. Olson warned Corman early about the importance of resisting what he called academic control of culture, which includes control of literary canons: "One cannot exaggerate the dangers (of the academy), given contemp. (t) mags, and general control (CONTROL) of culture by, not scholars, but academics (which is practicing poets, I mean, & critics . . . " (Evans 1:34). For Corman as for Olson, the university-affiliated little magazine was a contradiction in terms: "a little mag is only such when independent of . . . clear sponsorship by an institution" (*"Origin"* 242). In his view, by definition university magazines cannot radically disrupt, and will probably support, the academic poetry canon. According to this argument, if the academy is one of the main institutions by which canons are promoted and maintained, then academic literary organs are likely to further, or be forced to further, those institutional interests. Conversely, the little magazine's independence, combined with the fact that the editor and publisher are usually one, allows the magazine to propose an alternative canon without institutional mediation. From this point of view, one sees the broader implications of Corman's refusing an offer of sponsorship from Brandeis University, as he did when *Origin* began on the little magazine's typical shoestring budget. Brandeis offered Corman $10,000 to cover *Origin*'s first two years, a secretary, and an office. The university also proposed, however, "a four man board . . . to act as Censorship consultants," holding "veto power over material in order to protect any possibly damaging stuff"; and before long Corman was reporting, "faculty insists on editorial supervision" (Evans 1:50, 89). Tempted at first, after consulting with various friends and correspondents Corman turned the offer down.[16]

In the context of debates over whether academic institutions and critics or writers have more influence in shaping canons, the history of a little magazine like *Origin* is instructive. It shows writers operating outside of academic channels of canonization to create a mutually supportive and stable reading, writing, and publishing context for their work. Indeed, what I have called earlier the institutional model of canon formation—the argument that the academy shapes literary canons and, in doing so, will even accommodate a certain amount of polemically "anti-academic" work—only partly explains the impact on American poetry of a magazine like *Origin*. At least in its extreme form, that model assumes a definition of "canon" as "what is read, taught, and written about in the academy," a definition holding that, in Leslie Fiedler's words, " 'literature' is effectively what we teach in departments of English; or conversely, what we teach in departments of English is literature" (*What Was Literature?* 58). Writers, however, tend to have their own canons, those that they find useful for their own work, and that may or may not overlap with the canons of academic critics. The poetics represented in *Origin* was formulated outside of academic institutions, even if it was later accepted within them. Put another way, an institution may define the terms of that poetry's acceptance among scholars and students. It does not therefore define the terms of the poetry's practice or its relevance for other poets, its power to generate further poetic production.

To take writers' canons into account does not vitiate the notion of "canon" by defining it merely as "whatever work practicing writers value." Rather, it underscores the relevance of different, competing kinds of canon to discussions of canon formation. If the institutional model of canon formation does not help explain *Origin*'s initial influence, it *does* provide a way of situating later readings of *Origin*, including my own. What does it mean, after all, to accord *Origin* the status of the "best" or "most influential" little magazine of the postwar period? It means that the marginal has become canonized, via critical claims for that margin's centrality in a certain understanding of recent literary history. In other words, *Origin*'s first series, marginal in its time, now enjoys an academically determined and preserved canonical status: the status, in my own and in others' discussions, of an "important" little magazine. Any claims for *Origin*'s long-term impact on a public canon—claims for the public value of the poetry and poetics it represented—must acknowledge that that canon is in large part institutionally determined. Thus, like many avant-garde outlets (Allen's commercially and academically successful anthology is a directly relevant example), *Origin*, in opening up the American poetry canon, has become firmly lodged within the institution that it worked to resist. At the same time, close examination of *Origin*'s first series takes us beyond the unsurprising argument that some marginal work does, eventually, become accepted—because it shows interchange with academic journals to have been present from the very first, in ways that are usually overlooked. In this sense, then, *Origin* was a prophetic magazine: Corman anticipated, perhaps unwittingly, the degree of commerce with the academy that any little magazine would eventually be forced to have.

I do not intend this argument as an effort to coopt or diminish the force of the little magazine. From the skeptic's point of view, *Origin*'s status as a historically important magazine merely reflects the academy's powers of assimilation, and renders problematic the very possibility of an alternative poetics or of any noninstitutional definition of canon formation. From another point of view, however, *Origin*'s current canonical status reflects the little magazine's ability to expand or shift the center (just as *Kenyon* did before it *became* the center), rather than merely being assimilated passively to a center that remains unchanged. In 1951, *Kenyon* was considered—at least by academic critics—a more "important" journal than *Origin*. Indeed, most of those critics had not heard of *Origin*. But if we compare the 1951 *Origin* and *Kenyon* from the vantage point of the 1990s, *Origin* looks far more important to the subsequent development of American poetry.

Like *Origin* itself, this chapter has been more than a little self-divided from its beginning. The center/margin or inside/outside model that I have used reaches its limits when confronted with historical specifics that contradict it. But it also retains an overall descriptive value, reflecting real distinctions, for a period when, in broad terms, "center" and "margin" can be fairly clearly defined. The history of *Origin*'s first series reveals that the line separating "margin" and "center" was crossed from both directions. But that line—an appropriate metaphor insofar as it reflects one means by which marginal and centrist poets of the fifties defined their differences—remained mostly in place.

As Creeley rightly claims, "more than any other magazine of that period, *Origin* undertook to make place for the particular poets who later came to be called the Black Mountain School. . . . I am sure that Cid's consistent support of our writing had much to do with what became of it" ("On *Black Mountain Review*" 253). Nor is this solely a retrospective judgment from Creeley. After experiencing much initial anger, frustration, and disagreement with Corman, he wrote to Olson in September 1951, "let him be the one, I do damn well love. . . . I can't think of anyone else who wd do what he has done, for either of us" (*Olson-Creeley Correspondence* 7:196). If "what became" of the writing in *Origin* modifies the magazine's once-marginal status, we might remember that marginality (and centrality) are temporary, historically specific conditions. *Origin* can equally be said to have modified the once-central status of the *Kenyon Review,* itself marginal when it began in 1939. Whatever its critical and cultural place in the 1990s, and despite its voyages into the mainstream, from 1951 to 1957 *Origin* occupied the marginal position typical of the little poetry magazine. From that position, it successfully broadened the American poetry canon by publishing and providing a network of mutual support for a group of poets who went on to do significant work; by championing an oral or speech-based poetics against the dominance, in Olson's terms, of "that verse which print bred" (*Selected Writings* 15); by initiating the reemergence of the Pound-Williams tradition over that of Eliot; and by providing a model for later magazines that would broaden the influence of these poetics and this reading of the modern tradition. Appropriately, it is Olson who, in three different letters to Corman, summarized what the first series of *Origin* meant for the poets it published and for the development of recent American poetry: "because *Origin* exists, I write better, I write more"; "you have given me the *only* continuous audience I have ever had"; "you 'started' us all by magazine" (Evans 1:195, 301, 136).

5

"Provisionally complicit resistance"

Language Writing and the Institution(s) of Poetry

> What we need now is this unlikely / Challenger pounding on the gates of an amazed / Castle.
> —John Ashbery, "Self-Portrait in a Convex Mirror"

Through much of this study I have assumed that the university has become the central (though not the only) canon-making institution in contemporary American poetry. This situation follows partly from the professionalization of poetry criticism described in Chapter 3, and from the resulting split, represented in the establishment of creative writing programs, between poetry and criticism or theory. It is this split, and the related institutionalization of the univocal "workshop lyric" in university writing programs, university press poetry series, and classroom anthologies, that Language writing, the most visible and energetic avant-garde movement of the 1970s and 1980s, may be seen as addressing. To put this another way, the Language writers offer another example of poets critiquing and attempting to reshape canons, though not in terms that Helen Vendler or Harold Bloom would necessarily recognize. They confirm that poets can affect canon formation, but that they will often work with and through the mediating institution of the academy to do so.

I do not mean to suggest that Language writing began as a consciously constituted movement with a thought-out institutional critique in mind. Rather, like Olson, Creeley, et al., before they were critically reconstituted as the "Black Mountain school," I suspect the Language poets sought first to offer mutual support and response based on certain shared aesthetic and social principles. Nor do I mean that these writers conceived of the academy as a primary audience for their work, either individually or as a "group." At the same time, it is hard to overstate many of these poets' acute awareness of the background of institutionalized poetic and critical practice against which they were operating—an awareness that, because it is so fully theorized, goes far beyond the sense of contemporary "norms" that one would expect any poet to register. Language writing has had the effect of challenging almost every aspect of poetic canon formation as it has been historically practiced in the academy: the valorizing of the individual writer; the closural tendencies of more traditional ways of reading; the hierarchy of genre that privileges lyric; the presumed clear (more or less, most of the time) distinction between poetry and prose. These writers' collective practice posits alternative literary histories, alternative ways of reading, alternative conceptions of poetry—this is how they affect the American poetry canon. But insofar as they acknowledge, even embrace, the institutional component of this process, they refuse the purely aesthetic emphasis of Vendler's poet-centered model of canon formation. In the previous chapter, I noted some of the uneasy alliances and shifting boundaries that existed between an experimental little magazine, *Origin*, and the academy of the early 1950s. Here I want to suggest what the case of Language writing reveals about the likely, even necessary, relationship of a contemporary poetic avant-garde to the canon-making institutions of American poetry. How does Lionel Trilling's legitimization—or canonization—of the subversive, the production of what James Breslin calls "canonized revolutionaries" (2), work today, and how have some of our more experimental poets situated themselves in relation to that process?

Isn't Language writing merely set to occupy the very center that it claims to critique, set to become another "field" within the larger field of recent American poetry? A succinct statement of this commonly held objection comes from Norman Finkelstein:

In a paradoxically self-promoting move, [the Language poets] have lambasted the academy, which has been all too eager to lionize them and admit some of them into its ranks. Such is the nature of modern avant-gardes in relation to modern universities . . . I suspect that for all its subversive claims, language poetry is gradually (and happily) being absorbed by the university, the dominant institution which mediates nearly all literary activity in the latter part of our century. (*Utopian Moment* 103–4)

This criticism of Language writing—couched in a crisp summary of the cooption process—is sufficiently widespread that it needs addressing. But even when offered, as it is here, by one of our more sophisticated and independent critics of contemporary poetry, it is less persuasive—because too generalized and insufficiently historicized—than it first appears. The Language writers' critique of certain canonical ways of reading and writing (a goal rather more limited, even modest, than "lambasting the academy") may well have helped earn them whatever attention they are receiving. But to see this critique as a "paradoxically self-promoting move" is to take effect for intention. And even if the intention *were* self-promotion, even if we could attribute a common intention to such a diverse group of writers, this fact would merely locate the Language writers in a twentieth-century tradition of self-promoters going back to Pound and Stein. Thus Finkelstein's wry and accurate comment on the relation of modern avant-gardes to universities is more historically descriptive than it is rhetorically damning. Highly self-conscious about their institutional relations, many of the Language writers take these relations as a given social condition and work from there.

Further, as Finkelstein himself implies, nearly all poetry is absorbed by the university. While Finkelstein concludes that the academic absorption of Language writing (much less general and pervasive than he suggests, despite the undeniable interest in a handful of individual writers) vitiates its claims to subversiveness, I think it more useful to examine Language writing in terms of its possibilities for changing the mediating institution of the academy from within. In this regard it is worth recalling Raymond Williams' comments on hegemony, that term and concept that guides so much current discussion of canons. Williams stresses that

a lived hegemony is always a process. It is not, except analytically, a system or a structure. . . . It has continually to be renewed, recreated, defended, and modified. It is also continually resisted, limited, altered, challenged by pressures not at all its own.

It is this process, Williams continues, that makes possible "the concepts of counter-hegemony and alternative hegemony, which are real and persistent elements of practice" (112–13). Without this possibility of alteration and challenge within the university, *all* poetry, not only Language writing, becomes merely another processed food item in the curricular cafeteria, another way to fulfill "breadth" or "general education" requirements.

Having invoked Raymond Williams, I should add that Language writing can usefully be thought of in terms of "formations": "those effective movements and tendencies, in intellectual and artistic life, which have significant and sometimes decisive influence on the active development of a culture, and which have a variable and often oblique relation to formal institutions" (Williams 117). A literary formation like Language writing might simultaneously construct its own alternative institutions and both oppose and occupy a place within the dominant literary institution of the academy. In Williams' terms,

within an apparent hegemony, . . . there are not only alternative and oppositional formations (some of them, at certain historical stages, having become or in the process of becoming alternative and oppositional institutions) but, within what can be recognized as the dominant, effectively varying formations which resist any simple reduction to some generalized hegemonic function. (119)

As Ron Silliman argues along similar lines in assessing "the double-edged relationship of language poetry to the academy," "the university is not a monolith, but rather an ensemble of competing and historically specific discourses and practices." Hence "the academy is a ground, a field for contestation" ("Canons and Institutions" 165).

Linda Reinfeld rightly argues of the Language writers that "the movement of their poetry makes sense as a mode of resistance to institutional or critical demands for fixed aesthetic value and direction" generated by the authoritative center of the academy (148). These writers seek to "empty that center of its authority, to rescue that authority from itself" (149). This gesture gets complicated, of course, if the writers come to be seen as *occupying* the center that they claim to be emptying—that is, filling it with themselves. It is true that in the current treatment of Language writing, we are seeing the canonization of an avant-garde in progress. This process manifests itself in all the usual ways: an increasing number of critical articles on and references to Language writing and individual writers; the presence of Language writing as a subject on conference programs, and the poets' presence as speakers; books and book chapters, and dissertations that have become or are becoming books; in a few cases, publication with mainstream or academic presses. At the same time, criticism of Language writing's assimilation into the academy rests on an impossible, ahistorical wish for an ideologically pure, uncontaminated avant-garde that successfully resists cooption by the institution that it attacks—the wish, perhaps, for a radical otherness outside all considerations of "canon." The situation of *Origin* described in Chapter 4 shows that the boundary between academy and avant-garde was never entirely stable, and it is even less so now.

There are a number of reasons, then, why we need not swallow whole the argument that the assimilation of poetic and cultural critique into the academy negates or compromises entirely the force of that critique, especially when the last few years' culture wars suggest how many Americans see an academically based cultural criticism as threatening and potentially effective. First, a distinction should be made between the address, reception, and use of Language writing on the one hand and the institutional status of individuals on the other. To be specific: relatively few Language writers make a full-time living in English departments, and even fewer are employed *as poets*, to teach creative writing.[1] Second, "assimilation" is a matter of degrees. The Objectivist line, one of the traditions in American poetry from which Language writing stems, has received a certain amount of attention but has by no means been fully assimilated. Oppen, Zukofsky, and Niedecker, for instance, are hardly routine presences in anthologies of American literature or discussions of American poetry; as we have seen, Vendler's *Harvard Anthology of Contemporary American Poetry* simply erases without comment the whole Objectivist tradition. Meanwhile, Paul Hoover's *Postmodern American Poetry: A Norton Anthology* is the first anthology from a major trade press to contain a substantial number of Language poets. Third, at least some Language writers can be read as "assimilating" the academy as much as it is assimilating them. Charles Bernstein's *A Poetics*, for instance, uses the language and structure of conventional academic criticism as just one among many discourses, moving between that mode and others traditionally incompatible with it in the course of an essay.

Bernstein's example suggests that Language writing offers the best hope for breaking down the impasse between poetry and theory that has led to the marginalization of poetry within the academy and that is pushing poetry itself toward the status of a minor genre. As Ronald Wallace writes in his account of academic poetry publishing, meanwhile, university presses participate in the canonizing of a poetics that reinforces, even depends upon, the poetry-theory impasse: "With some important exceptions, most poets publishing with university and trade presses today reject modes of disruption, discontinuity, inconsistency, erasure, and incoherence that are valorized by recent theory" (32). The current situation of Language writing affords not merely another example of inevitable avant-garde cooption but an active critique both of the canonical poetics of the 1970s and 1980s and of what Finkelstein rightly calls the "dominant institution" in the shaping of poetic canons, the university. When an institution dominates the processes of canon formation in an art as thoroughly as the university does in poetry, then institutional and canonical critique become synonymous. To understand how this critique might work, however, it is necessary to review the debate over the historical claims made for Language writing's subversiveness and to reframe the nature of these claims and the terms of the debate.

Clearly enough, Language writing works primarily with the disintegration or disruption of three sets of conventions: narrative conventions, the grammatical and syntactic conventions governing the sentence, and the convention of lyric univocality. (In this way, such writing stands firmly in the tradition of twentieth-century avant-gardes for whom "rupture" has always been a central trope.)[2] Writers like Lyn Hejinian, Carla Harryman, and Ron Silliman break down story, argument, and autobiography into narratively and logically discontinuous juxtaposed sentences; they are particularly concerned with how narrative embodies certain ways of constructing the individual self or subject (and thus, implicitly, certain concepts of "life"), and with investigating Silliman's question "How do sentences integrate into higher units of meaning?" (*New Sentence* 76).

Different forms of disruption and discontinuity occur in Charles Bernstein, Susan Howe, Bruce Andrews, and Barrett Watten. They break down the syntax of sentences into the parataxis of phrases and shifting parts of speech. In David Melnick and P. Inman, words themselves are broken into their component syllables ("cocone, emble blems" [Inman, "From *Ocker*" 337]) and even letters, often rearranged and mixed with "nonsense" syllables. From Inman's *Ocker*: "(sbrim / m,nce // (nome,id // (armb,jor, // (droit,cur" (336).[3] Meanwhile, in Howe, Andrews, and Inman, as well as in Hannah Weiner's typographically mixed palimpsests, disruption of syntax also changes the customary appearance of the page; in work such as Johanna Drucker's *Bookscape*, typographical experimentation and visual design are among the work's central concerns. With regard to these writers, reading also becomes looking.

Enough general surveys of Language writing exist by now to make further summary of this kind unnecessary. I am more concerned here with the much-debated claims that some Language writers have made for the ideological import of their work—claims that call to mind the work of Julia Kristeva, the most influential recent theorist to connect

experimental language use with subversive politics in the manner of
the historical avant-garde, and a figure who has been important to
the thinking of many of the Language writers on poetics.[4] What do
these linguistic disruptions have to do with ideology, with the politics
of the sentence, of "voice," of narrative? One whole section of *The
L=A=N=G=U=A=G=E Book*, an anthology of theoretical/critical writ-
ings, is titled "Writing and Politics." The work in this section makes
it clear that one focus of many Language writers' political attention,
especially in the early years of the "movement," has been the place and
the nature of writing under capitalism. One of the best-known—per-
haps, by now, notorious—statements of the position represented
throughout these essays comes from Ron Silliman:

What happens when a language moves toward and passes into a capitalist stage
of development is an anaesthetic transformation of the perceived tangibility
of the word, with corresponding increases in its expository, descriptive and
narrative capacities, preconditions for the invention of "realism," the illusion
of reality in capitalist thought. These developments are tied directly to the func-
tion of reference in language, which under capitalism is transformed, narrowed
into referentiality. (*New Sentence* 10)

Developing this position, a number of Language writers have dis-
cussed "reference" and an easily packaged "meaning" as commodity
fetishes of language use within a capitalist system, as linguistic
products with their mode of production suppressed. As Silliman puts
it, "the commodity fetish in language becomes one of description, of
the referential, and has a second higher-order fetish of narration"
("Disappearance" 126). For many of these poets, then, to expose or fore-
ground linguistic "means of production" through techniques of dis-
ruption has been, by analogy, to expose the repressed, and repressive,
features of capitalist thought.

These arguments depend on the premise that, in Silliman's words,
"capitalism has its own mode of reality which is passed through the
language and imposed on its speakers" ("Disappearance" 131—Silli-
man drops this statement when he reprints this essay in *The New
Sentence*). This premise allows Steve McCaffery to call narrative "the
paradigm art form of the capitalist system" ("Intraview" 189), and to
argue: "Grammar is a huge conciliatory machine assimilating elements
into a ready structure. This grammatical structure can be likened to
profit in capitalism, which is reinvested to absorb more human labour
for further profit. Classical narrative structure is a profit structure. . . .
Grammatically centered meaning . . . is that fetish in which the sen-

tence completes itself" ("Notebooks" 160). Charles Bernstein puts it more generally: "use of standard patterns of syntax and exposition effectively rebroadcast, often at a subliminal level, the basic constitutive elements of the social structure" (*Content's Dream* 59–60).

Like any socioliterary category, "Language writing" has never been a homogeneous entity, and the "movement" itself has always contained dissenting voices on matters of politics and poetics. Indeed, I am tempted to adapt Luce Irigaray here and refer to "this movement which is not one," and I am aware of the risks involved in implying that a few individuals can speak, politically or in any other way, for a so-called "school." Many women writers associated with Language writing, for instance, have taken gender as a more central category in their thinking on poetics than capitalism. Johanna Drucker has argued that "representation is itself phallocentric" ("Women and Language" 64) as much as it is capitalist. And when Susan Howe asks, "Whose order is shut inside the structure of a sentence?" (*My Emily Dickinson* 11–12), she has in mind a patriarchal more than a capitalist order, without denying that the two may be related. As George Hartley reminds us, Barrett Watten rejects what we can call the "realism-as-reification" argument; Robert Grenier and Clark Coolidge disavow any connection with Marxist thought whatever. At the same time, enough Language writers *have* made detailed, forceful, controversial, and articulate claims about the ideological implications of conventional language use that these claims have predictably—because of their importance to an understanding of the Language project—elicited considerable debate among both apologists for and detractors of Language writing. Many of these arguments for the politics of rupture are more rhetorically than logically compelling—perhaps intentionally so. They arise from a literary-historical context even more thoroughly dominated then than now by the autobiographical free verse lyric and the presumed centrality of the authorial subject; and they arise from a desire to reintroduce politics into discussions of aesthetics. I doubt that today Silliman and McCaffery themselves would phrase their positions—positions that can now be seen as belonging to a particular stage of Language writing's development—as they once did. Nevertheless such arguments have come to structure much of the critical response to Language writing in the past decade. A review of this critical response will allow us to see how critics of very different ideological persuasions have assessed the poets' claims, and also provide a springboard for my own rather different assessment—one that reads the "politics" of Language writing as addressed to the canon-making institutions of contemporary poetry.

For Andrew Ross, echoing the discourse of Language theory, the poetry is important because it "attempts to *expose our patterns of consumption at the commodity level of meaning*" (373). Even more sympathetic is Jerome McGann, who summarizes perhaps too acceptingly the writers' own main arguments for what he calls their "textual activism" (266), and finds in the formal features of their work the "consciously antithetical political content" of Language writing (263). McGann concludes with the rather extreme assertion that "the politics of such writing—the theory and the practice of it alike—are plain for anyone to see" (276).

For Charles Altieri, on the other hand, these politics are anything but "plain to see," and he treats skeptically the view of description and referentiality as somehow intrinsically capitalist forms of language use. The conjunction of formal conservatism and oppositional politics in some non-Language poets, and of the opposite combination in others, leads Altieri to question the formal disruption–social disruption homology on which McGann's argument rests. Seeing the Language writers as themselves reifying language, Altieri further objects that their allegedly radical views of reader participation and freedom "can easily be recast to support or reflect basic capitalist practices. Why is the process of audience freedom not best understood along the lines of neoconservative economics: is not such freedom to recast inherited materials a perfect exemplar of the right to treat language as a commodity to be manipulated in whatever ways I can get away with?" ("Without Consequences" 305).[5]

Despite his critique of presumed homologies between textual and economic production in *The Political Unconscious* (43–46), one might expect that Fredric Jameson's Marxism—with its Althusserian bent that the poets share—would align him more closely than many critics with the Language writers' ideological project. His well-known essays on postmodernism, however, show this not to be the case. In these essays, "Postmodernism and Consumer Society" and "Postmodernism, or The Cultural Logic of Late Capitalism," Jameson finds in Language writing two formal features that he thinks especially characteristic of postmodernism in general: stylistic pastiche, and a quasi-schizophrenic "breakdown of the relationship between signifiers" ("Consumer Society" 119). On the relationship that he sees between capitalism and the postmodern, both as a period and as a style, Jameson is quite explicit:

I believe that the emergence of postmodernism is closely related to the emergence of this new moment of late, consumer or multinational capitalism. I believe also that its formal features in many ways express the deeper logic of that particular social system. (125)

Structurally, Jameson echoes the Language writers' own claims about an analogy between language forms and socioeconomic systems, while revising the terms of the analogy. In direct contrast to the poets themselves, Jameson reads the stylistic disruptions of Language writing as merely symptomatic of, rather than critical of, consumer capitalism.

Marjorie Perloff occupies yet another point on this spectrum of possible stands on the Language poetics–ideology connection. In an early, influential essay-review on Language writing, Perloff, one of our best readers of this work, attends almost exclusively to formal matters, and raises the topic of politics only to give it rather short shrift in a couple of paragraphs. Nevertheless she asks the same question that Altieri and Jameson, in their different ways, ask: "whether the calling into question of 'normal' language rules, or received discourses . . . is a meaningful critique of capitalism" (233). And Lee Bartlett, another mainly sympathetic reader, echoes Perloff in his overview of Language poetry, asking, "are the Language poets in fact naive in their failure to question the practical aspects of their political rhetoric" (750)?

Any reader of Language writing must confront this question. But what many of these critics seem to share, among their differences, is a usually unstated assumption that the Language writers' ideological claims for their project are best measured instrumentally, in terms of direct results in the "real" world. Altieri's title is most explicit on this point: "Without Consequences Is No Politics." Our dominant models for reading American poetry politically tend to be instrumental in just this way, and when most critics talk of "political" poetry, they talk of a poetry that uses language instrumentally: the work, for instance, of Rich, Forché, Baraka.[6] But Bernstein, for one, resists the direct or pragmatic connection between the literary and the political that his critics tend to look for:

A person's political responsibilities cannot be fulfilled by any kind of writing no matter how popular or how obscure. It's a mistake to superimpose political or ethical responsibilities—the necessity for social organizing—onto textual practices in any kind of literal way; it's a confusion of realms. (*Content's Dream* 421)[7]

Similarly, Barrett Watten, in a 1988 interview, questions the proposed connection between form and ideology: "I don't see any essential connection between what kind of writing [you] are doing—whether dissociative or hierarchically subordinated—and the power imbalance in a communicative act" ("Poetry and Politics" 200). In response to his interviewer's remark that "there isn't a privileged form in a political sense," he answers, "right, I reject that" (200).

What the critics whom I have cited do not sufficiently acknowledge is that, in postmodern culture, any ideological struggle gets carried on in highly mediated form; indeed, the Language writers take this very mediation and its mechanisms as a central subject. On the poetry-politics question, Jed Rasula reminds us of the obvious: that from any directly instrumental viewpoint "the nature of American politics precludes poetry as a significant social discourse, and the choice of poetry as a medium instantly sidelines the poet as a voice of any political consequence" (315). He sees Language writing as devoting itself mainly to the politics *of*, not *in*, poetry, offering an aesthetic and what I would call an institutional critique of contemporary writing and reading habits.

Justification for this position—which I see not as a move away from the political so much as a move toward a particular form of it—can be found in an essay that has been central for many Language writers, Louis Althusser's "Ideology and Ideological State Apparatuses." For Althusser, the function of ideology is to interpellate or socially constitute individuals as subjects. Practically speaking, in his words, "ideologies [are] *realized* in institutions, in their rituals and their practices, in the ISAs" (184). He argues that educational institutions are the dominant ideological state apparatus of our time. The ways in which the university, as one part of the educational ISA, interpellates subjects, however, can be contested within the institution—for any ISA is a site of class struggle and competing discourses. For a theorist such as Althusser, then, the problem becomes this: "From within ideology we have to outline a discourse which tries to break with ideology" (173). Similarly, from within what Silliman calls the "inescapable mediating institution" governing American poetry ("Poets and Intellectuals" 122), the academy, Language writing seeks to outline a discourse that breaks with the dominant discourses of that institution. For Bernstein, "resisting the institutionalization of interpretation is a motivation for both poetics and poetry" (*A Poetics* 157). But the sites of that resistance, if it is to make a difference, must include the institution itself, as Bernstein himself implicitly acknowledges by making this argument first in the pages of *Critical Inquiry* and then in a book published by Harvard University Press.

Central to any discussion of the institutional politics of poetry is the relative consensus among otherwise different Language writers on the idea of the reader as co-producer, rather than consumer, of the text. This, much more than the place of writing under capitalism, constitutes one of the few points of general agreement in a movement that is otherwise much more diverse and self-divided than has been acknowledged. To some degree, of course, the reader is always a co-producer of meaning; this is one of the basic insights of reader-response criticism. So what exactly does this mean for Language writers, "the reader as co-producer of the text"? It is already a commonplace among poets and critics to observe that the formal disruptions of Language writing seek to create, in Bruce Andrews' words, a condition of " 'unreadability'—that which requires new readers, and teaches new readings" ("Text" 31). As Andrews goes on to argue, the poems demand from readers active participation, the relinquishment of passively unself-conscious reading habits: "READING: not the glazed gaze of the consumer, but the careful attention of a producer, or co-producer" (36). Or Steve McCaffery: the poetry requires "a productive attitude to text," "a writerly stance on the reader's part" ("Notebooks" 162).

The terms in which Andrews and McCaffery discuss the relation of reader to text derive, of course, from Roland Barthes's well-known distinction between the *lisible* (readerly) and the *scriptible* (writerly) in S/Z—where Barthes also argues that "the goal of literary work (of literature as work) is to make the reader no longer a consumer, but a producer of the text" (4). These ideas can be glossed further via Barthes's essay "From Work to Text," written in 1971 (the year also of Robert Grenier's manifesto "I HATE SPEECH," sometimes regarded as a kind of founding document for Language writing). In that essay Barthes associates the "work" (more or less analogous to the "readerly") with interpretive closure and privileging of the signified; with writing as the creation of an object; with reading as consumption (*Image-Music-Text* 160). Conversely, he associates the "text" (the "writerly") with interpretive openness and "the infinite deferment of the signified"; with writing as movement within "a methodological field"; with reading as production (more of which below).[8] Barthes's "text" has all the features of Language writing. "The Text is that which goes to the limit of the rules of enunciation (rationality, readability, etc.)," he writes. It is "without closure," "plural," a "weave of signifiers," "woven entirely with citations, references, echoes, cultural languages (what language is not?), antecedent or contemporary, which cut across it through and through in a vast stereophony" (157–60).

Barthes stresses that the Text "*is experienced only in an activity of pro-duction*" (*Image-Music-Text* 164, 156)—by writer and, just as important for the purposes of my argument, by reader. Thus "it asks of the reader a practical collaboration" in "play, activity, production, practice," to the point where Barthes can describe Mallarmé as "wanting the audience to *produce* the book" (162–63). An effective summary of Language writing seen from this perspective comes from Bernstein (who also speaks in terms of "text"):

The text calls upon the reader to be actively involved in the process of constitut-ing its meaning, the reader becoming a neutral observer neither to a described exteriority nor to an enacted interiority. The text formally involves the process of response/interpretation and in so doing makes the reader aware of herself or himself as producer as well as consumer of meaning. It calls the reader to action, questioning, self-examination: to a reconsideration and remaking of the habits, automatisms, conventions, beliefs through which, and only through which, we see and interpret the world. (*Content's Dream* 233)

It is worth adding what Bernstein says elsewhere about these "conven-tions": "conventions, which are enacted at every level, can best be understood institutionally" (*A Poetics* 225).

In response to such arguments, Tenney Nathanson wonders "whether what readers confronting [Language writing] in fact experi-ence is the liberating effect of being able to produce rather than con-sume meaning. It is at any rate far from obvious what it might mean to produce a reading of one's own here" (311).[9] (Nathanson himself turns not to Barthes but to Kristeva's "necessary interpenetration of the registers she calls the semiotic and the symbolic," "a useful antidote to the possible misuse of the analogy between linguistic standardiza-tion and commodity reification" [313–14].) What invites objections such as Nathanson's is that "the reader" in Language theory tends to remain a rather monolithic category. Any attempt to situate this reader in fact leads one toward the academy: the institution that has most often shaped the reading habits of poetry readers, that is the site where much contemporary American poetry gets written and read, and that is a primary target of the Language writers' ideological critique. The reader most likely and most equipped to "produce" readings of these texts is an "experienced," "educated" poetry reader, one conscious of the con-ventions that the writing subverts, a reader with a high tolerance for opacity and somewhat informed about the poststructuralist views of language that the poetry itself embodies. As Steve McCaffery puts it in *Panopticon*, "THE TEXTUAL INTENTION PRESUPPOSES READERS WHO

KNOW THE LANGUAGE CONSPIRACY IN OPERATION." Like McCaffery, Bernstein assumes the existence of such a readership (and the increasing visibility of Language writing in conference programs, critical journals, and syllabi would seem to bear him out): "readers can be expected / to enjoy a device that ruptures the 'commodification' / of reading insofar as this fulfills / their desire for such a work" (*A Poetics* 65). In the remainder of this chapter, then, I will shift the terms of debate and suggest that actually the ideological implications of Language poetry are most usefully discussed in institutional rather than more globally political terms.

But first, some caveats and some distinctions. If certain male Language-affiliated poets have metaphorized reading in terms of consumption, their female peers more often see passive reading and the blurring of the roles of reader and writer in gender terms.[10] I raise this issue because, on the surface, the widespread acceptance of French poststructuralist theory would seem to mean that the academy no longer inscribes a predominantly male model of readership. But as Teresa de Lauretis argues, the influential work of Foucault, for instance, excludes (though it does not *preclude*) any substantive discussion of gender, while Althusser does not consider "the possibility—let alone the process of constitution—of a female subject" (6). The move that I have made from the instrumental to the institutional politics of Language writing has the virtue of locating readers for that work specifically. It risks, however, bracketing the relationship of gender, reading, and writing. To discuss Language writing as an autonomous entity recognizable mainly by its formal features—generally, the features of a nongendered *écriture féminine*—raises similar problems, as Bernstein points out: "The identity formed as / a result of an antiabsorptive autonomism / threatens to absorb differential groupings / within it" (*A Poetics* 20). Women writers' concern with questions of gender, that is, can get subsumed into the "larger" category of the aesthetic or the experimental. But from another angle, women's Language writing represents the very "theoretical-historical convergence of the female and avant-garde traditions" (77) that Marianne DeKoven simultaneously argues for and regrets the absence of. To resist the absorption of this "differential grouping," DeKoven suggests, it is necessary "to establish [women] as an 'ambiguously nonhegemonic' group *in relation to male avant-garde hegemony,* simultaneously within it and subversive of it" (79). In this view, experimental women writers would stand in the same relation to the avant-garde as the avant-garde does to the university.

In a valuable essay on "cooptation," Gerald Graff traces that concept from Trilling's "legitimization of the subversive" through Marcuse's "repressive desublimation" and "repressive tolerence" to the New Historicist and late Foucauldian view that "power operates not by repressing dissenting forces but by organizing and channeling them" ("Cooptation" 169). Graff's argument bears directly both on the emergent canonization of Language writing and on issues of canonicity more generally. Describing the terms in which experimental writing typically gets discussed, he observes that "today, certain theories or textual practices are predefined as *inherently* subversive—e.g., any 'rupture' of conventional realism or narrative closure, any decentering of the subject, any refusal to read for authorial intentions or determine meaning" (174). To focus on the institutional matrix of Language writing's production and reception, however, enables us to defer dubious claims for the poetry's "*inherently* subversive" nature in favor of more tenable claims for its *contextual* subversiveness. For as Graff argues, "the political valence of theory, idea, or textual practice is *conjunctual*—it does not inhere in the theory or practice *in itself*, but is a function of how the theory or practice is used or appropriated in specific contexts" (175).

Silliman, the poet who has written most explicitly on the inescapability of the academy as the central mediating institution (or ideological state apparatus) in American poetry, confronts directly the social positionality both of Language writing and of its audience. He describes this writing as

the grouping together of several, not always compatible, tendencies within "high bourgeois" literature. The characteristic features of this position within literature have been known for decades: the educational level of the audience, their sense of the historicity of writing itself, the class origin of its practitioners (how many, reading this, will be the children of lawyers, doctors, ministers, professors?), &, significantly, the functional declassing of most persons who choose such writing as a lifework. ("If by 'Writing'" 168)

If this confession of Language writing's bourgeois roots and audience seems surprising (or seems to contradict the work's announced political project), we might remember three things: that earlier avant-gardes have had comparable class origins; that they too can be defined by their attack on the institutions of their own class, especially, in Peter Bürger's term, "the institution Art"; and that, as Silliman has put it elsewhere, "regardless of the type of poet one is, the writer's relationship to her or his audience must now be negotiated with an awareness of the academy's institutional reach over the entire field of literature" ("Poets and Intellectuals" 122). As Silliman argues, "the function of a truly political writing is to, first, comprehend its position (most explicitly, that of its audience) . . ." ("If by 'Writing'" 168). The function of the high bourgeois literature called Language writing, in this argument, is to address the intellectual institutions of the bourgeoisie. Much of Silliman's theoretical writing has this institutional thrust: "a poetics must be concerned with the process by which writing is organized politically into literature," the "process of bureaucratization through which writing is transformed into the canon of Literature" (*New Sentence* 4, 15). Even more directly, in his important essay "Canons and Institutions" Silliman argues for rethinking questions of canonicity and exclusion in American poetry to a degree that "is possible only through the concerted *and collective* effort on the part of not just a half dozen committed individuals, but virtually an entire generation of outsider poets and their allies, an institutional intervention that has virtually no precedent in American literary history" (169).

Language writing has been criticized for its allegedly mandarin sense of audience, and for a supposed self-regarding cliquishness and defensiveness in the face of criticism from "outsiders." Such arguments typically take the form and tone of this attack from Tom Clark, who contrasts Language writing with the work of a poet whom many Language writers take as an important predecessor, William Carlos Williams: "Williams's historic decision to base his writing on the spoken American language . . . was the great democratic gesture of poetry in this century, expanding its audience to fulfill the grandly inclusive aims of Walt Whitman. The language school has set out to draw back the perimeters of that audience, contracting poetry until it fits only around themselves" ("Stalin" 304). This claim that Williams democratically expanded the audience for poetry to a range that can be described as "grandly inclusive" is far-fetched, to say the least. But what is of most interest here is the terms of the attack: the Language writers (set, through a highly partial reading of Williams, in specific contrast to him and Whitman) are antidemocratic, and they talk only to themselves.[11] In Clark's view, it seems, either poets address everybody or they address only themselves, and the former is what they *ought* to do. What is absent in his argument is the sense of a middle ground. That middle ground is occupied by what is in fact the main audience for poetry today, the academy—an audience neither grandly inclusive on the one hand nor miniscule or self-regarding on the other.

Linda Reinfeld makes this assumption about audience throughout her recent book on Language writing. While Michael Palmer "shakes

the structures of conventional [poetic] practice," "it takes some famil-
iarity with those structures to see what the process of destabilizing the
structures might mean" (89). While Bernstein's poetry might at first
deter "the uninitiated (and therefore all too vulnerable) reader" (74),
Language writing "is in fact not too difficult for an audience accus-
tomed to reading the experimental writing and critical theory of our
time" (50–51)—not too difficult, that is, for the initiated. Reinfeld's argu-
ment that Bernstein "refuses to hand over his writing to custodial
makers of meaning, philosophical or otherwise" (63), is compromised
by the fact that those same "custodial makers of meaning" constitute
the informed readership whom she invokes. More to the point is her
reminder that "the will to make sense of radical poetries and alternate
approaches is not inborn but inscribed" (41)—and it is inscribed and
maintained primarily in the academy.

As Bob Perelman argues in a 1988 essay, attacks on Language writing
are finally based on "institutional definitions, not language"—institu-
tional definitions that tend to hold "the roles of writer, critic, and audi-
ence . . . strictly separated out" and that promote an individualistic
conception of the poet.[12] This conception is preserved and defended,
in Perelman's view, by "the workshops' commitment to voice as imme-
diate subjectivity," which "masks the institutional circuits, the networks
of presses, reviews, jobs, readings, and awards that are the actual
sounding board of voice." If Perelman is right, then in response, as
Andrews observes, "writing can recognize its social ground by contest-
ing its establishment, its institutionalization" ('Poetry as Explanation"
28). In his own writing, Andrews seeks "to make as visible as possible
the limits & norms & operations of the machinery" (28). For Andrews,
and for most Language theory, this "making visible" refers mainly to
the machinery of meaning production that grammar and syntax are.
But there is another, equally relevant level of machinery—the machin-
ery of interpretation and of institutions. Andrews consistently stresses
the importance of context in discussing literary production, and the
main context for the reading and writing of poetry, once one moves out-
side the Language writers' own self-created network of presses and
magazines, is a set of university-affiliated institutions: classrooms,
writing workshops, critical journals, university presses and literary
magazines, reading series.[13] This is the context, that is, where the
reading of poetry mainly takes place—an institution dedicated to the
making of meaning and to the maintenance and dissemination of read-
ing conventions. But, to turn to Andrews again, this "context needs a
Contest: & so writing contextualizes as it contests the limits—which

are bonds and bounds of allegiance, of worth, of normal comprehensibility" ("Poetry as Explanation" 29). Contesting the limits of reading, and thus redefining its contexts, Language writing brings into the heart of this reading institution what Bernstein calls an "impermeability" or "anti-absorptiveness" created by forms of radical rupture—"a certain illegibility *within* the legible" (Andrews, "Poetry as Explanation" 25).

For a specific example of how formal rupture in Language writing combines with or represents institutional critique, I will turn to two poems by Bernstein published in, of all places, the September/October 1989 issue of *American Poetry Review*. Although *APR*, that national organ of the workshop lyric, has sometimes carried the work of writers such as Leslie Scalapino, and did run an early essay by Marjorie Perloff on Language writing, Bernstein is the first poet fully identified with Language writing to appear there. (Susan Howe, with a sequence of thirteen poems entitled "Silence Wager Stories" in the March/April 1991 issue, is the second; and selections from Howe's "Melville's Marginalia" appeared in the January/February 1993 issue.) Bernstein has specified *APR* as one of the quintessential organs of what he calls "official verse culture":

Let me be specific as to what I mean by 'official verse culture"—I am referring to the poetry publishing and reviewing practices of *The New York Times*, *The Nation*, *American Poetry Review*, *The New York Review of Books*, *The New Yorker*, *Poetry* (Chicago), *Antaeus*, *Parnassus*, Atheneum Press, all the major trade publishers, the poetry series of almost all of the major university presses. . . . (*Content's Dream* 247)

Critics in general routinely invoke APR as representing the antithesis of Language poetics: "Certainly when contrasted with much of American verse written in the past twenty years or so, such as that which appears in *American Poetry Review* (a verse which poses the poem as the expression of a significant and often personal experience of the individual poet), then Language Poetry might appear quite new" (Hartley 1–2). Lee Bartlett argues that "many of the Language poets insist on a poetry which resists any 'normative standardization in the ordering of words in the unit or the sequencing of these units'; resists, that is, the *APR* poem" (748).[14] Given the poetics that *APR* represents, then, Bernstein's publishing in it can easily be read as a consciously anti-institutional gesture (just as Stephen Berg's move from editing *Naked Poetry* and *The New Naked Poetry* to founding *APR* could serve as one way of marking the genealogy and institutionalization of the free verse lyric).

In the first poem, "The Age of Correggio and the Carracci," Bernstein simultaneously addresses, exploits, and breaks with the institutionalized rhetorical norms of current mainstream poetics. Here it is:

> Thanks for your of already some
> weeks ago. Things
> very much back to having returned
> to a life that
> (regrettably) has very little in
> common with, a
> totally bright few
> or something like
> it. Was
> delighted to get
> a most remarkable & am assuming
> all continues, well
> thereabouts. Fastens
> the way of which spirals
> fortuitously by leaps
> & potions, countering thingamajig
> whoseits. Contending, that is, as
> fly-by-night succumbs to
> dizzied day. Bright
> spot, stewed
> proclivity, over carousels of
> indistinguishable sub-
> limation. Say, grab
> the crack, secure the
> figs: monumentality rings
> only once, then pisses
> its excess into the subverbal
> omnipotence of a clogged
> throat (smote). Haze knows
> a different diffidence
> which dares not
> expire
> like the Generals who know something
> we won't cotton
> to, but swing on the trees
> just the same: an ant's blood
> crazy for canasta (my aunt
> with the cherry-blossomed chemise
> & cockamamy schemes, praying for
> Zoroaster).

The title seems to set up a poem that will be in some sense "about" art; as it turns out, however, that is not Bernstein's concern, except obliquely. In this poem, Bernstein is less interested in art works than art institutions. The Carracci set up an influential Renaissance art academy, a canon-making institution with the power to exclude a Correggio as a minor artist, an institution strongly committed to the classical tradition and where "the means for assimilating the canons of Emilian and Venetian art into the mainstream of Italian and European art were first discovered and their efficacy established beyond any power to resist" (Dempsey 254; the final clause is particularly pregnant). Poetically, Bernstein suggests, we are very much in an "age of the Carracci" now—an age of academies, an age of institutionally enforced norms and traditions, an age that promotes in poetry, as the Carracci did in painting, the values of "verisimilitude," "directness," "simplicity."

This is partly, then, a poem about art institutions and tradition. Moreover, beginning as a letter from an unnamed speaker to an unnamed recipient, it recalls a Renaissance art patron much better known to readers of twentieth-century poetry, Sigismundo Malatesta. Thus Bernstein invokes his own tradition, that of Pound (in a displaced form—he sounds like Pound sounding like Malatesta) and Zukofsky (the line breaks isolate "it. Was," possibly an allusion to the Zukofsky short story of that title). But as soon as Bernstein establishes his identification with these earlier writers, he playfully breaks out of this assertion of continuity, just as his speaker writes "[I] am assuming / all continues, / well / thereabouts": the break is announced partly by the ungrammatical comma between "continues" and "well." He also announces his simultaneous alignment with and divergence from Pound through varying degrees of ellipsis: ellipses that, like Pound's, can be completed quite easily in context ("thanks for your [letter]," "things / very much back to [normal]," "[I] was / delighted"), but also ellipses that, unlike Pound's, *cannot* be completed, that remain lacunae ("very little in common with ———," "a most remarkable ———").

At this point in the poem, Bernstein shifts abruptly out of the initial epistolary mode (itself here a sly combination of the superficially personal and the vacuously formulaic) and into a mode less sanctioned by tradition, one "the way of which spirals / fortuitously by leaps / & potions, countering thingamajig / whoseits. Contending, that is." One concern of the poem, and of Language writing generally, is with the use of "countering" or "contending" idioms that form what Bernstein calls "a multidiscourse text, a work that would involve many different types and styles and modes of language in the same 'hyperspace.' Such a textual practice would have a dialogic or polylogic rather than monologic method" (*Content's Dream* 227). It's no accident, of course, that Bernstein stitches together this "multidiscourse text" in a publishing context that generally stands as a monument to univocality and the "monologic method." The contending discourses in "The Age of Correggio" include different kinds of cliché (the empty "thingamajig / whoseits" that functions as the signifying equivalent of the earlier ellipses; the dead metaphors of "fly-by-night" and "something we won't cotton to"); they include the twisting of cliché ("leaps / & potions" instead of the expected "leaps and bounds"); they include arch poeticisms ("succumbs to / dizzied day"); they include elegant Latinate formations ("carousels of / indistinguishable sublimation") and playfully clumsy ones ("different diffidence"); they include mild obscenity ("pisses . . . into . . . a clogged throat"); and they include the flat biographical details of the last few lines' contemporary period style. P. Inman captures the effect of a poem like this when he praises Bernstein's "stylistic indeterminacy" as a form of "subject disruption"—"a constant defusion of the idea of 'voice.' Style becoming, not a matter of authorial signature, not even a style, but a tactic, a strategy to get into the text" ("One to One" 224).

Appearing in an outlet that has done much to canonize a poetics of small epiphanies couched in blandly biographical, univocal personal narratives, "The Age of Correggio and the Carracci" parodies and subverts those conventions by foregrounding its own artifice. No sooner does Bernstein seem to establish a "voice" for the poem than he drops it. Beyond mixing idioms, he also toys with prosodic convention (an iambic pentameter enjambed over three lines in "as / fly-by-night succumbs to / dizzied day"); with rhyme (the consciously clunky "canasta"—"Zoroaster"); and with alliteration (the dominance of hard *c*s to no deliberate end). He frames the poem with gestures toward the personal, beginning in the epistolary and ending in the autobiographical mode: "crazy for canasta (my aunt / with the cherry-blossomed chemise / & cockamamy schemes, praying for / Zoroaster)." But nothing *within* that frame can be construed as "personal" in any conventional sense; these gestures frame not a narrative but the contention of discourses that I have described, to the point where the frame itself forms another part of that contention.

Just as this appearance in *APR* is a characteristic Bernstein gesture, "taking a position of protest at the dead center of things" (Reinfeld 10), so "The Age of Correggio" is in many ways a "typical" Bernstein poem. (The quotation marks are designed to register my sense that

Bernstein himself resists the idea of a typical Bernstein poem by pub-
lishing self-divided books that move through many contradictory
registers, so that the polylogic method is extended to the shaping of
a whole volume.)[15] Less typical, but worthy of brief comment, is the
poem with which it appears, "Freud's Butcher":

> Many folks are in a snit
> They say the new poetry's not a kick
> They pout and pester from academic writing posts
> About emotions turned into ghosts of ghosts
>
> Hejinian, Silliman—the tide is over
> Andrews, McCaffery—abandon your mowers
> You're before your time then out of date
> It's not market forces nor fate
>
> A friend of mine named Edith Jarolim
> Told me a story from before meats were frozen
> Seems her mother's uncle kept the beef supplied
> To the distinguished family of Sig Freud's bride
>
> Frau Freud kept kosher, so Sigi too
> The mind might wander but the diet laws must do
> Art and religion don't always agree
> The one's by the rule, the other sometimes free

This is a deliberately bad occasional poem, addressed to—well, to many
readers of and contributors to *APR*. (It is also fairly clear, and in that
sense could be read as a sardonic second-guessing of readers who have
already made up their minds about the supposed opacity of much Lan-
guage writing.) These readers are the "folks" who "are in a snit," who
"say the new poetry's not a kick," who "pout and pester from academic
writing posts / About emotions turned into ghosts of ghosts." The poem
is parodically orthodox in its *abcc* quatrains (concluding in two rhymed
couplets for closure), in its strong terminal caesurae, in its sententious
epigrams. Its prosody is comically erratic, shifting unpredictably back
and forth between an iambic tetrameter and pentameter base. Appro-
priately enough, the poem has also appeared in Bernstein and Susan
Bee's pamphlet of parodies, *The Poems of the Nude Formalism*.

   Even if this poem is something of a throwaway—cheerfully announc-
ing, through all sorts of clues, its own planned obsolescence—it makes
a point similar to that of "The Age of Correggio." While it tells a story

about ideological purity (and coercion), how "Frau Freud kept kosher, so Sigi too," it does so in an utterly contaminated form and style (the exaggerated alliteration of the line just quoted, for instance). Thus it too reflects Bernstein's "dialogic" method. And it too is partly about literary institutions and canons. The poem concludes, "Art and religion don't always agree / The one's by the rule, the other sometimes free." Characteristically for Bernstein, the references for "the one" and "the other" are left somewhat unclear. But assuming that "the one" that works "by the rule" is religion, we might remember that another word for "rule" is "canon," and that the concept of a canon is originally religious. And if art is "sometimes free," I'd stress the qualifying adverb in that phrase. If it is sometimes *not* free, Bernstein suggests, "it's not market forces nor fate" that controls that freedom, that controls the reception and canonical status of "Hejinian, Silliman . . . / Andrews, McCaffery," or even that controls the reading paradigms of the "folks" in the first stanza. What controls that freedom to a significant degree is the whole complex of writing and reading institutions for which *APR* can stand as a synecdoche—a complex of institutions whose ideological implications Language writing, more than any other form of contemporary writing, successfully addresses, and whose hold it seeks to break.

As I argued in Chapter 2 with regard to John Berryman's self-conscious adoption of the cultural outsider stance, subject positions can be canonized too, and official verse culture canonizes that of the unitary lyric voice. To the extent that this undisturbed sense of voice and self is a synecdoche for stability, authority, the idea of a center, then to problematize that singularly constituted voice is to problematize the rhetorical and institutional authority sustaining it—an authority, as mentioned earlier, represented by a nationwide network of university presses, magazines, reading series, competitions, and granting agencies. Language writers attack this privileging of the singular "voice," which buttresses the concept of a canon made up of individual poets, partly through their collaborative work. Examples include *Leningrad* (by Michael Davidson, Lyn Hejinian, Ron Silliman, and Barrett Watten); *Rational Geomancy* (Steve McCaffery and b. p. Nichol); *Legend* (Andrews, Bernstein, Ray DiPalma, McCaffery, Silliman); *The Wide Road* (Hejinian and Carla Harryman). Indeed, this threat to individualistic ideas of literary production, Peter Bürger argues, is one feature of the historical avant-garde. By this means, as well as by the kinds of formal rupture discussed in this chapter, the Language writers have sought to reshape canonical ways of reading, and thus by extension to foreground, question, and disrupt poetry's relationship to its primary governing institution, the academy.

The appearance of "groupiness" that annoys such critics as Tom Clark actually forces some reassessment of the terms in which we think about canons. In a group manifesto, "Aesthetic Tendency and the Politics of Poetry," six Language writers stress the group nature of their project as a counter to the institutionalized individualism of mainstream poetics, and suggest that they are seen as threatening because they make the social constitution of the group so explicit. In their view, defense of the idea of the individual poet also serves as a defense of the category of the "literary" and of a canon defined narrowly in terms of individual authors. Conversely, "we are arguing for the significance of a group against the canonical individual of the 'expressivist' tendency, itself a social movement" (Silliman et al., "Aesthetic Tendency" 273). They are arguing, that is, for a shift in thinking about canons. As Alvin Kernan observes, literary institutions, like any ideological formation, survive by maintaining the illusion of their naturalness. Thus any demystifying of the poet's status becomes a threat to Literature:

Because the poet is so central to our conception of literature, one of its primary objectifications, a guarantee in his role and person of the special nature and value of literature, any attempt to demystify the role or the person who occupies it by calling his powers into question endangers the status of literature itself. (43)

From the more collectivist point of view of many Language writers, the transparent, quasi-realist rhetoric of the contemporary free verse lyric can be seen not only as a canonical aesthetic but as an ideology, designed to appear natural and to conceal its own constructedness. Walter Kalaidjian argues that this institutionalization of the private self as the center of poetry parallels the social dominance of a particular stage of bourgeois individualism.[16] In contrast to those writers whom Kalaidjian describes as "academics whose poetry typically seeks to repress and transcend their institutional lives" (27) in favor of adopting a supposedly individualistic subject position, Language writers often foreground group and institutional context in their thinking about poetry. Thus debates over the contemporary canon in poetry are also (or at bottom) debates over competing views of the self and of authorship.[17] Silliman proposes that "the collective literature of the community, an ensemble of 'scenes,' is gradually emerging as more vital than the production of single authors" (*New Sentence* 61). Similarly, Bernstein argues that "poetry gets shaped—informed and transformed—by the social relations of publication, readership, correspondence, read-

ings, &c. (or, historically seen, the 'tradition'), and, indeed, that the
poetry community(ies) are not a secondary phenomenon to writing but
a primary one" (*Content's Dream* 346). The Language writers' commit-
ment to various forms of group collaboration in a self-reinforcing net-
work of little magazines, small presses, talk series, and reading series
shows their awareness of all this and gives their institutional interven-
tion more force: in Silliman's words, "aesthetic practice raised to an
institutional strategy" ("Canons and Institutions" 169).[18]

Institutional interventions have their risks, of course. The skeptic
might see Bernstein's and Howe's appearance in *APR*, the increased
visibility of Language writing in scholarly journals and conference
programs, the occasional academic job, the publication of Bernstein's
essay collection *A Poetics* with Harvard, as signs of cooption. The
publication by Southern Illinois University Press of Watten's *Total
Syntax*, Perelman's *Writing/Talks*, and Andrews and Bernstein's *The
L=A=N=G=U=A=G=E Book* might merely represent the temporary
commitment of one academic press to the work, rather than a wide-
spread acceptance. But we can note also the recent appearance of Linda
Reinfeld's *Language Poetry* with Louisiana State University Press, a press
generally more conservative in its poetry interests; and the centrality
of Language writing in *Contemporary Literature*'s 1992 special issue
"American Poetry of the Eighties."

Not surprisingly, some writers within the Language community have
objected to what Silliman calls the "shifting from the canonical to the
institutional strategy" ("Canons and Institutions" 171)—by which he
means a shift from discussing canons in terms of who is in and who
is out to discussing their institutional basis and attempting to make
institutional interventions. Responding to Silliman's fall 1988 talk at the
New School for Social Research, Alan Davies said, "I see you institu-
tionalizing yourself as you think and as you communicate in the way
that you do, as you generate ideas in the way that you do, and as you
present them in this place to this body of people. And I don't like to
see that happen." Similarly, Andrew Levy questioned,

What is the value or efficacy of the kind of exposition that you are using tonight?
So much of the theor[e]tical writing that is being published in different public
forums such as your collaborative piece in *Social Text* is basically very tradi-
tional discursive essays. It's the same style that you can read almost anywhere:
it's just that the subject is different. (Silliman, "Canons and Institutions" 172)

These comments address what Bernstein also notes as the risk in-
volved in adopting institutional discourses: "insofar as you seize these

authoritative modes, you become them. There's no way to use them without reproducing them. So it's always an ambivalent thing, and I don't think it's possible not to err when you do this. You err on the side of power" (*A Poetics* 153). Silliman justifies his approach by an appeal to an audience that he sees as either academic or at least theoretically informed (or both).[19] The basis for Davies' and Levy's responses is style: to argue for an anti-institutional poetics in an institutionalized discourse is to undercut oneself from the beginning. Silliman himself, an articulate proponent of oppositional institutional strategies but also a self-confessed skeptic, asks,

if . . . the integration of . . . poets into the academy is interpreted as the loss of critical oppositionality, and at the same time the university system is perceived to be far more of a dominant social agent than it was just twenty years ago, what is to prevent "language poetry" from going into the kind of terminal blue funk that characterized the later Frankfurt School? ("Poets and Intellectuals" 124)

One could answer, "Nothing." But one can also argue that the next step after establishing a set of counterinstitutions is to go beyond preaching to the converted and intervene in mainstream institutions. As his 1979 essay "The Conspiracy of 'Us' " shows, Bernstein has long been aware that any group, including the Language writers, is susceptible to commodification: "group (family, aesthetic, social, national) is merely another part of our commoditized lives—for we consume these formations, along with most other things, as commodities, & are ourselves consumed in the process" (*Content's Dream* 343); "names become packages through which a commodity is born" (*A Poetics* 7).[20] Barrett Watten, commenting on $L=A=N=G=U=A=G=E$ magazine, puts it succinctly: "The radical poetics of *Language* are mediated by the commonsense functionalism of a professional role. Perhaps this is symptomatic of a cultural fact—that the intellectual is himself commoditized, by the university system" ("Method and $L=A=N=G=U=A=G=E$" 605).

In this situation, the goal for any avant-garde becomes not to avoid commodification or institutionalization so much as to use it. Andrew Ross puts the success of Language writing most accurately, then, when he observes that "the achievement of these [writing] practices is that they are making an art of the constantly assimilated position in which they find themselves" (378). All avant-gardes become assimilated to some degree; Barthes defines the avant-garde as "that restive language which is going to be recuperated" (*Pleasure of the Text* 54). Paradoxically

Language writing may gain its ideological impact, and its long-term effects on American poetry, out of its very assimilation into the institutions that govern poetry:

The primary ideological message of poetry lies not in its explicit content, political though that may be, but in the *attitude toward reception* it demands of the reader. It is this "attitude toward information," which is carried forward by the recipient. It is this attitude which forms the basis for a response to other information, not necessarily literary, in the text. And, beyond the poem, in the world. (Silliman, *New Sentence* 31)

An institutionalized aesthetics is one mechanism for the interpellation of subjects, which is why an aesthetics has ideological implications. The institutions of American poetry, that is, like any other social institutions, shape social subjects, make a certain range of subject positions (or "attitudes toward information") possible and available. As a complicating presence within these institutions, Language poetry seeks to affect how the ideological state apparatuses mediating American poetry shape poetry readers as social subjects; it seeks to broaden the range and nature of subject positions the American poetry "establishment" makes available. However, this effect will have to be achieved within, even while in conflict with, the governing institutions of American poetry. This is why, in her 1987 book of poems *Tabula Rosa*, Rachel Blau DuPlessis writes, "if *the laws / of language are / socio- / logical laws* then poetry / is provisionally / complicit resistance" (74). These lines capture nicely the ambivalent relationship of experimental writing to the canons of contemporary poetry: a resistance whose complicity (or whose resistance?) is only provisional, complicit resistance as only a provisional, contingent definition of a poetry that tries to stay one step ahead of canonizing institutions (or perhaps, to adapt Frank O'Hara, a step away from them). The situation of poetry today is such that Language poetry, more than any earlier avant-garde, has been forced to address its "complicity" with the canon-making institutions that it would reshape, and a number of poets have folded that address effectively into their work. To return to this chapter's epigraph, today the "unlikely challenger" has to "pound" from *within* the gates of the "amazed castle."

Notes
Works Cited
Index

Notes

Introduction

1. While Carafiol's examples are actually Stowe and Douglass ("New Orthodoxy" 632), I think the point stands. Carafiol develops his argument as to how and why "revisionist criticism of American writing has already produced a predictable critical rhetoric and canon" (*American Ideal* 14) in *The American Ideal* 10–38.

Chapter 1. A History of American Poetry Anthologies

1. In this chapter I limit myself largely to anthologies of American poetry written in English, and to some that collect American and English poetry. These chosen limitations exclude miscellanies earlier than Smith's like *Collection of Poems. By Several Hands* (1744), which contained almost solely the Rev. Mather Byles's poetry; and the Latin/English miscellanies *Pietas et gratulatio collegii cantabrigiensis apud novanglos* (1761) and *Epistolae familiares* (1765). For discussion of these collections, see Boys.

2. For brief discussion of some dissenting voices, see Mott, A *History of American Magazines, 1741–1850* 176, 185–88. Mott agrees, however, that the period generally was one of critical puffery. For more on the *Monthly Anthology*'s critical position, see Simpson.

3. For thorough discussion of the kind of women's poetry that mid-nineteenth-century anthologists ignored, see Watts, chaps. 3–4. A flurry of women's poetry anthologies in the late 1840s, coinciding with the 1848 Seneca Falls Convention, serves to counter rather than further any gains made during the preceding decade of organized activity in the women's movement. Among poems not anthologized that treat women's issues in an overt (rather than coded) way, Watts specifies work by otherwise popular women poets such as Lydia Huntley Sigourney, Mary Hewitt, Maria Brooks, Elizabeth Oakes Smith, and Frances Sargent Osgood.

Exceptions to Wheatley's neglect by white editors are Caroline May's *The American Female Poets* (1848), Rufus Griswold's *Female Poets of America* (1849), and Evert A. and George L. Duyckinck's *Cyclopedia of American Literature* (1855). The first white editor of an American poetry anthology to include "Some

Specimens of Negro Melody" as a distinctive category seems to have been the Englishman W. J. Linton (discussed later in this chapter) in 1878.

4. Preservation remained a central goal of poetry anthologies for at least another forty years after Smith's collection. In 1829 Samuel Kettell compiled his anthology "to rescue from oblivion the efforts of native genius" "by calling into notice and preserving a portion of what is valuable and characteristic in the writings of our native poets" (1:iii). In 1840 John Keese, editor of *The Poets of America*, described the usual circumstances of publishing poetry in America: "The main part of our poetical literature . . . has been occasional and fugitive. It has usually come before the public eye in small detached portions, with slight pretension to permanence in the form of its publication." Beginning with Smith's, the earliest American anthologies responded to these circumstances by presenting a coherent body of work in a more lasting format. For the early history of American magazines, see Wood.

5. In his introduction to the reprint edition of Smith's *American Poems*, Bottorff discusses the poets' attempt to influence the Constitutional Convention (xvi). On Smith's own Federalism, see Bailey 55–56.

6. For examples of this tendency and of its longevity, see Hazlitt, who stated that "by leaving out a great deal of uninteresting and common-place poetry, room has been obtained for nearly all that was emphatically excellent" (vii); Palgrave, who used "the best original Lyrical pieces and Songs in our language . . . and none beside the best" (xxv); and Quiller-Couch, who set out "to choose the best" and deliberately did not "search out and insert the second-rate" (vii, x).

7. The most widely read of these collections were George B. Cheever's *The American Common-place Book of Poetry* (1831); Sarah Josepha Hale's *The Ladies' Wreath: A Selection from the Female Poetic Writers of England and America* (1837); and William Cullen Bryant's *Selections from the American Poets* (1840).

8. That rectitude was defined partly by the church: Kettell, Griswold, and Cheever were all ministers. On the ministers' role as preservers of culture in mid-nineteenth-century America, see Douglas.

9. Despite Griswold's opinions of women's poetry, the lure of the marketplace kept him anthologizing it. After *Gems from American Female Poets* (1842), he also edited *Female Poets of America* (1849) to compete with Caroline May's *The American Female Poets* (1848) and Thomas Buchanan Read's *The Female Poets of America* (1849). The market offered handsome profits to editors who presented their books not just as literary products but as gift items. In 1837 Hale's *Ladies' Wreath* had been sold as a one-dollar duodecimo; in 1848 Read could sell a morocco-bound octavo edition of *The Female Poets* for $6.75. On Griswold's commercial intentions, see Bayless 144, and Pattee, *Feminine Fifties* 99. An excellent overview of nineteenth-century (white) American women poets remains Walker, *Nightingale's Burden*, especially chapters 2–3.

Graham's Lady's and Gentleman's Magazine 20 (June 1842), the *Southern Quarterly Review* 1 (July 1842), and *Magnolia*, n.s. 1 (Aug. 1842) all commented on

Griswold's regional biases. Poe gently noted both this bias and Griswold's partiality toward friends in the *Boston Miscellany* 2 (Nov. 1842). Bayless documents Griswold's views both of Transcendentalism (39) and of women writers (60).

As I noted earlier in this chapter, Griswold's tendency to disguise an essentially *regional* (Atlantic seaboard) canon as a *national* canon dates back to Elihu Hubbard Smith. It continues into the late nineteenth century. This habit stimulated a spate of openly regional anthologies designed (mostly without success) to broaden the geographical base of the accessible canon. As early as 1841 William D. Gallagher had edited *Selections from the Poetical Literature of the West* in response to "the apparently studied determination of our Atlantic neighbors to do nothing which will have a tendency to bring us into competition with them" (6). William T. Coggeshall waxed less militant in *The Poets and Poetry of the West* (1860), but still wanted to "enhance respect for [western] literature," and apparently addressed the eastern literary community in his proudly defensive assertion that western poetry lacked "the more pretending styles, which are wrought by elaborate culture" (vii, vi).

10. Also worth noting is Griswold's early support of the long neglected Jones Very. When Yvor Winters championed Very in *Maule's Curse* (1938), he thought Very's poetry still so hard to obtain that he ended the book with a selection of that poetry. And as late as 1952, Louis Untermeyer lamented in *Early American Poets* (1952) that "Very's poetry is little known and practically unread" (xv). Griswold had reprinted some of Very's poetry in every edition from the first.

11. Kenneth Price quotes Whitman's anonymously published response to this exclusion:

Will it not prove a pretty page of the history of our literature a couple of decades hence, that in 1874–5 Emerson, Bryant and Whittier each made great Omnibus-gatherings of all the current poets and poetry—putting in such as Nora Perry and Charles Gayler and carefully leaving Walt Whitman out? (79)

12. See the essays by Park Benjamin, Parke Godwin, and H. T. Tuckerman, and the anonymously authored "American Poetry," all published in the *United States Magazine and Democratic Review* between 1839 and 1845. On the influential critical judgments of the *Democratic Review,* see Stafford 95–121 and P. Miller, *Raven and the Whale.*

13. See Mott, *History of American Magazines, 1865–1885* 237–38.

14. Of this group, Emerson (as usual) is the most complicated case, and certainly one who cannot be represented as one-sidedly conservative: the avid student of European writers who lamented American interest in them, the unwitting preceptor to Whitman who was embarrassed by his "pupil," the innovative essayist and formally conventional poet. Further, to seem to equate an interest in the European literary tradition with cultural conservatism is, I realize, already a heavily overdetermined position within the longstanding nationalism-internationalism opposition in American poetry. Some of the most significant developments in American writing of the mid-nineteenth century,

the postbellum period, and the early modern period were inspired by a cosmopolitan interest in European models: de Stael, Coleridge, Zola, Flaubert, Baudelaire, and so on. At the same time, in the modernist moment especially, cultural conservatism and aesthetic innovations conducted in a cosmopolitan spirit often went hand in hand. Despite their extreme aesthetic differences from the earlier writers, and despite the differences in their historical situations, poets like Eliot and Pound share with Longfellow and Bryant the impulse to invoke a highly canonical sense of Eurocentric tradition as a stay against perceived threats to cultural continuity.

15. Rossetti had been Whitman's first English editor, editing a selection of his poems in 1868. He concluded an 1870 notice on Longfellow by saying that "the real American poet is a man enormously greater than Longfellow or any other of his poet compatriots—Walt Whitman" (quoted in *The Diary of W. M. Rossetti* 4 n. 3).

16. Stedman considered that the poetry of his own time was "somewhat timorous," that he lived in an "intermediary lyrical period" that offered at best "a hopeful prelude to whatsoever masterwork the next era [had] in store." But in representing his own period he allowed historical considerations more weight than with earlier periods, collecting that poetry "as an expression and interpretation of the time itself" (xxx, xxvi, xxii).

17. Analyzing Monroe's and Untermeyer's anthologies and Marguerite Wilkinson's successful *New Voices* (1919) and *Contemporary Poetry* (1921), Craig S. Abbott discusses the developing gulf between high modernism and what he calls these texts' popular modernism, based on popular reception and espoused by schools and colleges in the 1910s and 1920s. Since Monroe and Untermeyer incorporate elements and examples of both modernisms, they occupy an ambiguous place in my own discussion—especially Untermeyer, often cited by the New Critics as a symbol of uninformed popular taste. On the one hand, Untermeyer was representing nearly all the first- and second-generation high modernists (including Allen Tate and Robert Penn Warren) by the time of his fourth edition (1930); on the other, he grants the most space to Frost, Sandburg, and Lindsay. As a group, the Monroe, Untermeyer, and Wilkinson anthologies represent the chief modern American poets as Frost, Lindsay, Masters, Sandburg, Robinson, Lowell, and Teasdale. And when Fred Lewis Pattee added modern American poetry to the second (1926) edition of his *Century Readings for a Course in American Literature*, he added Masters, Robinson, Lowell, Frost, and Sandburg. The move toward a stronger favoring of some of these writers marks one difference between the 1919 and 1921 editions of Untermeyer's *Modern American Poetry*. (While Eliot was also admitted into the 1921 edition, he did not make it into Untermeyer's *Modern American and British Poetry* until 1939.) According to Abbott, Untermeyer's 1926 survey of 150 high school teachers found Frost (the only unanimous choice), Millay, Lizette Reese, Sandburg, and Teasdale the major twentieth-century American poets. In this survey, the poem voted "most likely to survive" was Joyce Kilmer's "Trees,"

later used by Brooks and Warren in *Understanding Poetry* as a negative contrast to "The Love Song of J. Alfred Prufrock" and characterized by Allen Tate as simultaneously "the 'favorite poem' of the American people" and "surely one of the preposterously bad lyrics in any language" (*Essays* 160–61). Abbott cites *Understanding Poetry* as the single "most directly influential document" (218) in shifting the curriculum away from this popular modernist canon, and notes Brooks's related effort in *Modern Poetry and the Tradition* to counter, in Brooks's words, "the history of modern American poetry as written by the Untermeyers and Monroes" (*Modern Poetry* 69). See Chap. 3 for more detailed discussion of *Understanding Poetry* and *Modern Poetry and the Tradition*, and of the different canons of American poetry proposed by the New Critics and by editors of American literature textbooks.

The developing gap between a popular and a high American modernism had its parallel in English poetry anthologies of the time. Edith Sitwell published her annual *Wheels* anthology, starting in 1916, in reaction to Edward Marsh's biannual anthologies of Georgian poetry. Marsh was the first modern English anthologist to try and win attention for younger poets by collecting their recent work, and his first two volumes (1911–12, 1913–14) especially enjoyed considerable prestige. But his aesthetic conservatism and closeness to popular taste prompted sharp reactions not only from Sitwell but also from T. S. Eliot, who as "Apteryx" penned a less than flattering 1918 review in the *Egoist*.

18. One anthology deserves mention that *did* attend more to reshaping the established nineteenth-century canon than to promoting the modernist (much of which was still a few years away from being written): Edith Rickert and Jessie Paton's *American Lyrics* (1912). Because their revaluation of the New England poets anticipates later critical opinion so accurately, it deserves quoting at length. The "New England School . . . had an immediate success out of all proportion to its merit"; Longfellow "has been deposed from his throne because . . . he had almost nothing to say"; Whittier wrote "merely undistinguished verse"; "Holmes . . . was no poet at all"; "Lowell . . . never got away from consciousness of himself as a versifier, from the necessity, so to speak, of keeping an eye on the technique of his work"; "Bryant . . . rarely escapes entirely from the meshes of his journalistic career." Rickert and Paton shift toward favoring Whitman and Emerson most highly, and toward acknowledging Dickinson's importance; and they call Poe "our first great American poet" (xv–xvii).

Robert McDowell notes how anthologies of the last twenty years have perpetuated the rhetoric of the "new" and the "young," but with a descriptive rather than polemical purpose. Even as Donald Allen edited *The New American Poetry*, the idea of "newness" was starting to lose its combative edge; Allen's mainstream competitor was *The New Poets of England and America*.

19. The reputations of Whitman (especially) and Dickinson were furthered by a group of early 1930s anthologies: Kreymborg's *An Anthology of American Poetry: Lyric America, 1630–1930* (1930); Untermeyer's *American Poetry from the*

Beginning to Whitman (1931); and two teaching anthologies, Frederick C. Prescott and Gerald D. Sanders' *An Introduction to American Poetry* (1932) and Mark Van Doren's *American Poets, 1630–1930* (1932). While Whitman is the most fully represented poet in each book, however, this still does not reflect universal agreement on his importance, as I show in Chapter 3's analysis of his exclusion from a poetry canon being (re-)shaped by the New Critics.

20. Changes between the 1939 and 1973 Oxford Books of *English* verse, edited by Sir Arthur Quiller-Couch and Dame Helen Gardner respectively, parallel the changes between Carman's and Matthiessen's collections in ways that show the transatlantic reach of New Critical principles recommending revaluation of much nineteenth-century poetry. As George Woodcock writes of Gardner's *New Oxford Book of English Verse, 1250–1950* (1973), "in the period from the beginning of the nineteenth century down to 1918, there is a positive massacre of Victorian and Edwardian innocents: ninety-seven vanish, and there are only three new names: Edward Lear, Lewis Carroll, and Oscar Wilde" (127). Also like Matthiessen, Gardner expands the Palgrave-influenced lyric emphasis of earlier editions to include selections from long poems and satirical and light verse.

21. Examples of such anthologies from the 1980s alone would include:

1981: Erlene Stetson, ed., *Black Sister: Poetry by Black American Women, 1746–1980*

1982: Toni Empringham, ed., *Fiesta in Aztlan: An Anthology of Chicano Poetry*; Peter Wild and Frank Graziano, eds., *New Poetry of the American West*

1983: Joseph Bruchac, ed., *Breaking Silence: An Anthology of Contemporary Asian American Poets* and *Songs from This Earth on Turtle's Back: Contemporary American Indian Poetry*; Jason Shinder, ed., *Divided Light: Father and Son Poems, A Twentieth-Century American Anthology*

1985: Robert Dodge and Joseph McCullough, eds., *New and Old Voices of Wah'kon-tah*

1986: Joseph Baird and Deborah Workman, eds., *Toward Solomon's Mountain: The Experience of Disability in Poetry*

1988: Leatrice Lifshitz, ed., *Her Soul beneath the Bone: Women's Poetry on Breast Cancer*; Carl Morse and Joan Larkin, eds., *Gay and Lesbian Poetry in Our Time*; Duane Niatum, ed., *Harper's Anthology of Twentieth-Century Native American Poetry*; Gregory Orgalea and Sharif Elmusa, eds., *Grape Leaves: A Century of Arab American Poetry*

1989: Janice Canan, ed., *She Rises like the Sun: Invocations of the Goddess by Contemporary American Women Poets*; W. D. Erhart, ed., *Unaccustomed Mercy: Soldier Poets of the Vietnam War*; Michael Klein, ed., *Poets for Life: Seventy-Six Poets Respond to AIDS*; Christian McEwen, ed., *Naming the Waves: Contemporary Lesbian Poetry*; Maureen Honey, ed., *Shadowed Dreams: Women's Poetry of the Harlem Renaissance*

1990: Peter Oresick and Nicholas Coles, eds., *Working Classics: Poems on Industrial Life.*

Much of this information derives from Jed Rasula's forthcoming *The American Poetry Wax Museum*.

22. Allen's association of the "raw" not just with the marginal but with the potentially ephemeral is now well-known: "Only a fraction of the work [in this anthology] has been published, and that for the most part in fugitive pamphlets and little magazines" (xiv). On the role of one such magazine in canonizing the New American poets, see my discussion of *Origin* in Chap. 4. Even the preservative power of books is easily taken for granted. Brad Westbrook, manuscript librarian at UC San Diego, which owns the production files for *The New American Poetry*, *In the American Tree*, and several Jerome Rothenberg collections, writes of these anthologies' "almost ephemeral nature as books. Many of the anthologies we have simply were not made to last" (personal letter, 17 Nov. 1993).

23. See, for instance, Dudley Randall's *The Black Poets* (1971).

24. I intend the categories into which I divide recent anthologies in the subsequent discussion to provide necessarily imperfect working distinctions that can facilitate analysis. Their boundaries are inevitably unstable, however, especially as the university classroom becomes the main place where anthologies are read, and as the last year or so has brought revisionist collections (by Eliot Weinberger, Paul Hoover, and Douglas Messerli) specifically *designed* for classroom use. Weinberger's revisionist *American Poetry since 1950: Innovators and Outsiders* shares numerous features of its apparatus—though not contents—with A. J. Poulin's more overtly textbookish *Contemporary American Poetry*. Hoover's *Postmodern American Poetry: A Norton Anthology*, discussed briefly later in this chapter, and Messerli's *From the Other Side of the Century: A New American Poetry, 1960–1990* complicate my schema further even as I write.

25. While they do not claim to represent the full range of contemporary activity, some important revisionist anthologies have themselves been highly selective not just aesthetically (which is their point) but also socioculturally. Witness the paucity of female and minority writers in *The New American Poetry* and, more recently, in *American Poetry since 1950*. On the other hand, *Postmodern American Poetry* includes at least thirty-three female and minority writers, while Barone and Ganick's *The Art of Practice* is the first fully gender-equitable anthology of innovative work, containing twenty-three women poets out of forty-five.

26. Weinberger's tone and phrasing invite such listing of "oversights." After generating my own list I encountered John Yau's much more comprehensive one, not limited to the counting of "heads according to race and gender" but mostly—not always—fitting Weinberger's chronological criteria: "Ted Berrigan, Sterling A. Brown, Joseph Ceravolo, Kathleen Fraser, Barbara Guest, Robert Hayden, Lyn Hejinian, Bob Kaufman, Philip Lamantia, Ron Padgett, James Schuyler, Gertrude Stein, Wallace Stevens, Melvin Tolson, Paul Violi, Ann[e] Waldman, Rosmarie Waldrop, Keith Waldrop, Philip Whalen, John Wieners, Jay Wright" (46). Elsewhere in his review Yau mentions Rachel Blau DuPlessis,

Henry Dumas, Stephen Jonas, Etheridge Knight, Larry Neal, Lorenzo Thomas, Bernadette Mayer, Alice Notley, and Marjorie Welish as candidates for inclusion. Burton Hatlen notes the absence of numerous women writers whom Yau also names, along with Helen Adam, Rae Armantrout, Gwendolyn Brooks, Carla Harryman, Fanny Howe, Joan Retallack, Leslie Scalapino, and Diane Wakoski (154). Again, to be fair to Weinberger, not all of these fit his chronological criteria; but enough do that Hatlen's point stands. In an emerging debate over the book Weinberger responds to Hatlen's review in a letter to the editor, *Sagatrieb* 12.1 (1993): 153-55. For Weinberger's response to Yau, and Yau's response to the response, see their letters to the editors in *American Poetry Review* (July/Aug. 1994): 43-44.

27. Recent anthology editors use or cite *The New American Poetry* as a model more than any other single anthology. To begin the introduction of *In the American Tree*, Ron Silliman locates Language writing both within and as a break with "the broader movement of 'New American' poetry"—"a break within a tradition in the name of its own higher values" (xv); Douglas Messerli makes the same point in introducing his *"Language" Poetries*. Like Allen, Silliman uses a regional division ("East" and "West") and a concluding section ("Second Front") of statements on poetics. Paul Hoover, in *Postmodern American Poetry*, echoes Allen's breakdown into "poetry" and "poetics" sections, beginning each with Olson and kicking off his introduction with Olson's early use of the term "postmodern." In *From the Other Side of the Century: A New American Poetry, 1960-1990*, Messerli invokes Allen in his use of four groups or "gatherings"; in his starting date (1960—Allen's ending date); and in his subtitle, carefully revised to read *A*, not *The*, *New American Poetry*. Philip Dow's title similarly both recalls Allen's and makes a key change, from "poetry" (with its implied emphasis on a kind of poetic practice) to *19 New American Poets* (with its implied emphasis on individual careers). Andrei Codrescu begins and ends his introduction to *Up Late* with a homage and reference to Allen: "The 1960 Grove Press anthology of 'New American Poetry' . . . has been one of the most influential books in the history of American poetry," and "we have all stayed up late in the particular faith of New American Poetry" (xxxi, xxxviii). Sometimes Allen's text appears as the focus of sympathetic disagreement. For example, Jerome Rothenberg and Pierre Joris, who place themselves among those "associated with the so-called 'New American Poetry' & its offshoots," distance themselves from the New Americanists' "frequent rejection of an international view" ([14]). Meanwhile Philip Dacey and David Jauss set out to "[do] for contemporary traditional verse what Donald Allen's *New American Poetry* . . . did for contemporary free verse" (2), showing how *The New American Poetry* has become a kind of Rorschach blot for later editors who invoke its strategies or example in the interests of promoting a very different poetics.

28. To expand on some of these issues: first, Weinberger's chosen chronology also makes the collection largely, though not exclusively, a record of the years 1950-80, again because it leads to reduced representation of younger

"innovators and outsiders." The anthology includes only one poet under fifty. (After completing this chapter, I found John Yau making the same observation: "It's as if Weinberger's anthology stopped in 1979" [46–47].) More than that of other recent anthologists of innovative work, Weinberger's revisionism is directed less at the present than at the mid-century past—or at the present's *version* of that past. Second, despite the anti-academicism of his complaints against Language poetry, Weinberger includes more writers who are or have been full-time literary academics than either Silliman or Messerli.

For development of Weinberger's views on Language writing, and for a statement of the needs that *American Poetry since 1950* addresses, see his exchange with Michael Davidson in *Sulfur* 22 (1988). Weinberger also explains here why he does not consider Coolidge, Howe, and Palmer (or Mac Low) Language poets, and thus why he can later comfortably include them in his anthology. For a detailed, evenhanded review of *American Poetry since 1950* that lays out its many virtues, see Hatlen; for an extremely critical one, see Yau, who, in terms of the taxonomy of anthologies that I am arguing for, seems to wish that Weinberger had produced a far more identity- and issue-based text than it was his intention (rightly or wrongly) to produce. Since I have mostly quarreled with Weinberger here, I should go on record as also sharing Hatlen's sense of the anthology's strengths: its "detailed challenge to the still-standard narrative of American literary history since World War II" (149); its recognition of "the centrality of the Objectivists and of Kenneth Rexroth to our poetic heritage" (151); its emphasis on the long poem; its effort—idiosyncratic and thus partial, to be sure—to provide a "comprehensive . . . survey of the 'counter-canon' " (151).

29. For example: nine of Allen's poets and of Hall, Pack, and Simpson's poets appear in *The New Oxford Book of American Verse*; twelve of Allen's and of Hall, Pack, and Simpson's in *The Norton Anthology of Poetry*, third edition; and twelve of Allen's and fourteen of Hall, Pack, and Simpson's in *The Norton Anthology of Modern Poetry*, second edition.

30. Since in the following pages I go on to critique some of these same Norton anthologies as symptomatic of certain limitations in mainstream publishing, I should say that Norton does represent the New American Poetry tradition more effectively—or less inadequately—than other trade publishers. The company also deserves credit for being the first such publisher to issue an anthology like Hoover's.

Eight of the nine poets I name here (Baraka is the exception) also make up the only overlaps between what Thom Gunn calls J. D. McClatchy's "establishment anthology," *The Vintage Book of Contemporary American Poetry*, and Weinberger's "anthology of intransigence." Gunn rightly points out that "some kind of a détente took place in the late Sixties, and that as a result many of the poets in previously opposed camps have been listening to each other ever since." He observes that "these eight, all starting as rebels against the establishment, are now part of it, from sheer fame: those still alive are respected teachers and have received prizes; all are widely read, as they should be. They are no longer outsiders" (6). If the acceptance of this core group marks the extent of Gunn's "détente," however, differences between McClatchy and Weinberger mark its limits: if the editors can agree on eight poets that they share, they disagree on eighty-four poets that they do not share (fifty-seven in McClatchy, twenty-seven in Weinberger).

31. Along with *The Norton Anthology of American Literature*, these seven textbooks include Macmillan's *Anthology of American Literature*; Harcourt Brace Jovanovich's *Heritage of American Literature*; McGraw-Hill's *The American Tradition in Literature*; *The Heath Anthology of American Literature*; *American Literature: A Prentice-Hall Anthology*; and *The Harper American Literature*. Levertov's appearance in all seven texts dates only from her inclusion in the second edition of the *Harper* in late 1993, an edition to which Olson and Duncan were also added. In contrast to their representation of the countercanon that I am discussing, these textbooks promote a much stronger consensus about a more mainstream mid-century canon: Roethke, Bishop, Lowell, Wilbur, Sexton, Rich, Plath, and James Wright appear in all seven.

32. See Daniel Halpern, ed., *The American Poetry Anthology* (1975); Jack Myers and Roger Weingarten, eds., *New American Poets of the Eighties* (1984) and *New American Poets of the Nineties* (1991); Dave Smith and David Bottoms, eds., *The Morrow Anthology of Younger American Poets* (1985); Robert Pack, Sydney Lea, and Jay Parini, eds., *The Bread Loaf Anthology of Contemporary American Poetry* (1985); J. D. McClatchy, *The Vintage Book of Contemporary American Poetry* (1990). Any list of recent poet-edited mainstream survey anthologies should also include Stuart Friebert and David Young, eds., *The Longman Anthology of Contemporary American Poetry 1950–1980* (1st ed. 1983; 2d ed. 1989); Ronald Wallace, ed., *Vital Signs: Contemporary American Poetry from the University Presses* (1989); Ed Ochester and Peter Oresick, eds., *The Pittsburgh Book of Contemporary American Poetry* (1993); Michael Collier, ed., *The Wesleyan Tradition: Four Decades of American Poetry* (1993). Such a list foregrounds the extent to which the editing of mainstream surveys, like that of their revisionist other, has tended to be dominated by men.

33. For more detailed commentary on the mainstream survey anthology, see Hudgins and McDowell. Both evaluate the anthologies that they review in terms of pedagogical usefulness, assuming a mostly student audience for the texts. Along similar lines, Christopher Clausen argues that the "proliferation of university writing programs" makes such anthologies viable commercial propositions: "All of these volumes are intended for the textbook market. What other market is there?" (132). Hudgins, Weinberger, and Michael Heller all argue that as anthologies of "the kinds of poems that are now being produced by the yard at MFA factories across the land" (Heller 156–57), these texts tend to offer aesthetic sameness in the guise of breadth:

Anthologies of the contemporary sort suggest or impose pattern in a far more heavy-handed manner than those which survey a [past] period or attempt a summing up of some historical depth. Paradoxically, the anthologizer of the contemporary is often far more conservative, far more narrow, not in a sense of preserving tradition but in validating a particular version of the present, than the sifter of the centuries. (Heller 156-57)

Given the difficulties of producing a genuine survey, all anthologists are open to Heller's charge of "suggesting or imposing a pattern." Revisionist editors tend to state their positions openly, however; editors of mainstream surveys often claim for their texts a diversity that does not stand up to scrutiny.

34. See also Clayton Eshleman's essay with the pointed title "The Gospel According to Norton." The critical habit of invoking "Norton" almost as a brand name synonymous with canonical status similarly reflects these anthologies' perceived centrality. Thus, for example, Jane Marcus looks forward to the time when Inanna, heroine of the "first written female epic," "becomes flesh in the hearts and minds of readers or on the pages of a Norton Anthology of Literature" (83); Elaine Showalter assumes even before its publication that *The Norton Anthology of Literature by Women* "will establish a feminist canon for the next generation" (40).

35. On the social and critical forces that have kept Native American work outside the poetry canon, see Krupat. In particular, Krupat shows that, despite late-nineteenth-century ethnographers' interest in Native American cultures, the poetry did not appear in white-edited anthologies until Mark Van Doren's *Anthology of World Poetry* (1928) and Untermeyer's *American Poetry from the Beginning to Whitman* (1931). The first collection that can properly be described as an anthology of Native American poetry is George Cronyn's *The Path on the Rainbow* (1918), although Krupat remarks that "no 'authoritative' collection appeared before Margot Astrov's [*The Winged Serpent*] in 1946; it might also be said that no 'authoritative' collection has yet appeared" (110).

Chapter 2. Poets Canonizing Poets

1. Before going further, I should distinguish between the model of canon formation that I am discussing here and the commonly held view of literature as itself an institution. These are related, but by no means identical, ideas. Literature as an institution is constituted by, maintained by, and included in a larger network of institutional forces. Put another way, the institution of literature is a subcategory of, and not to be identified with, literary institutions.

2. For an excellent discussion of the construction of Hawthorne's reputation in his own lifetime, see Brodhead.

3. As Gary Taylor shows, however, readers did not necessarily find Shakespeare great literature for literary reasons. Taylor provides a thorough historical exposition of the various ideological uses to which Shakespeare has been put. Driven to defend Shakespeare's greatness, some critics responded to Taylor's work with the argument that other artists found value in Shakespeare long

before literary institutions as we recognize them today were founded. That "Shakespeare" himself was an institution by the time that Coleridge, for example, got to him, and that Taylor's critics are defending the institution or the idea "Shakespeare" as much as the writer, are issues that I must bypass in the interests of concentrating on my own argument.

4. Historically, even the *maintenance* of canons cannot be attributed solely to the academy. Again as Taylor shows, the eighteenth and nineteenth centuries found ways to "maintain" Shakespeare without the help of an academy.

5. See Shusterman 106–13 for an effective critique of the narrow professionalism of Fish's theory of readership.

6. Most of these commentators hold to some modified version of the aesthetic model. Perhaps the *least* modified formulation, one that explicitly opposes creative writers and academic critics, is this from Christopher Ricks:

> The crucial constituting of what is tendentiously called the canon is effected not by academics and critics but by creative writers . . . , and the crux is the conviction that works of literature most live, not in the formation of the cunning canon or the candid curriculum, but in their fecundating of later works of literature. (44)

Here, good literature is that which generates more literature (as distinct, in the institutional model, from more commentary). William Phillips, longtime editor of *Partisan Review*, comes close to sharing this position, but with a final twist that accords some power to critics (though not necessarily academics):

> The so-called canon, or I'd prefer at this point to use the word tradition, has been created by creators in the field . . . the tradition of poetry and the notion of the great poets of the past has been carried forward by writers of poetry and by great practicing critics. ("Changing Culture" 381)

While Charles Altieri claims to argue for a middle position, against "false oppositions between an aesthetic framework and an existential one" (*Canons* 57), he seems to favor the former model: "Works have claims on us because we want to understand how they could have mattered so much for those writers who we think still speak to us from the past or whose contemporary stances engage us." Unlike Vendler, however, Altieri argues that writers respond more to each other's content and "wisdom" than their style (*Canons* 56–57). While Henry Louis Gates is far more inclined toward an institutional model, tracing some of his comments on the issue allows us to see him moving toward a more centrist position. In an essay first delivered as an April 1987 conference paper, he states flatly that "scholars make canons" ("Canon Formation" 38). In a later version of the same essay, however, he adds that "just as often, writers make canons, too, both by critical revaluation and by reclamation through revision" (*Loose Canons* 102). For further variations on the aesthetic model, see Nemoianu, and a number of essays in the 1985 special issue of the *John Donne Journal* that discuss "the ways in which presently canonical Romantic and Victorian poets in their own writing interpret, evaluate, appropriate, and imitate the work of seventeenth-century authors whose position in the literary canon was in the nineteenth century uncertain or largely marginal" (Harrison 163). Meanwhile, to complicate matters, one can find a poet, Ron Silliman, taking the institutional view: "Questions of canonicity, of the survival of poets and poetry, are determined institutionally, rather than between texts or aesthetic principles" ("Canons and Institutions" 157). I discuss in my last chapter how certain Language writers hold to an institutional as much as an aesthetic understanding of contemporary poetics.

7. Annabel Patterson provides an alternative account of poetic relationships, self-canonization, and the long-term preservation of tradition that accords poets a central role in these processes without depending either on Vendler's aestheticism or on Bloom's theories of oedipal struggle. (On this latter point, she says, "there is no evidence . . . that Milton suppressed overt allusions to Spenser in some type of influence anxiety. On the contrary, it appears that Spenser was, to Milton, only one among many influences" [779].) Patterson's approach to the question of "how and why authors have themselves contributed to canon-formation" (774) stresses poets' selective representations of their predecessors in "account[s] of literary relationship that [are] manifestly not to be trusted" (776); her main example involves "how Milton constructed his Spenser" (783). She also analyzes, however, how the habit of pairing writers in relationships implying causality and/or influence functions institutionally, examining the place "Spenser-and-Milton as a couple have come to occupy in the academic canon—that is to say, [as representing] an effective conveyance of certain traditional values, including the value of tradition itself" (777).

8. Given Stevens' longstanding and generally accepted status among poets and critics (though not among general readers), the idea that in 1985 he should *need* such energetic promotion at the expense of other poets is odd, to say the least. In his recent reception history of the poet, John Timberman Newcomb considers Stevens' reputation "perhaps more secure than that of any American poet of this century" (*Wallace Stevens* 3–4).

9. As the current book goes to press, a second edition of the *Harper American Literature* has appeared. Assuming that Vendler remains the contemporary poetry editor, she shows admirable flexibility in her representation of the evolving contemporary canon, cutting seven poets from the earlier "Literature of Contemporary America" section and adding seventeen, including fourteen female and minority writers. The excisions include poets whom Vendler has praised elsewhere (Amy Clampitt), and the additions include poets on whom she has written critically (Sharon Olds). At the same time, the effect is that in poetry the *Harper's* second edition smacks more of selection by committee than the first, with less of Vendler's distinctive stamp on it. Unusually for Vendler, her revised introduction now suggests a heavy dependence on institutional criteria for selection, on "who has studied with whom in one of the many writing programs, or who reads with whom on the poetry circuits," on "how the major prizes are bestowed," and on "which of the contempo-

rary poets consistently are taught" ("Literature of Contemporary America" 2d ed. 2394).

10. Given his now apparently secure canonical status, as measured by critical attention and inclusion in a wide range of anthologies, O'Hara may seem a surprising inclusion in this list. The first critical book on O'Hara, however, Marjorie Perloff's *Frank O'Hara: Poet among Painters*, did not appear until 1977. As Perloff shows, before the 1970s brought the first surge of critical interest in O'Hara, his work and reputation had been kept alive chiefly by other poets and artists, in poet-edited little magazines and anthologies such as Ron Padgett and David Shapiro's *Anthology of New York Poets*, and then by an editor, Donald Allen, best known for his championing of then-marginal poetics in *The New American Poetry*.

11. As he does with Fish, Richard Shusterman demonstrates persuasively how thoroughly Bloom's model of reading is embedded in academic concepts of the reading and interpretive process (88–89). He notes how often Bloom, despite his valorizing of poets' readings, "makes the common error of conflating reader with professional critic or interpreter, and thus equating the act of reading with the critical performance of formulating or presenting a critical formulation" (88).

12. Bloom did write on both A. R. Ammons and John Ashbery before they became nationally known (though both were well published and hardly neglected). See his chapter on Ammons in the 1971 *The Ringers in the Tower* (257–90), and his 1973 essay "John Ashbery: The Charity of the Hard Moments"; he reinforces his canonizing judgments on these poets in the last chapter of *A Map of Misreading* (1975). To the extent that this early work on Ashbery and Ammons helped their reputations, it provides evidence of the very canonizing power that Bloom usually (though not always) denies to critics and attributes to poets. On the whole, however, Bloom shows a remarkably orthodox and unadventurous sense of the recent canon, as when he lists as "the strongest of our contemporaries—Robert Penn Warren, Elizabeth Bishop, A. R. Ammons, James Merrill, W. S. Merwin, John Hollander, James Wright and John Ashbery" (*Agon* 288). He shared early academic skepticism about Allen Ginsberg in a 1961 review of *Kaddish*, commenting that Ginsberg's "major efforts, 'Howl' and 'Kaddish,' are certainly failures, and 'Kaddish' a pathetic one," due to the "baleful influences on recent verse fashion" of Pound and Williams (*Ringers* 213–14).

13. Compare Wendell V. Harris' argument that canons comprise not texts but readings, that "although a canon is nominally made up of texts, it is actually made up not of texts in themselves but of texts as read." In this view, canon formation occurs "not through a work's acceptance into a severely limited set of authoritative texts but through its introduction into an ongoing critical colloquy" (117, 111).

14. Those points in his work at which Bloom elevates criticism to the status of prose poetry and elides the roles of critic and poet, each of whom produces strong misreadings of poems, serve to finesse the institutional issue further.

If one can talk of critics as poets, one can avoid discussing the ways in which their "misreadings" might be institutionally determined. For a useful discussion of these often-noted points of slippage between "critic" and "poet" in Bloom, see Finkelstein, "Sage of New Haven."

15. On the relationship between Bradstreet's "firstness" and her gender, see Caldwell, who draws some extended, provocative analogies between the search for a female and for an American voice in poetry. As a woman, Bradstreet is "forced by her gender into a confrontation with urgent problems of poetic expression" (28) that also produce a nascent American voice "suited to the experience of a New World not yet fully accessible to the consciousness of its inhabitants" (25).

16. Just as Berryman's "rebel poet" stance joins in a long-standing American literary tradition, so this poetic self-begetting through a female muse/lover joins a long-standing patriarchal one. Mary K. DeShazer usefully reviews the poet-muse relationship, including its sexual aspects, in *Inspiring Women* 1–44. Especially relevant to this passage of "Homage" is her reminder that "the poet's desire for his muse has been depicted through the ages as a sexual passion, and from his coitus with her, in reversal of natural biological functions, he, not she, begets their offspring, poetry" (2).

Eileen Margerum argues that, in "The Author to Her Book," Bradstreet uses the trope of parthenogenesis—the child/book has "no father"—to declare herself "free of the protection and influence" of male poets (158).

17. See Stanford. It is worth remembering that, five years after the book publication of *Homage* and without mentioning Berryman, Roy Harvey Pearce makes an influential statement of this view when he locates the continuity of American poetry in the very antinomian impulse that Berryman finds in Bradstreet.

18. While feminist praise of Bradstreet as an early role model may seem to follow Berryman, these critics characteristically focus on her achievement specifically as a *woman* poet in her culture, which is not Berryman's emphasis. For feminist readers, Bradstreet has been marginalized as a woman poet in a patriarchal culture; for Berryman, she has been marginalized by virtue of being a poet at all in an antipoetic culture. Berryman's claim to be interested in Bradstreet as a woman rather than as a poetess (that revealing term) is both true and a little misleading. He is interested in *the idea of Bradstreet as poet,* but not in her poetry. Similarly, to be interested in her as a woman, as the poem shows, is not necessarily to be interested in questions of gender.

19. Compare Elizabeth Wade White's tactful understatement that "curiously, but perhaps explicably too, since he is a man and, so to speak, a rival poet, Mr. Berryman balks at granting any homage whatsoever to Anne Bradstreet's verse" (547).

20. On the surface, Berryman's turn to an early precursor as a means of evading a more recent one is itself a very Bloomian move. By the poet's "introjecting . . . earliness," as Berryman does with Bradstreet, Bloom's key trope

of "metalepsis or transumption . . . becomes a total, final act of taking up a poetic stance in relation to anteriority." I stress again, however, Berryman's indifference to Bradstreet's poetry. For Berryman the issue of "the anteriority of poetic language, which means primarily the loved-and-feared poems of the precursors" (Bloom, *Poetry and Repression* 20), crucial to Bloom's theory of influence and thus of canon formation, does not arise with regard to Bradstreet.

21. Bawer discusses "Homage" specifically as an Eliotic poem (131–32), and Stephen Matterson reads it as "the poem with which Berryman sought explicitly to evade the influence of T. S. Eliot" (5).

22. Berryman began a May 1952 reading at Wayne (now Wayne State) University with "Easter 1916" and parts of "Ash Wednesday" before moving on to his own work. In the same month, he preceded his Eliot lecture at the University of Cincinnati with a reading of "Gerontion" (Mariani, *Dream Song* 247).

23. Compare Berryman's 1968 comment on impersonality as "an idea which [Eliot] got partly from Keats (a letter) and partly from Goethe (also a letter)" ("Interview" 5).

Chapter 3. The New Criticism and American Poetry in the Academy

1. This lack of attention to poetry in what Richard Ohmann calls non-academic "gatekeeper journals" that help shape canons in contemporary fiction means that Ohmann's otherwise valuable model of canon formation applies much less readily to poetry than to fiction. See Ohmann, *Politics* 68–91.

2. The first-generation New Critics denied their enterprise the status of a coherent "movement" on various occasions. But while internal disagreements certainly existed, they ran less deep than certain divisions among Marxist critics about first principles, divisions that probably explain why Marxist criticism developed or presented a less organized front than New Criticism in battles for institutional dominance. V. F. Calverton and Granville Hicks, for instance, admitted the importance of but frequently deferred discussion of aesthetics; in the preface to *The Liberation of American Literature*, Calverton writes, "I have intentionally avoided the problem of aesthetic analysis and evaluation" (xii). Meanwhile, other Marxist literary intellectuals—James T. Farrell, Bernard Smith, writers affiliated with the early *Partisan Review*—criticized Hicks for insufficient attention to aesthetics.

3. Evan Watkins shows how, more than competing methodologies, New Criticism also answered the simultaneous need for expanded recruitment and rigorous certification procedures created by the growth of literary studies in the university, and thus why English departments found it an effective tool in "*internal competition* with other disciplines for university funding, [and] for scholarly prestige":

By isolating the reading of the literary text from the resources necessary to historical scholarship, from the "sensibility" and refinement of appreciation, and from the investment in conceptual understanding required by Marxist or Freudian interpretation, for example,

New Criticism could appear to recruit "democratically," across the entire university population. Everybody was positioned equally to read "the poem itself." (559)

In other words, the New Criticism seemed to provide the most efficient means available for the professional growth and self-perpetuation of English studies. Terry Eagleton similarly finds New Criticism an effective method for coping with a growing number of students because it did not require large resources (*Literary Theory* 50). Much has been written on the rapid expansion of higher education after World War II; but in the years 1900–1930, enrollment increased almost five-hundred percent and the number of institutions increased almost forty-five percent (Bledstein 297).

4. The appearance of R. S. Crane's 1935 landmark essay "History versus Criticism in the Study of Literature," from a subsequently influential critic who differed significantly from the New Critics, suggests that the history-criticism opposition was a matter of generational difference as well as "schools." Crane actually anticipated by some years Ransom's "Criticism, Inc.," the professional ambitions of the New Critics, and the gap in the profession that they saw themselves filling. Crane argues that the critic deals with "questions of literary values" (8) and focuses on "particular masterpieces considered as organic wholes" (10), while the historian eschews value judgments and focuses on persons. Criticism is "analytical and evaluative" (12); it is to be distinguished from psychology, history, sociology, "ethical culture," or autobiography; and one of its practical virtues is that it helps "to conserve, in the midst of a university dominated by science and history, the proper interests of art" (19). Like Ransom a few years later, Crane is explicit as to the institutional implications of his theoretical position, and as to his complaints about academic politics:

And it is no secret that the scholars in our departments who have attained the highest academic distinctions and who have had the greatest influence in the shaping of our programs have been with few exceptions men whose competence has been chiefly demonstrated by their contributions to historical learning. (21)

Again like Ransom, Crane goes on to recommend institutional as well as methodological changes, comprising "a thoroughgoing revision, in our departments of literature, of the policy which has dominated them—or most of them—during the past generation" (22).

Irving Babbitt anticipated both Crane and Ransom on the close connection between methodology and departmental hierarchies, complaining in 1908 that "the philologists . . . command the approaches to the higher positions through their control of the machinery of the doctor's degree" (131). As Gerald Graff shows in *Professing Literature* and his 1985 essay "The University and the Prevention of Culture," Babbitt's remarks from his defense of humanist criticism also serve notice that the New Critics and historians were enacting the latest in a series of institutional conflicts that had marked English studies since its inception.

5. One central survival strategy that I am unable to explore in depth here involved the New Critics' efforts to promote a more "scientific" criticism in the service of non- (and even anti-) scientific goals. The professional problem that they faced was this: how to overthrow the dominance of philology and the historical method and push the value of criticism while maintaining for English studies the prestige of a science? On the idea of poetry as itself an antitechnocratic social and political value, and of literature as "a whole alternative ideology," see Eagleton, *Literary Theory* 20–23.

6. The virulence of the academic antimodernism to which Brooks and Tate refer shows vividly in a text like *The New American Literature, 1890–1930* (1930), by Fred Lewis Pattee, one of the country's leading senior Americanists, who dismisses the modernist revolution in poetry as a "debacle." The poetic renaissance expired in aestheticized self-involvement, following that "leading eccentric of the period, [who] for a time was also a highly intoxicating element," T. S. Eliot (385).

Leslie Fiedler writes that when he entered graduate school in the late 1930s, twentieth-century literature was seen as the last refuge of an inadequate scholar, and even nineteenth-century literature was a suspect field (*What Was Literature?* 111). Gerald Graff, describing the history of course listings at Northwestern University, notes that in the academic year 1934–35 only four English courses came up to the nineteenth century, and that Arnold, Tennyson, and Whitman were the most recent poets taught. He speculates that 280 out of an estimated 360 students taking English at Northwestern read nothing published after 1850 ("Who Killed Criticism?" 339). In 1963 René Wellek still felt it necessary to plead for the inclusion of contemporary literature in an English Ph.D. program, and recalls that when he attended Princeton in 1927, no courses on modern literature or criticism were available ("New Criticism" 614). Finally, Gertrude Himmelfarb takes the remarkable (for 1990) position that the importance of historical collective opinion in identifying great books means that "contemporary literature should not be taught in schools and universities" (364).

7. As one exception to Brooks's generalization, in 1928 Laura Riding and Robert Graves argued that "*The Waste Land* has to be read as a short poem; that is, as a unified whole" (51). They did not venture a sustained reading of the poem, however.

8. In the year of this essay, 1940, Ransom wrote to Tate at Princeton that "[I] am much interested in the Princeton version of the war between creative writing and scholarship." Ever alert to opportunities for advancing the causes of poetry and poetry criticism within the academy, he continues:

About two weeks ago I wrote to Cleanth proposing that they and we run two parallel and hot-stuff symposiums at the same moment, next fall, calling attention each to the other's symposium, and get it into TIME's notice; then circularize the whole membership of M.L.A. with the matter, with an idea not only to the circulation of the periodicals but to some uproar at the next-Christmas meeting of the scholars in Boston; the rift has been steadily widening right in that body. (*Selected Letters* 268)

While Ransom was especially adept at institutional politics, Alan Filreis notes the same expertise in Tate (66–67).

9. See Chap. 5 for my assessment of the possibilities for contemporary poets (the Language writers) to effect such change.

10. In its early years *Partisan Review* took a different view of literary professionalism, with William Phillips (writing as "Wallace Phelps") and Philip Rahv anticipating many of the New Critical poet-professors' views on the functions of professional criticism. In their 1935 essay "Criticism," those functions include evaluation; training readers to make generic and evaluative distinctions; "influencing actual creation" of new works; and providing an alternative to historical scholarship, conceived as "pedantic treatment of minor ideas with the emphasis placed on 'data' rather than on analysis" (17). See Leitch 109–14, however, for a summary of how *Partisan* became a particularly vocal organ for the view that criticism, by establishing itself in the university, was reneging on its cultural mission and losing touch with any possibility of a broad audience. Alfred Kazin, Irving Howe, Philip Rahv, and Delmore Schwartz, for instance, all took this view, and objected to what (confusing cause with effect) they saw as the resulting diminishment of literary journalism, to the identification of criticism with pedagogy, and to the academic cooption of the modernist avant-garde. (Lionel Trilling and F. W. Dupee, as academics who wrote regularly for *Partisan*, are exceptions to this view of criticism.) At the same time, the New York intellectuals associated with the magazine were (except for Schwartz) on the whole not much interested in poetry; as I argue in discussing *Origin* magazine, they were unreceptive to the poetic avant-garde of their own moment, the very active avant-garde that they saw as an antidote to academic bureaucratization.

Terry Eagleton reaffirms the *Partisan* equation of professionalization with social and cultural ineffectiveness in arguing that the university gave criticism an "institutional basis and professional structure" but separated it from the public realm, leading to "its effective demise as a socially active force" (*Function* 65). Prospective critics thus faced a choice between embracing "inchoate amateurism" and "socially marginal professionalism" (69).

11. The New Critics resolved the apparent contradiction between the ideal of professional disinterestedness and the responsibility of evaluation by claiming to base evaluation on supposedly objective aesthetic properties. The ideal of the disinterested professional is also closely tied to the New Critical resistance to literary nationalism discussed later in this chapter, in a way that, like the competing impulses toward cultural influence and transcendent disengagement, derives from Matthew Arnold. Like Arnold, the New Critics equated nationalism with provincialism, and advocated an international literary culture that could exist above and apart from the exigencies of daily life. In this view, nationalism inhibits disinterestedness, literary development, and breadth of critical vision, by limiting the critic's focus to the products of his or her own country. As Arnold put it, "all mere glorification by ourselves of ourselves, or our literature . . . is both vulgar, and, besides being vulgar, retarding" (279).

For the New Critics, then, an Arnoldian disinterestedness and commitment to aesthetic criteria that transcended historical and cultural differences were incompatible with a sustained interest in a specifically *American* poetry.

The issue of disinterestedness is further complicated by the deeply personal investment that professor-poets, like other poets, have in acts of canonizing that help promote, directly or indirectly, their own work. Late in his career, Allen Tate looked back on this situation quite frankly:

> I have never considered myself much of a literary critic, but rather a writer of program-matic essays covertly eliminating kinds of poetry that I was sure I did not want to write, and perhaps uncandidly, because unconsciously, justifying what I was attempting. (*Essays* 235)

12. As regards the other critics whom Ransom names, Empson had written *Seven Types of Ambiguity* before holding his first academic job (in Tokyo), and in 1940 was working for the BBC; Richards had left Cambridge and was living in China; and Eliot had resisted Richards' efforts to recruit him to Cambridge, in the conviction that, as he said in the first of his 1932–33 Norton lectures at Harvard, "I doubt whether it is possible to explain to . . . undergraduates the differences of degree among poets, and I doubt whether it is wise to try." Eliot concludes this lecture with "a large and difficult question: whether the attempt to teach students to *appreciate* English literature should be made at all; and with what restrictions the teaching of English literature can rightly be included in any academic curriculum, if at all" (*Use of Poetry* 35–36).

Neither Eliot nor most of his modernist contemporaries, we should remember, "majored in English" in the contemporary sense of that phrase. Eliot's largely elective undergraduate curriculum included thirteen courses in non-English literatures and only four English courses; as a philosophy graduate student, he also took five courses in Indic philology.

13. For similar comments, see also Bergonzi 143; Cain 159, 164; Fiedler, "Literature" 89; Gibbons 19; Lauter, *Canons* 133–53; Krieger 153–71; Pritchard 205; and Reichert 173–203. As regards classroom practice, Gerald Graff recalls that when he began attending graduate school at Stanford in 1959, questions of evaluation, of a work's place in "any larger system of values or ideas," of why it was worth reading, rarely arose ("Yvor Winters" 292). Smith's *Contingencies of Value* represents one substantial recent effort to reintroduce the topic of value to theoretical discussion, as does John Guillory's debate with her in chapter 5 of his *Cultural Capital*.

14. With the exception of F. O. Matthiessen's *American Renaissance* (1941) and perhaps Yvor Winters' *Maule's Curse* (1938), the first major revaluations of the American tradition to be informed in some way by New Criticism were written *after* that criticism was widely established, and after a certain rapprochement between New Criticism and American studies (discussed later in this chapter) had taken place. They also focused mainly on prose. I have in mind here such studies as Charles Feidelson's *Symbolism and American Literature* (1953);

R. W. B. Lewis' *The American Adam* (1955); Marius Bewley's The *Eccentric Design* (1959); Leslie Fiedler's *Love and Death in the American Novel* (1960); and Leo Marx's *The Machine in the Garden* (1964). For fuller discussion of this issue, and of New Critical influence on "self-reflexive theorists of American literature" (170), see Reising.

15. Dickinson's "transcending" of Victorianism will be severely modified for readers today by the many feminist discussions of Dickinson that locate her squarely in her time and see her as a poet who exploits and manipulates as much as she transcends Victorian conventions—see, for instance, Cheryl Walker and Paula Bennett. To be fair to Brooks, however, Dickinson exhibits little of what *he* means by "Victorianism": a "dull and sometimes pompous didacticism," the compulsion to provide an "edifying moral," and an unironized sentimentality (*Modern Poetry* 240). Dickinson's use of sentimental conventions is sufficiently mediated, apparently, to save her from Brooks's censure on this point. Later in this chapter I discuss briefly the implications in New Critical rhetoric of the term "sentimentality."

16. Elizabeth Hardwick's 1991 essay on the "Prairie Poets" (Sandburg, Masters, and Lindsay) in the *New York Review of Books* continues the New Critical association of their aesthetic failures ("hasty, repetitive, and formless verses") with a "futile parochialism" (16). Of Brooks's reading: on the surface, it seems that he *has* to accept the nationalistic reading of Whitman to be able to locate it as a problem. But this is hardly the case. Other possible Whitmans were available, including the leftist Whitman discussed later in this chapter whom the New Critics would also reject for political as well as aesthetic reasons. Brooks seems to allow the poets whom he wants to devalue to read Whitman for him.

17. For a useful overview that captures the complexity of Whitman's views on tradition, see Price. He confirms what New Critical readings of Whitman overlooked, the poet's invention of "a tradition in which Whitman himself became the past as he wrote and thus became the significant heritage for writers he imagined, the 'poets to come'" (4).

18. Compare with Tate's view of Whitman's prophetic stance Blackmur's dismissal of "the Apocalyptic or Violent school," in which he includes Lindsay, Jeffers, Roy Campbell, Sandburg, Patchen, Fearing, and Rexroth: "all of these stem poetically and emotionally from Whitman-Vates: and all are marked by ignorance, good will, solipsism, and evangelism." A few pages later, Blackmur devotes a similarly dismissive paragraph to Williams as a "neo-barbarian" (*Language* 432–33, 435).

19. I am indebted to Jerome McGann for this point.

20. Concluding his now-famous essay "Some Lines from Whitman" (first published in *Kenyon Review* in 1952), Jarrell—one of the earliest New Critically-trained readers to write sympathetically on Whitman—suggests that "it is ridiculous to write an essay about the obvious fact that Whitman is a great poet." But then, as he continues, "critics have to spend half their time reiterating whatever ridiculously obvious things their age or the critics of their age have found

it necessary to forget" (119). (Compare Ron Silliman's description of the processes of exclusion and marginalization in American poetry as "canonic amnesia," and his observation that "poetry, particularly in the United States, is a profoundly amnesiac discourse" ["Canons and Institutions" 169, 150]; and Michael Palmer's comment on the "willful amnesia" ["Shelley" 278] of Helen Vendler's *Harvard Book of Contemporary Poetry*.)

The term "willful amnesia" seems justified when we recall one of the numerous glaring absences in New Critical discussions of American poetry—that of African-American poets. And it seems justified because Tate, for one, knew of these poets, both through his reading and probably through his four-year sojourn in New York and his acquaintance with white writers on the fringe of the Harlem Renaissance like Gorham Munson and Waldo Frank. In 1924 he reviewed *An Anthology of Negro Poetry*, edited by Newman Ivey White and Walter Clinton Jackson. He knew enough to compare the volume to James Weldon Johnson's *The Book of American Negro Poetry*. He knew enough about what was both actually and potentially distinctive in black poetry to note the editors' overlooking of "Negro writing cast in the less conventional forms," especially Jean Toomer, and to mock their references to " 'finish' " and " 'good taste and conventional morality' " (*Poetry Reviews* 21–22). Beyond this review, and his ambivalent preface to Melvin B. Tolson's *Libretto for the People of Liberia*, however, neither Tate nor most other New Critics pay serious attention to black writing. One might think that a criticism concerned with the relationship of past and present, local and universal, as Tate's was, could find much to do with the internal conflicts and tensions of a poem like Countee Cullen's "Heritage"— the Keatsian rhetoric pulling against the nativist theme in measured tetrameters and, just occasionally, the rhythms of Lindsay's "Congo," the Africa that exists partly in the mind, partly in the veins, like a strange prophecy of Wallace Stevens' "an abstraction blooded, as a man by thought." See Nielsen 102–22 for a more detailed discussion of Tate and Robert Penn Warren on race that makes useful distinctions between them.

21. James Murphy complicates received views of the decade with the reminder that "in the mid-thirties, in [*New Masses* and the original *Partisan Review*] and in the American proletarian literature movement as a whole, the term *leftism* was employed as an epithet characterizing certain attitudes and practices that were considered unacceptable" (1). For my purposes, however, the term remains useful for denoting criticism of a generally Marxist or socialist persuasion.

22. To the extent that Whitman's status among leftist critics was *not* entirely secure in the 1930s, this was due to disagreement over the politics of his individualism. Even on this issue, however, the pro-Whitman voices heavily outnumbered their opponents, as leftist critics were driven to accommodate an apparently problematic aspect of a poet whom they wanted to enlist in their cause. A sampling of remarks from the decade can provide the flavor of this debate. Despite his general praise for the poet, V. F. Calverton still finds

Whitman a dated "prophet of the past and not of the future," one whose "conception of democracy was individualistic and not social"; "Whitman was not a believer in social revolution and was not a [b]ugleman of the proletariat" (297, 296). Far more commonly, however, critics seek to make Whitman's individualism compatible with socialist goals. Newton Arvin argues that "Whitman's individualism, unlike Emerson's, was profoundly modified by his gospel of comradeship and solidarity" ("Whitman's Individualism" 212). Granville Hicks asserts: "Despite his deep-seated individualism, he saw more and more clearly towards the end that these men he admired must organize themselves for the conquest of power" (25). Similarly, Philip Stevenson finds this individualism "triumphantly expressing the aspirations of the masses" (129), arguing "that in becoming the greatest poet of democracy Whitman came within an ace of being at the same time the first great poet of Socialism" (129, 131). Leonard Spier finds Whitman achieving a balanced view "of individualism within the social frame, freedom within limits," even if "he failed to realize that, in the main, individual emancipation can only be achieved through class emancipation" ("Walt Whitman" 77, 89). And one of the most influential cultural critics of the decade, V. L. Parrington, distinguishes Jacksonian individualism, with its "meanness," its "anarchism selfish and unsocial," from Whitman's, and stresses in Whitman the combination of individualism and "comradeship" or "solidarity" (76–77).

23. Harvey Teres shows *Partisan*'s editors, William Phillips and Philip Rahv, articulating an Eliotic critical position even in their early essays, in ways that anticipate both the magazine's post-Party aesthetic stand and its rapprochement with New Critical journals. Teres notes how in the 1934 essay for *Dynamo*, "Sensibility and Modern Poetry," "Phillips was not concerned with Eliot's or Crane's politics, in or out of their poetry" (134). All that separates Phillips' and Rahv's goals for "Criticism" (in the 1935 *Partisan* essay of that title) from New Criticism is the goal of "advancing proletarian art" (18).

24. See too Pound's 1917 characterization of James as a "crusader" in the cause of "internationalism," against (in the words of Pound's title) "Provincialism the Enemy" (*Selected Prose* 189).

25. Some of Eliot's statements about Whitman from this time are bafflingly contradictory, perhaps reflecting his ambivalence. In an 18 Dec. 1926 review, he focuses, like Pound, on Whitman as

a "man with a message," even if that message was sometimes badly mutilated in transmission; he was interested in what he had to say; he did not think of himself primarily as the inventor of a new technique of versification. His "message" must be reckoned with, and it is a very different message from that of Mr. Carl Sandburg. ("Whitman" 426)

Six months later, Eliot calls Whitman "a great master of versification," and adds, "it is, in fact, as a verse maker that he deserves to be remembered. . . . His political, social, religious, and moral ideas are negligible" ("[Tennyson]" 302). Only in 1946 could Eliot say that "I should now speak more respectfully of

Whitman," apparently for the same reason that he came to speak thus of Milton—the time had passed when, for Eliot or his contemporaries, either could be a dangerous influence ("Ezra Pound" 33). In 1951, Eliot could even praise Whitman as an "international" rather than "provincial" or "parochial" figure, though he was still too idiosyncratic to be a useful influence for anyone else (*To Criticize the Critic* 43–60).

26. Among many possible examples, see Broe and Ingram, Clark, Gilbert and Gubar, Lauter (*Canons*), Ostriker, and Scott.

27. Millay was a frequent object of New Critical attack. Tate wrote to Laura Riding in 1925 that "you are the one to save America from the Edna Millays!" (quoted in Wexler 10). In an otherwise quite sympathetic review of *Fatal Interview* in which Tate links Millay with Byron as "distinguished examples of the second order [of poet]," he describes her as "not an intellect but a sensibility"; she is not really a modernist because her poetry, unlike that of the "ignored and misunderstood" Eliot, "does not define the break with the nineteenth century" (*Reactionary Essays* 222–24). While granting that Millay "is entirely too good a poet within her limits to deserve curt dismissal," Brooks asserts that she "fails at major poetry" due to her "essential immaturity." Even "within her limits" "the themes . . . are conventional" and (predictably) "the poetry has nothing of Donne's exciting interplay of idea and emotion" ("Edna Millay's Maturity" 2–4).

28. Publication figures for *Understanding Poetry* and *An Approach to Literature* are derived from Grimshaw.

29. Specifically, the twenty-four American poets of the first edition include three women and no minorities. The second edition contains four women and no minorities in its thirty-three American poets, and the third edition six women and no minorities in its forty-one. It took until 1976 for Brooks and Warren (or their editor at Holt, Rinehart, and Winston) to include forty-five poems by women and twenty-four by African and Native Americans, along with a number of blues and spirituals. For concisely devastating statistical summaries of the historical Anglocentricity of the New Critical and Americanist canons, see Kelly; Franklin xiii–xxii; and Lauter, who uses an examination of modernist poetry anthologies, mid-century curricula, and text surveys (*Canons* 20–22), and his own 1981 survey ("Small Survey") to document how pervasive and long-standing the exclusions noted above have been.

30. In 1939 Warren saw Frost as "scarcely an influence on contemporary poetry," neither so engaged with the ideas of his time as to act as "a provoker of poetry in others" nor offering "any technical innovations which can be assimilated by other poets." If he lacks Whitman's cultural responsiveness and force as a "provoker," however, "this does not . . . imply a pejorative judgment." For "this type of importance is not necessarily to be correlated with the degree of absolute poetic excellence of the work; for Whitman's work, I believe, is inferior to Frost's" ("Present State of Poetry" 390–91).

31. In Brooks's view, Frost "dilute[s] his poetry" with statement, which is

"why he fails to realize full dramatic intensity"; his "metaphors are few and tame," and he "does not think through his images"; "much of Frost's poetry hardly rises above the level of the vignette of rural New England" (*Modern Poetry* 113, 111). He registers the same opinion in a 1939 review of Frost's *Collected Poems*—poems "almost devoid of metaphor" and thus "almost as diluted as prose" ("Poet or Sage?" 326). Brooks also reads "After Apple-Picking" as a symbolist poem, however, and finds some more "indirect" (325) poems of high quality, which partly explains Frost's prominence in *Understanding Poetry*.

32. The relative (and surprising) neglect of modern poetry in the first edition of *Understanding Poetry* is corroborated by a look at *An Approach to Literature*, which can be seen as a more general companion textbook to *Understanding Poetry*. In the 1938 edition of *Approach*, only 9 out of 121 poems are by twentieth-century American writers. The anthology contains only one poem each by Frost and Crane, and nothing by virtually all the major American modernists: Eliot, Pound, Stevens, Moore, or, more predictably, Williams (to name only those who show up later in *Understanding Poetry*)—this in contrast to, for instance, 6 Tennyson and 5 Milton selections.

33. Compare R. L. Morris' prophetic remark, in a review, that "I do not believe that *Understanding Poetry* will be the only book of its kind. Instead it has probably founded a dynasty" (94). One of the earliest texts modeled on *Understanding Poetry* is Wright Thomas and Stuart Gerry Brown's *Reading Poems*—Brooks and Warren's proposed title for their own book before they changed it at their publisher's request (Brooks, "Forty Years" 7).

34. The five anthologies are Norman Foerster, ed., *American Poetry and Prose* (Boston: Houghton Mifflin, 1934); Jay B. Hubbell, ed., *American Life in Literature* (New York: Harper, 1936); the *Oxford* (New York: Oxford UP, 1938); Milton Ellis, Louise Pound, and George Weida Spohn, eds., *A College Book of American Literature*, vol. 2 (New York: American, 1940); and Smith's *The Democratic Spirit: A Collection of American Writings from the Earliest Times to the Present* (New York: Alfred A. Knopf, 1941).

35. Craig S. Abbott summarizes survey data suggesting that the representation of modern American poets in high school anthologies through much of the century parallels that in college texts:

Surveying virtually all one-volume collections of literature published between 1917 and 1934 and designed for a year's work in grades nine through twelve, James Warren Olson found that the modern American poets most frequently anthologized were, in order, Sandburg, Robert Frost, E. A. Robinson, Sara Teasdale, Masters, Lowell, and Lindsay. . . . A similar study found that as late as 1960, the 72 multigenre high school anthologies then available presented a canon of Frost, Sandburg, Edna St. Vincent Millay, Teasdale, Robinson, Lindsay, Masters, Arthur Guiterman, Eliot, and Lowell—Frost with 136 appearances, Lowell with 20. (210)

36. For more detail on this narrowing trend in anthologies, see Tompkins 186–92.

Chapter 4. Little Magazines and Alternative Canons

1. It could be argued that the idea of marginalized opposition to some presumed aesthetic center has become *less* tenable but not untenable, that recent changes in American literary culture are changes more of degree than of kind. Note the complete absence of overlap among such recent anthologies as, on one hand, Helen Vendler's *Harvard Book of Contemporary American Poetry* and Dave Smith and David Bottoms' *Morrow Anthology of Younger American Poets*, and, on the other, Ron Silliman's *In the American Tree* and Douglas Messerli's *"Language" Poetries*. From this point of view, even allowing for its overall diversity, American poetry does have a stylistic or rhetorical center: that of the now widely critiqued autobiographical free verse lyric, what Charles Altieri has called the scenic lyric and Donald Hall the McPoem, "the product of the workshops of Hamburger University" (*Poetry and Ambition* 8), a style and mode institutionalized through MFA programs, writing workshops, federal grants, and an academically based network of magazines and presses. Systematic opposition to that center has existed most clearly and effectively in magazines like *Sulfur, Conjunctions, Temblor* (recently discontinued with its tenth issue), and the many little magazines associated with first- and second-generation Language writing. From a different direction, it exists too in the New Formalism and the New Narrative movements. Yet even writers associated with some of these oppositional magazines and movements question the applicability of the center-margin distinction to the current scene. Ron Silliman writes: "Neither the poetry of the center nor those of the peripheries are in any real sense homogenous. Rather than a struggle between clearly defined alternatives, we find instead ensembles of values which may overlap as much as they conflict with one another." Silliman goes on to describe "a decentralization in which any pretense, whether from the 'center' or elsewhere, of a coherent sense as to the nature of the whole of American poetry is now patently obvious as just so much aggressive fakery" (*New Sentence* 172).

For Altieri's discussion of this late 1970s and 1980s period style, see *Self and Sensibility*, especially 1–51. Recent critical commentary on the scenic lyric really begins with Robert Pinsky's introduction to *The Situation of Poetry* (3–12). See also Paul Breslin 118–35; Holden 3–21; Perloff 155–57; Golding, "Language-Bashing Again."

2. When it began *Origin* was not, of course, the *only* magazine of its kind. May's monograph *Twigs as Varied Bent* (1954), the earliest history of post–World War II little magazines, finds a quantity and diversity of little magazines in this period that are now usually overlooked. But *Origin* quickly distinguished itself from others in a number of ways. First, its relative longevity gave it the chance to have a more sustained impact than any of the typically short-lived littles among its contemporaries. To mention only a few that published *Origin* contributors, *Montevallo Review* ran from 1950 to 1953; *Goad* lasted only four issues (from summer 1951 to January 1953), and so too did *Poetry New York; Four Winds* lasted three issues. At the same time, longer-lived magazines were expiring:

Furioso in 1952, *Wake* in 1953, *Golden Goose* in 1954. Second, many of the little magazines that started within the few years preceding *Origin* and that lasted enjoyed academic sponsorship: *Chicago Review,* which published its first issue in winter 1946, *Epoch* (fall 1947), *Shenandoah* (spring 1950), *Beloit Poetry Journal* (fall 1950). In contrast, *Origin* stayed free of academic affiliation, and hence free of academic interference—a topic to which I shall return later. Third, the magazine's regular appearance—more or less quarterly publication sustained over six years—"closed the gap between the writing and the appearing" (Evans 1:215), in Olson's words, far more briskly than comparable outlets. (Creeley, for example, complains about Richard Wirtz Emerson at *Golden Goose* that "he's apt to close up shop for a time, . . . & they publish the mag abt once a yr as it is. . . . one Emerson jams the whole damn move" [*Olson-Creeley Correspondence* 4:66]).

3. As one representative, if retrospective, comment on the mainstream postwar quarterlies, see Robert Duncan's letter of 9 November 1967 to a Washington University librarian. Having had Duncan's "An African Elegy" typeset for *Kenyon Review,* John Crowe Ransom pulled the poem after reading Duncan's defense of homosexuality, "The Homosexual in Society." Summarizing his correspondence with Ransom on this issue, Duncan writes that it comprises "an interesting particular record of the problems my generation faced as writers with the editor of the *Kenyon Review.* And it was in extension the opposition we faced with *Partisan Review, Hudson Review, Southern Review, Sewanee Review*" (quoted in Faas 154). The lumping of these particular five magazines into one category is a recurrent rhetorical strategy among writers of *Origin* and related groups. Gilbert Sorrentino recalls that "the writing in the magazines I read [in the early fifties] seemed to be singularly stale, even though it was presented as a model of excellence. *Partisan Review, Hudson Review, Poetry* and others were publishing writers who, for some reason, seemed to me to be people who lived at another time in another country" (301). Seymour Krim specifies *Kenyon, Sewanee, Hudson,* and *Partisan* as influential magazines resistant to experimental writing and to work not characterized by "a kind of modern formalism" (326); commenting in an interview with David Ossman on his editing of *Yugen,* LeRoi Jones names the latter three in a similar complaint. In a February 1950 letter to Creeley, Williams diagnosed *Partisan* as suffering from "chronic constipation" (Mariani, *Usable Past* 187).

From a very different, and highly comic, perspective, Kenneth Koch echoes these views. In "Fresh Air" he writes:

> And supposing one writes to the Princess Caetani,
> "Your poets are awful!" what good would it do?
> And supposing one goes to the *Hudson Review*
> With a package of matches and sets fire to the building?
> One ends up in prison with trial subscriptions
> To the *Partisan, Sewanee,* and *Kenyon Review!*

(57)

Theodore Weiss recalls receiving, early in his editing of *The Quarterly Review of Literature*, a letter in which Kenneth Rexroth "excoriated our having anything to do with the, as he saw it, altogether decayed world of the academic. We must in no way resemble *The Kenyon Review* or *The Partisan Review*" (114). Finally, it is worth noting that criticism of these journals did not stem solely from a marginalized minority. See, for instance, the 1949 and 1950 essays of Alan Swallow and William Van O'Connor.

Perhaps the difference from *Origin* must be defined especially in the case of *Partisan*, since it began with many of the generally recognized features of a "little magazine" and is sometimes still seen as the best "little" of the last fifty years. (It and *Poetry* are the only two magazines of which Reed Whittemore offers extended portraits in his pamphlet *Little Magazines*.) From the beginning, its differences from such journals as the *Kenyon*, *Sewanee*, and *Southern Reviews* were more political than aesthetic, and they proved no barrier to literary and critical commerce between *Partisan* and these other journals. The four journals published many of the same critics and most of the same poets, and did so with some frequency. Allen Tate published more poems in *Partisan* (including one of his best-known, "Ode: To Our Pro-Consuls of the Air") than he ever did in the *Southern* or *Sewanee Reviews*; Philip Rahv had solicited his work for *Partisan* as early as 1938 (Cooney 209). Beyond Berryman, whose case I have discussed in Chapter 2, Grant Webster also lists among poets who can fairly be associated with *Partisan* in the years 1946–55 Shapiro, Wilbur, Bishop, Roethke, Snodgrass, and Hoffman—none of whom would appear out of place in the more overtly New Critical journals (221). Even allowing for the twenty-twenty vision of hindsight, then, Lionel Trilling's description of *Partisan* in 1946 as "a magazine of literary experiment" (*Liberal Imagination* 93) hardly seems accurate; as James Gilbert shows, far more easy to come by from the postwar years are complaints about the magazine's political and cultural orthodoxy (275).

Looking back on the early *Partisan*, its editor, William Phillips, allows that the magazine's effort to yoke radical politics and literary modernism "sometimes seemed to lead to contradictions—as in our publishing of the leading New Critics, who certainly did not represent our more historical sense of literature" ("On *Partisan Review*" 134). Those contradictions appear in some of Phillips' own remarks, which suggest a strangely ahistorical bent to *Partisan*'s "historical sense of literature." He observes, "Philip Rahv and I were the most dissident members of the John Reed Club, and *we were most concerned with keeping literature free of illegitimate political pressures*" (my emphasis); "our outlook was Marxist, and our sensibility had a radical bent, but we stressed the relative autonomy of writing" (133). Although Webster locates what he calls the "rapprochement . . . between the Intellectuals and the Formalists" (221) in the immediate postwar years, it began at least as early as 1939, when *Kenyon Review* published Rahv's "Paleface and Redskin," the essay that first laid out the terms in which the anthology wars of the late fifties would be couched. Cooney

(206–17) offers a particularly useful overview of the relationship between *Partisan* and the New Critics.

4. Corman learned rather quickly (and had probably not expected otherwise) that *Origin's* influence would not come through subscriptions and sales. While issue #1 was in the process of being printed, subscriptions stood at around 125 (Evans 1:134); by May 1952, Corman expected "that ORIGIN will be out of business by #7, if not before" (1:256). He printed 1,000 copies of issue #1, and reduced this number to 500 with #2. By the end of *Origin's* first series, with #20, he had brought the print run down to 400, and produced even fewer for the second series (14 issues from April 1961 to July 1964) and the third (20 issues from fall 1965 to January 1971). Remarkably and admirably, Corman gave away issues in the second series to anyone who contacted him expressing interest in and responding actively to the work *Origin* contained. He sold no subscriptions. Later, subscriptions for the third series, which ran at a time when the magazine had acquired some reputation, ranged between 50 and 75, "which was not very different," Corman notes, "from the first series" (*Gist* xxxvi). When this series ended, library subscriptions stood at around 70 and individual subscriptions at less than 25.

By contrast, according to Lionel Trilling the circulation of *Partisan Review* stood at 6,000 in 1946 and 10,000 by 1950 (*Liberal Imagination* 89). In four years *Partisan's* readership *increased* by more readers than *Origin* has had as a total in the five series between 1951 and the present. Even a little magazine comparable to *Origin* like *Furioso* enjoyed a larger audience. Reed Whittemore sold around 800 copies of *Furioso's* first postwar issue, and "of succeeding issues (which continued till 1953) we sold between 900 and 1,400 copies. At no time did the subscription list exceed 400, but our sales in bookstores and on newsstands was 'gratifying' in its small and completely unprofitable way" (*Boy from Iowa* 103). Aware that numbers in themselves tell very little about an audience, however, Whittemore continues, "I was disappointed to discover, slowly, that our circulation did not consist of 900 to 1,400 *interested* readers" but comprised many "publishers looking for new talent" and career-minded prospective contributors assessing the magazine as a possible outlet (104).

5. Felix Stefanile describes the little magazine as itself a form of correspondence, an "open letter to the world" ("Imagination of the Amateur" 338). He compares its circulation to that of the epistle among friends in the early eighteenth century, its audience to "that confraternity of peers which was the motive spirit of the epistle" (346). Editorship involves "seeking readers on an almost individual basis, a *correspondence*" (356). Similarly, Theodore Weiss stresses the value of the companionship created by correspondence among contributors in the early years of his *Quarterly Review of Literature* (102).

6. *Origin's* own origins dramatize this relationship between the instability of the typical single little magazine and the stability of the magazines' overall function. *Origin* arose out of the failure of Creeley's projected *Lititz Review*, and out of Corman's following up on Creeley's sense in 1950 that "for the past five

years it has occurred to me, regularly, that there is no little magazine that is what it could be, that none of them combine some apparent kind of literary, etc., 'policy' with an illustration of same in the editing, etc." (Leed 245). Between February and June 1950 Creeley and an old Harvard friend, Jacob Leed, corresponded intensively over the possibility of Leed's printing on a recently acquired used handpress a little magazine to be called the *Lititz Review*. Creeley went a long way toward making this vision a reality, gathering a number of contributions and receiving advice and support from Pound and Williams. He also enjoyed considerable help from Corman. As he wrote to Leed, "Cid . . . is knocking himself out on our venture. He's been responsible for god knows how many submissions" (Leed 251). When Leed's press broke down, so did the *Lititz Review*; but Corman, with financial help from Evelyn Shoolman, picked up the pieces. Many of the potential contributors with whom Creeley was in touch ended up in *Origin*: Williams, Olson, Levertov, Morse, Ferrini, Bronk, Constance Hatson, Corman himself.

7. For further comments on the influence on *Contact* of Corman, *Origin*, and, to an extent, Creeley, see Souster, and Gnarowski 3–14.

8. *Kenyon's* contents for 1953, the year that Donahoe wrote this letter to Ransom, further illustrate the background against which *Origin* was operating. In that year *Kenyon* published seventeen poems by eleven poets. These poets include three of the writers whom W. H. Auden elected as "Yale Younger Poets" in the fifties: W. S. Merwin (who had won the award in 1952), Edgar Bogardus (1953), and James Wright (1957). Meanwhile, most of the winter issue was devoted to a section from Robert Penn Warren's *Brother to Dragons*. The summer issue carried Robert Lowell's "Beyond the Alps" and two poems by his former teacher, Richard Eberhart; in the following issue Lowell reviewed *Brother to Dragons*. The thrust of Donahoe's comments on the representative nature of the *Kenyon* "Poem about Culture" is confirmed by Robert von Hallberg's using as an example of what he calls "culture poetry" Anthony Hecht's "The Gardens of the Villa D'Este"—first published in the *Kenyon Review* in spring 1953 and also alluded to in Donahoe's letter (*American Poetry* 72, 75). These poems punctuated and complemented essays by William Empson on Shakespeare and Dover Wilson; by Arnold Stein on Milton; by Richard Ellmann on Yeats; and by Lionel Trilling on Dickens. Reviewers included Arthur Mizener (on R. P. Blackmur), Cleanth Brooks (on Arnold Stein), John Crowe Ransom, and a number of younger poets: Lowell on Penn Warren, Merwin on "Four British Poets," Howard Nemerov on Dylan Thomas.

A similar "context analysis" of *Kenyon* for 1951, when the journal carried the Paul Goodman essay, "Advance-Guard Writing, 1900–1950," that Olson admired so, reinforces my point. For example, Goodman's piece appeared alongside a Blackmur essay on Flaubert and in counterpoint to Ransom's "The Poetry of 1900–1950." Here Ransom argues for Hardy, Yeats, Robinson, Eliot, and Frost as the century's "major" poets and puts Pound and Williams in the "minor" category, on the same level as Robert Bridges, Walter de la Mare, and

John Masefield. In the spring 1951 issue Creeley's story "The Unsuccessful Husband" sits amid Lowell's "The Mills of the Kavanaughs," which leads off the issue, and two essays on Donne. His story "The Boat," in the autumn 1953 issue, is followed by a Lionel Trilling essay, "*Little Dorrit,*" and by Merwin's "Canso"—Wade Donahoe's example of the "culture poem." Later in the issue comes Lowell's review of *Brother to Dragons*. (That same fall Corman was contemplating an editorial-review for *Origin* #12 of Olson's early *Maximus Poems*, "to set them against R. P. Warren's *Brother to Dragons*" [Evans 2:96].) Creeley's ambivalence about publishing in a context that ran counter to his own sense of writing community is reflected in his remark that "to be published in the *Kenyon Review* was too much like being 'tapped' for a fraternity. It was often all over before one got there, *and few if any of one's own fellow writers came too*" ("On *Black Mountain Review*" 255; my emphasis).

9. Corman apparently received numerous reader comments on Olson's alleged derivativeness from Pound, writing to Olson that "there are those who still claim you are nothing but thin Pound" and "I continue to get gripes from . . . those who speak of you as just another Poundling" (Evans 1:230, 279).

10. For Creeley's negative response to the internationalization of *Origin* #4, however, see his 10 Mar. 1952 letter to Olson: "Very disappointed with Cid's 4 . . . all that damn shit. Italian [&?] the French. SHIT" (*Olson-Creeley Correspondence* 9:173).

11. In fairness to Corman, I should note that he published no poems by Eberhart, Hatson, Hoskins, or Morse after issue #3.

12. Behind these alternative views of modernism, of course, lies Hugh Kenner's *The Pound Era*. For the more recent arguments to which I am alluding, see Perloff's "Pound/Stevens: whose era?" in *Dance of the Intellect* 1–32, and Beach's articulation of an anti-Bloomian theory of influence centered on Pound. Bloom's promotion of Stevens, consistent throughout his career, is most evident in *Wallace Stevens: The Poems of Our Climate*. Outside of her critical work, Helen Vendler argues for Stevens' centrality in a different way when, as I have noted in Chapter 2, she begins her *Harvard Book of Contemporary American Poetry* with Stevens while ignoring both his major contemporaries and most later poets in the Imagist/Objectivist tradition. Gelpi usefully reviews both similarities and differences between Stevens and Williams in his essay "Stevens and Williams: The Epistemology of Modernism," and at greater length in *A Coherent Splendor*. For discussions that seek to bridge the two traditions, see David Walker's *The Transparent Lyric* and my essay "Community of Elements."

13. Surprisingly, in a 1951 letter Olson had at first waxed enthusiastic about the prospect of Morse's issue-length essay on Stevens (the only poet he had ever gone to hear in the Morris Gray reading series at Harvard) (Evans 1:157–58). A year later, however, he characterized Stevens as a poet of "*ornamentation*" and "*decoration*" (1:266–67). Corman, for his part, apparently asked Stevens to look over and/or respond to Morse's essay, but the poet declined in a 19 Feb. 1952 letter (Stevens 750). While he also declined, in one of his last

204 Notes to Pages 137–140

letters, Corman's request for a poem, he observed of *Origin* that "the last few numbers have been particularly good" (889). Such comments may lie behind Corman's account of Stevens as "one who read *Origin* and an encourager" (Evans 2:161).

14. On the role of literary quarterlies in defending this concept of a literary and cultural center, see Spears. Specifying the *Sewanee, Partisan, Kenyon,* and *Hudson Reviews* as examples, Spears praises the quarterlies because "they act *as if* there were a profession of letters operating at the center of a unified culture," and "while other periodicals reflect the fragmentation of our culture into specialized groups, the quarterlies at least make an effort to keep the ideal of cultural unity alive." They "have the responsibility of maintaining literature as a unifying center for the culture" (39). Olson's increasing distance from this center can be measured by his late 1953 question to Corman: "Are Hudson, & Sewanee, still in existence?" (Evans 2:103).

15. Relevant here is the fact that, around the time *Origin* began, the definitional boundaries separating little magazines from university quarterlies looked, to some writers, much less clear than they do in hindsight (and, of course, less clear than they looked to the *Origin* writers themselves). When Ransom wrote "These Little Magazines" in 1946, he did so in a symposium comprising himself as representing *Kenyon Review,* Paul Bixler of the *Antioch Review,* and Delmore Schwartz of *Partisan.* In 1947 Malcolm Cowley included *Kenyon, Sewanee,* and *Partisan* in an essay on "ten little magazines"; in 1949 Russell Lynes proposed *Partisan, Kenyon,* and the *Virginia Quarterly Review* as the country's most important little magazines. While Gordon Hutner makes a strong case for the view that the *Kenyon Review* was more intellectually eclectic and ambitious than it is now given credit for, his argument does not extend in any detail to the poetry and poetry criticism that the magazine published.

16. Just as Gerald Graff has complicated the canon debate by proposing that academic institutions do not necessarily shape all their intellectual productions in their own ideological image, so one might question the argument that a university literary magazine is shaped by the values and interests of its sponsoring institution. That shaping is rarely direct or overt. At the same time, the history of university-based little magazines features numerous examples of interference from the sponsoring institution: *Chicago Review, Beloit Poetry Journal, Northwest Review, Prairie Schooner* (Pollak 37–38; Robinson 29–30). The *Chicago Review* provides perhaps the best-known example. After the spring and autumn 1958 issues, featuring a number of San Francisco writers and the first two chapters of Burroughs' *Naked Lunch,* had caused a minor outcry in the local press, the University of Chicago administration, apparently with faculty support, suppressed the next issue, which was scheduled to carry more of *Naked Lunch* and work by Dahlberg, Kerouac, and Corso. In response, editor Irving Rosenthal, poetry editor Paul Carroll, and four other editors resigned, and Rosenthal and Carroll published the whole suppressed issue as the first number of *Big Table* in spring 1959. Along similar lines, Karl Shapiro records his

experience with the University of Nebraska-sponsored *Prairie Schooner*, which he edited from 1956 to 1966:

I had a bitter experience at the *Prairie Schooner*, where I was fired—or, rather, urged to quit. (Now, that was interference, academic interference.) I had wanted to publish a story that mentioned a homosexual. It was set in galley proofs, but I went away, probably to Europe, and the acting editor held the galley proofs for a whole year. When I came back I demanded that the story be published. The staff went to the chancellor, who used to look over the galleys of the *Prairie Schooner*—which I didn't know—and his decision was to cut the story. So I resigned from the magazine and began to look for a job elsewhere. (Shapiro 203)

As regards more recent examples: Clayton Eshleman has told me in conversation that, as editor of *Folio* at Indiana University, he wanted to run thirty pages of Zukofsky's *Bottom* and a Ginsberg poem, "Paterson." The works were suppressed as incomprehensible and obscene, respectively. He replaced them with a different section of *Bottom* and another Ginsberg poem, "My Sad Self," but funding for the magazine was subsequently withdrawn. As recently as 1982, when Eshleman edited *Sulfur* at the California Institute of Technology, one corporate patron objected to a Paul Blackburn poem in *Sulfur* #4 and demanded that CalTech's name be removed from the magazine masthead. CalTech fulfilled its initial commitment of five years' funding to *Sulfur*, but the situation rendered any further sponsorship of the magazine impossible. The accumulation of such examples, along with those of the *Purple Sage* (University of Wyoming) and *New Mexico Quarterly* (University of New Mexico) cited by Mary Biggs, hardly supports Biggs's own contention that "overt suppression by university officials is rare" (7).

Chapter 5. "Provisionally complicit resistance"

1. As far as I am aware, even in 1994 only four of the twenty poets in Douglas Messerli's *"Language" Poetries: An Anthology* are full-time literary academics in tenured or tenure-track positions: Bernstein, Howe, Watten, and Perelman. Five of the forty poets in Ron Silliman's *In the American Tree* occupy that status: the four just named, and Michael Davidson. (David Bromige is retired from academic work.) Outside of these anthologies, admittedly one could compile a longer list of writers in the academy who could be associated with Language poetry to a greater or lesser degree, through aesthetic practice and/or social affiliation. At the same time, a number of these teach or have taught only part-time or on an occasional basis, while others are not affiliated with English departments (Bruce Andrews teaches in the Department of Political Science at Fordham University, Johanna Drucker in the Department of Art History and Archaeology at Columbia).

2. For recent discussions of the tradition of rupture, or "disjunctive poetics," in avant-garde writing, see Eysteinsson, Quartermain, and Suleiman.

3. One colleague has asked me of this passage the reasonable question, "What words are broken and rearranged here?" A partial list of the English, Latin, and French words lurking on or just beneath this fractured surface would include "brim(s)," "mince," "gnome" (and "no me"), "arm," "or," "armb[and]," "armor," "adroit," and the more obvious "id," "droit" (French for "right"), and "cur."

4. Peter Middleton discusses points of overlap and difference between Kristeva and Language writing, specifically Susan Howe, in "On Ice: Julia Kristeva, Susan Howe and Avant-Garde Poetics." In "Language Poetry and Linguistic Activism," he usefully reads these writers' "linguistic activism," as I have done briefly in this chapter, in terms of Raymond Williams' theory of cultural formations. Suleiman, chaps. 1 and 2, helpfully historicizes the issues by discussing two relevant features of the *Tel Quel* group that included both Kristeva and Roland Barthes in the late 1960s and 1970s: the centrality of the idea and trope of "rupture" to their thinking, and the association of avant-gardist technique, radical politics, and the feminine (what Suleiman calls "the'woman'/avant-garde/marginality trope" [16]). For a useful overview and critique of Kristeva's thinking on the language-and-politics issue, see Moi 150–73.

5. For similar skepticism registered from a Marxist perspective, see Terry Eagleton's satiric essay "The Revolt of the Reader" (*Against the Grain* 181–84). However, Altieri's criticism that some of Language writing's theoretical claims could be reinterpreted along neoconservative lines (as could Altieri's own argument for a centrist view of the canon in *Canons and Consequences*) seems more damning than it actually is. As Michael Palmer points out in a 1986 interview, "the potential (for distortion or appropriation) exists within anything you constitute as a mode. . . . It would be incredibly naive to think that one could constitute a form within which one would not be vulnerable to any kind of drift" ("Interview" 12). (A similar response applies equally well to Jameson's comments on Language writing: that there is no critique of capitalism in postmodern culture that is not also a symptom.) Meanwhile, Altieri's charge that the writers themselves reify language in the process of critiquing reification is anticipated by one of Language writing's senior fellow travelers, Jackson Mac Low. Mac Low realizes that the homology between reference and reification is "easily turned against its proponents. What could be more of a fetish or more alienated than slices of language stripped of reference?" (491–92). Hence, in this early (1980) essay about labeling the movement, Mac Low prefers the term "perceiver-centered" rather than "language-centered" or "nonreferential" to describe what came to be called Language poetry.

6. Michael Palmer addresses similarly this

problem of political poetry in the United States, which tends to become doctrinal or an occasion for self-display. You take the poets' Nicaragua shuttle and go down for ten days, then you return and become a hero or heroine of the Revolution—that ain't the way it works. . . . It's instructive to go to the poets for whom the political is not a "topic." ("Counter-Poetics" 15)

He makes the same anti-instrumentalist point, and in very similar words, in a 1986 interview where he criticizes

the more conventional "political poem"—which particularly in our current moment, when we have a sort of poets' shuttle down to Nicaragua and so on to get material, everyone acting like La Pasionara or something—which seems to me ultimately a complete betrayal of what is to be meant by the political. (" 'Dear Lexicon' " 12)

Many writers and critics have argued that such an "instrumental" use of language is appropriate for historically excluded or oppressed social groups whose most pressing socioliterary need is to have their voices heard and their stories told. In assessing the apparently competing claims of a content-centered transparency and innovation, Rita Felski summarizes the arguments for what she calls "autobiographical realism":

in the context of the women's movement, the necessity and importance of a feminist avant-garde must be balanced against an equal need on the part of oppositional movements for texts which address the particularity of their social experience more explicitly and unambiguously, a need that often resulted in a preference for realist forms which emphasize the denotative rather than aesthetic dimension of the text. (162)

Ron Silliman defends a politically oriented "transparency" in distinguishing it from the writing workshops' more privatized aesthetic:

The writer as well as the reader whose identification is with a social grouping that has, heretofore, been the object rather than the subject of history—for example, women of color or sexual minorities—has a manifest need to *have their stories told*. This is, in many circumstances, a truly liberating project open to the poetics of transparency, precisely by positing this new subject in an emphatic and unambiguous way. ("Poets and Intellectuals" 123)

One unwitting effect of this argument, however, can be to maintain experimentation as the preserve of white men. More women have been associated with Language writing than with any earlier American poetic avant-garde. Nevertheless, some experimental women writers have commented on the problem of double marginalization—by the women's movement on the basis of their aesthetics, and by avant-garde literary formations on the basis of gender. Rachel Blau DuPlessis argues that "the gender system of assymetry around femaleness" means that "a woman's work will . . . be less able to be assimilated either to the mainstream *or to the margins of our culture*" (*Pink Guitar* 52; my emphasis). As Susan Howe puts it with regard to Language writing, "Yet even here when the history of this sub sub group gets written even *here* women get shut up or out" ('Encloser' 193); "when articles are written about Language Poetry or when fights between the various covens occur, it's usually men who do the writing and fighting" (*Birth-mark* 168-69). See also Brooke-Rose; Drucker, "Contemporary Women Writers"; and Fraser, "Tradition of Marginality" and "Without a Net." Much of what Felski calls the "realism vs. modernism" debate has occurred in reference to fiction; for a recent application to and defense of experiment in contemporary women's poetry, see Armantrout, "Feminist Poetics and the Meaning of Clarity."

7. Bernstein echoes George Oppen's well-known pronouncement that he gave up poetry for political activism in the 1930s because "I didn't believe in political poetry or poetry as being politically efficacious . . . if you decide to do something politically, you do something that has political efficacy" (187).

8. A number of statements in *S/Z* anticipate "From Work to Text" in a way that justifies associating the work with the readerly and the text with the writer-ly, despite Barthes's denial of these equations. In *S/Z*, for instance, Barthes describes the readerly as "committed to the closure system of the West, . . . devoted to the law of the Signified" (7–8); and he contrasts readerly and writerly via degrees of "plurality" or "polysemy"—the "incompletely" or "moderately plural (i.e., merely polysemous)" against the "multivalent," "the reversible and frankly indeterminable," the "integrally plural" (6). This latter distinction resurfaces in "From Work to Text" in the description of the text as "an *irreducible* (and not merely an acceptable) plural" (*Image-Music-Text* 159).

9. Erica Hunt raises this question from within the Language community:

One troubling aspect of privileging language as the primary site to torque new mean-ing and possibility is that it is severed from the political question of for whom new mean-ing is produced. The ideal reader is an endangered species, the committed reader has an ideological agenda both open and closed, flawed and acute, that we do not address directly. (204)

10. Rachel Blau DuPlessis comments on the experience of reading the canon-ical male modernists:

I read them, dazzled, Pound, Williams, Eliot. They "read" me. Some me, anyway. I am, within their words, dug into habitual gender sites, repositioned from producer to pro-duced, from writer to written, from artist to inspiration. Or to blockage. And the works are difficult enough that their "mastery" is a challenge, so that separating from their assumptions is difficult; the reader is slid to scholiast, to epigone, to apologist. (*Pink Guitar* 47)

Elsewhere, in contrast, DuPlessis characterizes an experimental female aes-thetic by its eschewal of authoritative stances and collapsing of roles: "Not even seeking the authority of the writing. (Reader could be writer, writer reader. Listener could be teacher.)" (5–6). Kathleen Fraser comments on the response to male rhetorical authority of a woman who is simultaneously reader and emerging writer:

One may admire it and at the same time feel a sudden silence of resistance descending, if one is a woman trying to give shape to her own experiences, yet perceiving that almost all the models being held up to her have been created largely out of male privilege and assumed access to public speech. The confidence that existing poem forms cover the essential and important areas of human experience is a troubling barrier to the discov-ery of new formal possibilities. ("Line" 155)

Fraser goes on to point out the number of women writers who are drawn to the "notational form" of journal or daybook as "something not so finished and official as a poem, yet a site for *close reading* of the subject (the shifting self in relation to romance, politics, nature, culture, etc.)" (167; my emphasis). Beverly Dahlen's long work-in-progress, after all, which she describes as "theoretically open-ended, which turns out to be something like a journal" (3), is called *A Reading*.

11. On the adoption of different versions of Williams by the Language poets and the New Formalists, respectively, see my " 'Openness,' 'Closure,' and Recent American Poetry."

12. Compare Barthes:

Our literature is characterized by the pitiless divorce which the literary institution maintains between the producer of the text and its user, between its owner and its customer, between its author and its reader. This reader is thereby plunged into a kind of idleness—he is intransitive. (*S/Z* 4)

13. An *emerging* context, the impact of which is hard to assess at this early stage, involves the development of electronic poetry journals (the collectively edited *We Magazine*, John Fowler's *Grist*, Kenneth Sherwood and Loss Pequeño Glazier's *Rift*), reviews (Luigi-Bob Drake's *Taproot Reviews*), and discussion groups (Joe Amato's *Nous Refuse*). While the internet holds great potential for the extra-academic production and reception of poetry and poetics, however, at the time of writing access to it remains limited for writers and readers not affiliated with the academy or the corporate world.

Specific information on the "e-poetry circuit" derives from Bernstein, "Provisional Institutions."

14. From a very different perspective, Adrienne Rich, who contributed four columns to the early *APR*, comments on appearing in that context:

Early [I] came to mistrust the "liberal" policy which could accom[m]odate my feminism, or occasional utterances by black writers, to a predominantly white and sexist content, and a pervasive lack of purpose—poetic or political. . . . women's words, even where they are not edited, can get flattened and detonated in a context which is predominantly masculine and misogynist, and . . . the attempt to "reach" readers through such a context can be a form of self-delusion. (107)

In recent years, however, Rich has once again started to publish regularly in *APR*.

15. Compare Reinfeld: Bernstein "organizes his books to frustrate attempts to read into them patterns of organic growth and development." This extends to the shape of his career, Reinfeld argues, as "each of his collections includes both recent and not-so-recent work" and thus none of them can be read "as a testament to some form of 'growing awareness' " (78). Bernstein himself comments on his systematically building contradictory registers into a poem, in terms directly relevant to "The Age of Correggio":

In much of my own work: working at angles to the strong tidal pull of an expected sequence of a sentence—or by cutting off a sentence or phrase midway and counting on the mind to complete where the poem goes off in another direction, giving two vectors at once—the anticipated projection underneath and the actual wording above (*Content's Dream* 38)

16. While Kalaidjian's point is well taken that much recent American poetry shows high romanticism's potential for cultural criticism reduced to "a narrow introspective rhetoric" (27), the equation of poetry with lyric predates the university's mediation of poetry by well over a hundred years. Thus the academy institutionalizes in particularly influential form—but does not *originate*—an already extant ideology of the poetic.

17. For a more developed statement of this position than I can undertake here, see Lazer.

18. The nature and extent of collaboration in the history of American poetry remain largely unexplored, and it is not confined to avant-gardes. Amy Lowell felt that she should hang out a shingle that read "Lowell and Russell, Makers of Fine Poems."

19. Bernstein makes a comparable appeal to audience and rhetorical situation in describing his desire to employ conventional expository modes that "appear to be invested with greater social power," "to access the power in these high-status forms. . . . This social dynamic is something I consider when determining what writing style to deploy in a given circumstance" (*A Poetics* 152).

20. In *Paradise* Silliman writes, only half ironically, that "becoming identified with an inaccurate but provocative name enabled the Language Poets to rapidly deepen market penetration and increase market share" (18).

Works Cited

Aaron, Daniel. *Writers on the Left.* New York: Avon, 1965.

Abbott, Craig S. "Modern American Poetry: Anthologies, Classroom, and Canons." *College Literature* 17 (1990): 209-21.

The Age of Correggio and the Carracci: Emilian Painting of the Sixteenth and Seventeenth Centuries. New York: Cambridge UP, 1986.

Aiken, Conrad, ed. *American Poetry, 1671-1928.* New York: Modern Library, 1929.

Aiken, Conrad, ed. *Twentieth-Century American Poetry.* New York: Modern Library, 1944.

Allen, Donald M., ed. *The New American Poetry.* New York: Grove, 1960.

Allen, Gay Wilson. "Walt Whitman—Nationalist or Proletarian?" *English Journal* 26 (1937): 48-52.

Allison, Alexander W., et al., eds. *The Norton Anthology of Poetry.* New York: W. W. Norton, 1970. 2d ed. 1975; 3d ed. 1983.

Althusser, Louis. *Lenin and Philosophy and Other Essays.* Trans. Ben Brewster. New York: Monthly Review, 1971.

Altieri, Charles. *Canons and Consequences: Reflections on the Ethical Force of Imaginative Ideals.* Evanston: Northwestern UP, 1990.

Altieri, Charles. *Self and Sensibility in Contemporary American Poetry.* New York: Cambridge UP, 1984.

Altieri, Charles. "Without Consequences Is No Politics: A Response to Jerome McGann." In von Hallberg, *Politics and Poetic Value* 301-7.

"American Poetry." *United States Magazine and Democratic Review* 8 (Nov.-Dec. 1840): 399-430.

Anania, Michael. "Of Living Belfry and Rampart: On American Literary Magazines since 1950." In Anderson and Kinzie 6-23.

Anderson, Elliott, and Mary Kinzie, eds. *The Little Magazine in America: A Modern Documentary History.* Yonkers: Pushcart, 1978.

Andrews, Bruce. "Poetry as Explanation, Poetry as Praxis." In Bernstein, *Politics of Poetic Form* 23-43.

Andrews, Bruce. "Text and Context." In Andrews and Bernstein 31-38.

Andrews, Bruce. "Writing Social Work and Political Practice." In Andrews and Bernstein 132-36.

Andrews, Bruce, and Charles Bernstein, eds. *The L=A=N=G=U=A=G=E Book*. Carbondale: Southern Illinois UP, 1984.

Apteryx [T. S. Eliot]. "Verse Pleasant and Upleasant." *Egoist* 3 (1918): 43–44.

Arac, Jonathan. *Critical Genealogies: Historical Situations for Postmodern Literary Studies*. New York: Columbia UP, 1987.

Armantrout, Rae. "Feminist Poetics and the Meaning of Clarity." *Sagetrieb* 11.3 (1992): 7–16.

Armantrout, Rae. " 'Why Don't Women Do Language-Oriented Writing?' " In Silliman, *In the American Tree* 544–46.

Arnold, Matthew. "The Literary Influence of Academies." *Poetry and Criticism of Matthew Arnold*, ed. A. Dwight Culler. Boston: Houghton Mifflin, 1961.

Arpin, Gary Q. "Mistress Bradstreet's Discontents." *John Berryman Studies* 1 (1975): 2–7.

Arvin, Newton. "Report from the Academy: The Professor as Manager." *Partisan Review* 12 (1945): 275–78.

Arvin, Newton. *Whitman*. New York: Macmillan, 1938.

Arvin, Newton. "Whitman's Individualism." *New Republic* 71 (1932): 212–13.

Ashbery, John. *Rivers and Mountains*. New York: Ecco, 1966.

Ashbery, John. *Self-Portrait in a Convex Mirror*. New York: Penguin, 1976.

Babbitt, Irving. *Literature and the American College: Essays in Defense of the Humanities*. Boston: Houghton Mifflin, 1908.

Bailey, Marcia Edgerton. *A Lesser Hartford Wit, Dr. Elihu Hubbard Smith, 1771–1798*. University of Maine Studies, 2d ser. 11, Orono: U of Maine P, 1928.

Barrett, William. "A Present Tendency in American Criticism." *Kenyon Review* 11 (1949): 1–16.

Barrett, William. "The Resistance." *Partisan Review* 13 (1946): 479–88.

Barrett, William. "Temptations of St. Yvor." *Kenyon Review* 9 (1947): 532–51.

Barthes, Roland. *Image-Music-Text*. Sel. and trans. Stephen Heath. New York: Hill and Wang, 1977.

Barthes, Roland. *The Pleasure of the Text*. Trans. Richard Miller. New York: Hill and Wang, 1975.

Barthes, Roland. *S/Z*. Trans. Richard Miller. New York: Hill and Wang, 1974.

Bartlett, Lee. "What Is 'Language Poetry?' " *Critical Inquiry* 12 (1986): 741–49.

Bawer, Bruce. *The Middle Generation: The Lives and Poetry of Delmore Schwartz, Randall Jarrell, John Berryman, and Robert Lowell*. Hamden, CT: Archon, 1986.

Bayless, Joy. *Rufus Wilmot Griswold, Poe's Literary Executor*. Nashville: Vanderbilt UP, 1943.

Beach, Christopher. *The ABC of Influence: Ezra Pound and the Remaking of American Poetic Tradition*. Berkeley: U of California P, 1992.

Benét, Stephen Vincent. *Burning City: New Poems*. New York: Farrar and Rinehart, 1936.

[Benjamin, Park.] "Recent American Poetry." *United States Magazine and Democratic Review* 5 (June 1839): 523–41.

Bennett, David. "Periodical Fragments and Organic Culture: Modernism, The Avant-Garde, and the Little Magazine." *Contemporary Literature* 30 (1989): 480–502.

Bennett, Joseph. "Five Books, Four Poets." *Hudson Review* 4 (1951): 133–43.

Bennett, Paula. *Emily Dickinson: Woman Poet.* Iowa City: U of Iowa P, 1990.

Benstock, Shari, ed. *Feminist Issues in Literary Scholarship.* Bloomington: Indiana UP, 1987.

Bercovitch, Sacvan. *The Puritan Origins of the American Self.* New Haven: Yale UP, 1975.

Berg, Stephen, and Robert Mezey, eds. *The New Naked Poetry: Recent American Poetry in Open Forms.* Indianapolis: Bobbs-Merrill, 1976.

Berg, Temma. "Psychologies of Reading." In *Tracing Literary Theory,* ed. Joseph Natoli. Urbana: U of Illinois P, 1987. 248–77.

Bergonzi, Bernard. *Exploding English: Criticism, Theory, Culture.* Oxford: Clarendon, 1990.

Bernstein, Charles. "The Age of Correggio and the Carracci" and "Freud's Butcher." *American Poetry Review* (Sept.–Oct. 1989): 14.

Bernstein, Charles. *Content's Dream: Essays, 1975–1984.* Los Angeles: Sun and Moon, 1986.

Bernstein, Charles. *A Poetics.* Cambridge: Harvard UP, 1992.

Bernstein, Charles. "Provisional Institutions: Alternative Presses and Poetic Innovation." Unpublished essay, 1993.

Bernstein, Charles, ed. *The Politics of Poetic Form: Poetry and Public Policy.* New York: Roof, 1990.

Bernstein, Charles, and Susan Bee. *The Poems of the Nude Formalism.* Los Angeles: Sun and Moon, 1989.

Berryman, John. "A Peine Ma Piste." *Partisan Review* 15 (1948): 826–28.

Berryman, John. "The Art of Poetry: An Interview with John Berryman." With Peter Stitt. In Thomas 18–44.

Berryman, John. *Collected Poems, 1937–1971.* Ed. Charles Thornbury. New York: Farrar, Straus and Giroux, 1989.

Berryman, John. *The Freedom of the Poet.* New York: Farrar, Straus and Giroux, 1976.

Berryman, John. "An Interview with John Berryman." With John Plotz et al. In Thomas 3–17.

Berryman, John. *Stephen Crane.* New York: Sloane, 1950.

Bérubé, Michael. *Marginal Forces/Cultural Centers: Tolson, Pynchon, and the Politics of the Canon.* Ithaca: Cornell UP, 1992.

Biggs, Mary. "Academic Publishing and Poetry." *Scholarly Publishing* 17 (1985): 3–23.

Blackburn, Paul. "The Grinding Down." *Kulchur* 3.10 (1963): 9–18.

Blackmur, R. P. *Language as Gesture: Essays in Poetry.* 1952. New York: Columbia UP, 1981.

Blackmur, R. P. *The Lion and the Honeycomb: Essays in Solicitude and Critique.* New York: Harcourt, Brace, 1955.

Blackmur, R. P. "The Situation in American Writing: Seven Questions (Part 2)." *Partisan Review* 6.5 (1939): 117–20.

Bledstein, Burton J. *The Culture of Professionalism: The Middle Class and the Development of Higher Education in America.* New York: Norton, 1976.

Bloom, Harold. *Agon: A Theory of Poetic Revisionism.* New York: Oxford UP, 1982.

Bloom, Harold. *The Breaking of the Vessels.* Chicago: U of Chicago P, 1982.

Bloom, Harold. "Criticism, Canon-Formation, and Prophecy: The Sorrows of Facticity." *Raritan* 3.3 (1984): 1–20.

Bloom, Harold. *Figures of Capable Imagination.* New York: Seabury, 1976.

Bloom, Harold. "Interview with Robert Moynihan." In Robert Moynihan, *Recent Imaginings: Interviews with Harold Bloom, Geoffrey Hartman, J. Hillis Miller, Paul de Man.* Hamden, CT: Archon, 1986. 1–47.

Bloom, Harold. "John Ashbery: The Charity of the Hard Moments." In *Contemporary Poetry in America: Essays and Interviews,* ed. Robert Boyers. New York: Schocken, 1974. 110–38.

Bloom, Harold. *A Map of Misreading.* New York: Oxford UP, 1975.

Bloom, Harold. *Poetry and Repression: Revisionism from Blake to Stevens.* New Haven: Yale UP, 1976.

Bloom, Harold. *The Ringers in the Tower: Studies in Romantic Tradition.* Chicago: U of Chicago P, 1971.

Bloom, Harold. *Wallace Stevens: The Poems of Our Climate.* Ithaca: Cornell UP, 1977.

Bly, Robert. "Award." *The Sixties* 5 (1961): 91.

Bogan, Louise. "The Situation in American Writing: Seven Questions (Part 2)." *Partisan Review* 6.5 (1939): 105–8.

Bontemps, Arna, ed. *American Negro Poetry.* New York: Hill and Wang, 1963.

Boys, Richard C. "The Beginnings of the American Poetical Miscellany, 1714–1800." *American Literature* 17 (1945): 127–39.

Bradstreet, Anne. *The Works of Anne Bradstreet: In Prose and Verse.* Ed. John Harvard Ellis. 1867. New York: Peter Smith, 1932.

Breslin, James. *From Modern to Contemporary: American Poetry, 1945–1965.* Chicago: U of Chicago P, 1984.

Breslin, Paul. *The Psycho-Political Muse: American Poetry since the Fifties.* Chicago: U of Chicago P, 1987.

Brodhead, Richard H. *The School of Hawthorne.* New York: Oxford UP, 1986.

Broe, Mary Lynn, and Angela Ingram, eds. *Women's Writing in Exile.* Chapel Hill: U of North Carolina P, 1989.

Brooke-Rose, Christine. "Illustrations." In Friedman and Fuchs 55–71.

Brooks, Cleanth. Contributions to "The Changing Culture of the University" symposium. *Partisan Review* 58 (1991): 305.

Brooks, Cleanth. "Edna Millay's Maturity." *Southwest Review* 20.2 (1935): [Book Section] 1–5.

Brooks, Cleanth. "Forty Years of *Understanding Poetry.*" *CEA Forum* (1980): 5–12.

Brooks, Cleanth. *Modern Poetry and the Tradition.* 1939. New York: Oxford UP, 1965.

Brooks, Cleanth. "The New Criticism." *Sewanee Review* 87 (1979): 592–607.

Brooks, Cleanth. "Poet or Sage?" *Kenyon Review* 1 (1939): 325–27.

Brooks, Cleanth. *A Shaping Joy: Studies in the Writer's Craft.* New York: Harcourt Brace Jovanovich, 1971.

Brooks, Cleanth. *The Well-Wrought Urn: Studies in the Structure of Poetry.* New York: Harcourt, Brace, 1939.

Brooks, Cleanth, and Robert Penn Warren. *Understanding Poetry: An Anthology for College Students.* New York: Henry Holt, 1938. 2d ed. 1950; 3d ed. New York: Holt, Rinehart and Winston.

Bryant, William Cullen, ed. *A Library of Poetry and Song.* 20th ed. New York: J. B. Ford, 1871.

Bryant, William Cullen, ed. *Selections from the American Poets.* New York: Harper, 1840.

Buell, Lawrence. "Henry Thoreau Enters the American Canon." In *New Essays on Walden*, ed. Robert F. Sayre. New York: Cambridge UP, 1992. 23–52.

Burgess, Anthony. "The Writer among Professors." *TLS* (10 Dec. 1982): 1357.

Burklund, Carl Edwin. "A Chant for America." *Rebel Poet* (Oct. 1932): 8.

Cain, William E. *The Crisis in Criticism: Theory, Literature, and Reform in English Studies.* Baltimore: Johns Hopkins UP, 1984.

Cain, William E. *F. O. Mattiessen and the Politics of Criticism.* Madison: U of Wisconsin P, 1988.

Caldwell, Patricia. "Why Our First Poet Was a Woman: Bradstreet and the Birth of an American Poetic Voice." *Prospects* 13 (1988): 1–35.

Calverton, V. F. *The Liberation of American Literature.* New York: Charles Scribner's Sons, 1932.

Canby, Henry Seidel. "The American Scholar Ninety Years Later." *Saturday Review of Literature* (23 June 1928): 1–3.

Canby, Henry Seidel. *Classic Americans: A Study of Eminent American Writers from Irving to Whitman.* New York: Russell and Russell, 1939.

Carafiol, Peter. *The American Ideal: Literary History as a Worldly Activity.* New York: Oxford UP, 1991.

Carafiol, Peter. "The New Orthodoxy: Ideology and the Institution of American Literary History." *American Literature* 59 (1987): 626–38.

Carman, Bliss, ed. *The Oxford Book of American Verse.* New York: Oxford UP, 1927.

Cheever, George B., ed. *The American Common-place Book of Poetry.* Boston: Carter, Hendee and Babcock, 1831.

Ciardi, John. "The Researched Mistress." *Saturday Review* (23 March 1957): 36–37.

Clark, Tom. "'Stalin as Linguist.'" *Partisan Review* 54 (1987): 299–304.

Clark, Suzanne. *Sentimental Modernism: Women Writers and the Revolution of the Word.* Bloomington: Indiana UP, 1991.

Clausen, Christopher. "Packaging Poems." *Sewanee Review* 96 (1988): 131–36.

Codrescu, Andrei, ed. *American Poetry since 1970: Up Late*. New York: Four Walls Eight Windows, 1987.

Coggeshall, William T. *The Poets and Poetry of the West*. Columbus, OH: Follett, Foster, 1860.

Committee on the College Study of American Literature and Culture. *American Literature in the College Curriculum*. Chicago: National Council of Teachers of English, 1951.

Conarroe, Joel. *John Berryman: An Introduction to the Poetry*. New York: Columbia UP, 1977.

Cooney, Terry A. *The Rise of the New York Intellectuals: Partisan Review and Its Circle, 1934–1945*. Madison: U of Wisconsin P, 1986.

Corman, Cid. "Communication: Poetry for Radio." *Poetry* 81 (1952): 212–15.

Corman, Cid. "In the Word Was the Beginning." *Origin* 1st ser. 20 (1957): 1–3.

Corman, Cid. "A Note on the Founding of *Origin*." *Serif* 5.1 (1968): 29–30.

Corman, Cid. "*Origin*." In Anderson and Kinzie 239–47.

Corman, Cid. "The Voice as the Instrument of Verse." *Origin* 1st ser. 9 (1953): 1–6.

Corman, Cid, ed. *The Gist of Origin, 1951–1971*. New York: Grossman, 1975.

Cowley, Malcolm. "Ten Little Magazines." *New Republic* (31 May 1947): 30–33.

Crane, Hart. *The Complete Poems and Selected Letters and Prose of Hart Crane*. Ed. Brom Weber. Garden City, NY: Doubleday, 1966.

Crane, R. S. *The Idea of the Humanities and Other Essays Critical and Historical*. 2 vols. Vol. 2. Chicago: U of Chicago P, 1967.

Creeley, Robert. *The Collected Essays of Robert Creeley*. Berkeley: U of California P, 1989.

Creeley, Robert. "On *Black Mountain Review*." In Anderson and Kinzie 248–61.

Crews, Frederick. *The Critics Bear It Away: American Fiction and the Academy*. New York: Random House, 1992.

Culler, Jonathan. *Structuralist Poetics: Structuralism, Linguistics, and the Study of Literature*. Ithaca: Cornell UP, 1975.

Cutrer, Thomas W. *Parnassus on the Mississippi: The Southern Review and the Baton Rouge Literary Community, 1935–1942*. Baton Rouge: Louisiana State UP, 1984.

Dacey, Philip, and David Jauss, eds. *Strong Measures: Contemporary American Poetry in Traditional Forms*. New York: Harper and Row, 1986.

Dahlen, Beverly. "Forbidden Knowledge." *Poetics Journal* 4 (1984): 3–19.

Daly, Robert. *God's Altar: The World and the Flesh in Puritan Poetry*. Berkeley: U of California P, 1978.

Dana, Charles A., ed. *The Household Book of Poetry*. 1858. 11th ed. New York: D. Appleton, 1866.

Davey, Frank. "Introducing *Tish*." In Gervais 150–61.

Davie, Donald. *Trying to Explain*. Ann Arbor: U of Michigan P, 1979.

DeKoven, Marianne. "Male Signature, Female Aesthetic: The Gender Politics of Experimental Writing." In Friedman and Fuchs 72–81.

de Lauretis, Teresa. *Technologies of Gender: Essays on Theory, Film, and Fiction.* Bloomington: Indiana UP, 1987.

Dell, Floyd. "Walt Whitman, Anti-Socialist." *New Review* (15 June 1915): 85–86.

de Loach, Allen. "Little Mags/Small Presses and the Cultural Revolution." *Intrepid* 21–22 (1972): 106–39.

Dempsey, Charles. "The Carracci Reform of Painting." In *Age of Correggio* 237–54.

DeShazer, Mary K. *Inspiring Women: Reimagining the Muse.* New York: Pergamon, 1986.

Dicker, Harold. "From the Notebook: Poetic Analysis." *Origin* 1st ser. 9 (1953): 8–13.

Donahoe, Wade. "A Letter." *Origin* 1st ser. 14 (1954): 54–58.

Douglas, Ann. *The Feminization of American Culture.* New York: Knopf, 1977.

Drucker, Johanna. "Contemporary Women Writers and the Legacy of the Avant-Garde." Unpublished essay, 1990.

Drucker, Johanna. "Women and Language." *Poetics Journal* 4 (1984): 56–68.

Duberman, Martin. *Black Mountain: An Exploration in Community.* Garden City: Anchor/Doubleday, 1973.

Duncan, Robert. "Africa Revisited." *Origin* 1st ser. 6 (1952): 16–22.

Duncan, Robert. "Note to Olson." *Origin* 1st ser. 12 (1954): 18–19.

DuPlessis, Rachel Blau. *The Pink Guitar: Writing as Feminist Practice.* New York: Routledge, 1990.

DuPlessis, Rachel Blau. *Tabula Rosa.* Elmwood, CT: Potes & Poets, 1987.

Eagleton, Terry. *Against the Grain: Essays, 1975–1985.* London: Verso, 1986.

Eagleton, Terry. *The Function of Criticism from the Spectator to Post-Structuralism.* London: Verso, 1984.

Eagleton, Terry. *Literary Theory: An Introduction.* Minneapolis: U of Minnesota P, 1983.

Eliot, T. S. "Ezra Pound." In *An Examination of Ezra Pound*, ed. Peter Russell. Norfolk, CT: New Directions, 1950. 25–36.

Eliot, T. S. "Introduction: 1928." In Ezra Pound, *Selected Poems*, ed. Eliot. London: Faber and Faber, 1928.

Eliot, T. S. *Selected Prose of T. S. Eliot.* Ed. Frank Kermode. New York: Harcourt, Brace and Jovanovich, 1975.

Eliot, T. S. "[Tennyson and Whitman]." *The Nation and Athenaeum* (4 June 1927): 302.

Eliot, T. S. *To Criticize the Critic, and Other Writings.* New York: Farrar, Straus and Giroux, 1965.

Eliot, T. S. *The Use of Poetry and the Use of Criticism.* London: Faber and Faber, 1964.

Eliot, T. S. "Whitman and Tennyson." *The Nation and Athenaeum* (18 Dec. 1926): 426.

Ellis, George, ed. *Specimens of the Early English Poets.* 3 vols. 1790. 5th ed. London: Henry Washbourne, 1845.

Emerson, Ralph Waldo, ed. *Parnassus.* Boston: Houghton Mifflin, 1874.

Eshleman, Clayton. "Doing *Caterpillar.*" In Anderson and Kinzie 450–71.

Eshleman, Clayton. "The Gospel According to Norton." *American Poetry Review* (Sept.–Oct. 1990): 33–41.

Eshleman, Clayton, ed. *A Caterpillar Anthology: A Selection of Poetry and Prose from Caterpillar Magazine.* Garden City, NY: Doubleday, 1971.

Evans, George, ed. *Charles Olson and Cid Corman: Complete Correspondence, 1950–1964.* 2 vols. Orono: National Poetry Foundation, 1987–91.

Eysteinsson, Astradur. *The Concept of Modernism.* Ithaca: Cornell UP, 1990.

Faas, Ekbert. *Young Robert Duncan: Portrait of the Poet as Homosexual in Society.* Santa Rosa: Black Sparrow, 1983.

Farrell, James T. "The Situation in American Writing: Seven Questions." *Partisan Review* 6.4 (1939): 30–32.

Fekete, John. *The Critical Twilight: Explorations in the Ideology of Anglo-American Literary Theory from Eliot to McLuhan.* London: Routledge and Kegan Paul, 1977.

Felski, Rita. *Beyond Feminist Aesthetics: Feminist Literature and Social Change.* Cambridge: Harvard UP, 1989.

Fiedler, Leslie. "Literature as an Institution." In *English Literature: Opening Up the Canon. Selected Papers from the English Institute, 1979,* ed. Fiedler and Houston A. Baker, Jr. Baltimore: Johns Hopkins UP, 1981.

Fiedler, Leslie. "Toward an Amateur Criticism." *Kenyon Review* 12 (1950): 561–75.

Fiedler, Leslie. *What Was Literature? Class Culture and Mass Society.* New York: Simon and Schuster, 1982.

Filreis, Alan. *Wallace Stevens and the Actual World.* Princeton: Princeton UP, 1991.

Finkelstein, Norman. "The Sage of New Haven." *Criticial Texts* 6 (1989): 1–22.

Finkelstein, Norman. *The Utopian Moment in Contemporary American Poetry.* Rev. ed. Lewisburg, PA: Bucknell UP, 1993.

Fischer, Michael. *Does Deconstruction Make Any Difference? Poststructuralism and the Defense of Poetry in Modern Criticism.* Bloomington: Indiana UP, 1985.

Fish, Stanley. *Is There a Text in This Class? The Authority of Literary Communities.* Cambridge: Harvard UP, 1980.

Foster, Hal, ed. *The Anti-Aesthetic: Essays on Postmodern Culture.* Port Townsend, WA: Bay, 1983.

Fowler, Alastair. *Kinds of Literature: An Introduction to the Theory of Genres and Modes.* Cambridge: Harvard UP, 1982.

Fox, Willard. "Two Rooms: A History and Analysis of Little Magazine Collections at Buffalo, New York, and Madison, Wisconsin." *Literary Research* 11 (1986): 141–58.

Franklin, H. Bruce. *The Victim as Criminal and Artist.* New York: Oxford UP, 1978.

Fraser, Kathleen. "Line. On the Line. Lining Up. Lined with. Between the Lines. Bottom Line." In *The Line in Postmodern Poetry,* ed. Robert Frank and Henry Sayre. Urbana: U of Illinois P, 1988. 152–74.

Fraser, Kathleen. "The Tradition of Marginality." *Frontiers* 10 (1989): 22–27.

Fraser, Kathleen. "Without a Net: Finding One's Balance along the Perilous Wire of the New." Unpublished essay, 1992.

Fraser, Russell. "R. P. Blackmur at Princeton." *Sewanee Review* 89 (1981): 540–59.

Freeman, Joseph. *An American Testament: A Narrative of Rebels and Romantics.* New York: Farrar and Rinehart, 1936.

Freneau, Philip. *The "Poems" (1786) and "Miscellaneous Works" (1788) of Philip Freneau.* Ed. Lewis Leary. Delmar, NY: Scholars' Facsimiles and Reprints, 1975.

Friedman, Ellen G., and Miriam Fuchs, eds. *Breaking the Sequence: Women's Experimental Fiction.* Princeton: Princeton UP, 1989.

Friedman, Susan Stanford. "Exile in the American Grain." In Broe and Ingram 87–112.

Fuson, Ben W. *Which Text Shall I Choose for American Literature? A Descriptive and Statistical Comparison of Currently Available Survey Anthologies and Reprint Series in American Literature.* Parkville, MO: Park College P, 1952.

Gallagher, William D. *Selections from the Poetical Literature of the West.* Cincinnati: U. P. James, 1841.

Gates, Henry Louis, Jr. "Authority, (White) Power, and the (Black) Critic: It's All Greek to Me." In *The Native Context of Minority Discourse,* ed. Abdul R. Jan Mohamed and David Lloyd. New York: Oxford UP, 1990. 72–101.

Gates, Henry Louis, Jr. "Canon Formation, Literary History, and the Afro-American Tradition: From the Seen to the Told." In *Afro-American Literary Study in the 1990s,* ed. Houston A. Baker, Jr., and Patricia Redmond. Chicago: U of Chicago P, 1989. 14–39.

Gates, Henry Louis, Jr. "Good-bye, Columbus? Notes on the Culture of Critricism." *American Literary History* 3 (1991): 711–27.

Gates, Henry Louis, Jr. *Loose Canons: Notes on the Culture Wars.* New York: Oxford UP, 1992. 17–42.

Gates, Henry Louis, Jr. "The Master's Pieces: On Canon Formation and the African-American Tradition." *South Atlantic Quarterly* 89 (1990): 89–111.

Gelpi, Albert. *A Coherent Splendor: The American Poetic Renaissance, 1910–1950.* New York: Cambridge UP, 1988.

Gelpi, Albert. "Stevens and Williams: The Epistemology of Modernism." In Gelpi, *Wallace Stevens* 3–23.

Gelpi, Albert, ed. *Wallace Stevens: The Poetics of Modernism.* New York: Cambridge UP, 1985.

Gerhardt, Rainer M. "Letter for Creeley and Olson." *Origin* 1st ser. 4 (1951–52): 1–7.

Gervais, C. H., ed. *The Writing Life: Historical and Critical Views of the Tish Movement.* Coatsworth, Ont.: Black Moss, 1976.

Gibbons, Reginald. "Academic Criticism and Contemporary Literature." In Graff and Gibbons 15–34.

Gilbert, James Burkhardt. *Writers and Partisans: A History of Literary Radicalism in America.* New York: Wiley, 1962.

Gilbert, Sandra M., and Susan Gubar. *The War of the Words.* Vol. 1 of *No Man's Land: The Place of the Woman Writer in the Twentieth Century.* New Haven: Yale UP, 1988.

Ginsberg, Allen. *Allen Verbatim: Lectures on Poetry, Politics, Consciousness.* Ed. Gordon Ball. New York: McGraw, 1974.

Ginsberg, Allen. "From an Early Letter." In Berg and Mezey 84–87.

Gioia, Dana. "Can Poetry Matter?" *Atlantic Monthly* (May 1991): 94–106.

Gnarowski, Michael. *Contact, 1952–1954: Notes on the History and Background of the Periodical and an Index.* Montreal: Delta Canada, 1966.

[Godwin, Parke.] "Bryant's Poems." *United States Magazine and Democratic Review* 6 (Oct. 1839): 273–86.

Gold, Michael. "Ode to Walt Whitman." *New Masses* (5 Nov. 1935): 21.

Golding, Alan. "The 'Community of Elements' in Wallace Stevens and Louis Zukofsky." In Gelpi, *Wallace Stevens* 121–40.

Golding, Alan. "Language-Bashing Again." *Mid-American Review* 8.2 (1988): 93–100.

Golding, Alan. " 'Openness,' 'Closure', and Recent American Poetry." *Arizona Quarterly* 47 (1991): 77–91.

Goodman, Paul. "Advance-Guard Writing, 1900–1950." *Kenyon Review* 13 (1951): 357–80.

Graff, Gerald. "Co-optation." In *The New Historicism*, ed. H. Aram Veeser. New York: Routledge, 1989.

Graff, Gerald. *Professing Literature: An Institutional History.* Chicago: U of Chicago P, 1987.

Graff, Gerald. "The University and the Prevention of Culture." In Graff and Gibbons 62–82.

Graff, Gerald. "Who Killed Criticism?" *American Scholar* 49 (1980): 337–55.

Graff, Gerald. "Yvor Winters of Stanford." *American Scholar* 44 (1975): 291–98.

Graff, Gerald, and Reginald Gibbons, eds. *Criticism in the University.* Evanston: Northwestern UP, 1985.

Grimshaw, James A., Jr. *Robert Penn Warren: A Descriptive Bibliography, 1922–79.* Charlottesville: UP of Virginia, 1981.

Griswold, Rufus Wilmot. *Passages for the Correspondence and Other Papers of Rufus W. Griswold.* Ed. W. M. Griswold. Cambridge: Harvard UP, 1898.

Griswold, Rufus Wilmot. *Readings in American Poetry: For the Use of Schools.* New York: J. C. Riker, 1843.

Griswold, Rufus Wilmot, ed. *Gems from American Female Poets.* Philadelphia: H. Hooker, 1842.

Griswold, Rufus Wilmot, ed. *The Poets and Poetry of America.* Philadelphia: Carey and Hart, 1842. 8th ed. 1847.

Guillory, John. *Cultural Capital.* Chicago: U of Chicago P, 1983.

Gunn, Thom. "The Postmodernism You Deserve." *Threepenny Review* 57 (1994): 6–8.

Haffenden, John. *The Life of John Berryman.* London: Ark, 1983.

Hale, Sarah Josepha, ed. *The Ladies' Wreath: A Selection from the Female Poetic Writers of England and America.* Boston: D. Appleton, 1837.

Hall, Donald. *Poetry and Ambition: Essays, 1982–1988.* Ann Arbor: U of Michigan P, 1988.

Hall, Donald, Robert Pack, and Louis Simpson, eds. *New Poets of England and America.* New York: New American Library, 1957.

Hardwick, Elizabeth. "Wind from the Prairie." *New York Review of Books* (9 Sept. 1991): 9–16.

Harris, Wendell V. "Canonicity." *PMLA* 106 (1991): 110–21.

Harrison, Antony H. "Reception Theory and the New Historicism: The Metaphysical Poets in the Nineteenth Century." *John Donne Journal* 4 (1985): 163–80.

Hartley, George. *Textual Politics and the Language Poets.* Bloomington: Indiana UP, 1989.

Haskell, Thomas L. "Professionalism *versus* Capitalism: R. H. Tawney, Emile Durkheim, and C. S. Peirce on the Disinterestedness of Professional Communities." In *The Authority of Experts: Studies in History and Theory,* ed. Haskell. Bloomington: Indiana UP, 1984. 180–225.

Hatlen, Burton. Review of Eliot Weinberger, ed., *American Poetry Today. Sagetrieb* 11.3 (1992): 149–55.

Hazlitt, William, ed. *Select Poets of Great Britain.* London: Thomas Tegg, 1825.

Heller, Michael. "Slitting Box Tops at the Anthology Mart." *Parnassus* 7 (1978): 146–59.

Hemenway, Robert. "In the American Canon." In *Redefining American Literary History,* ed. A. LaVonne Brown Ruoff and Jerry W. Ward, Jr. New York: Modern Language Association, 1990. 62–72.

Hicks, Granville. *The Great Tradition: An Interpretation of American Literature since the Civil War.* 1933. Chicago: Quadrangle, 1969.

Himmelfarb, Gertrude. Contribution to "The Changing Culture of the University" symposium. *Partisan Review* 58 (1991): 360–64.

Hoffman, Daniel, ed. *Harvard Guide to Contemporary American Writing.* Cambridge: Belknap P of Harvard UP, 1979.

Holden, Jonathan. *The Rhetoric of the Contemporary Lyric.* Bloomington: Indiana UP, 1980.

Hoover, Paul, ed. *Postmodern American Poetry: A Norton Anthology.* New York: W. W. Norton, 1994.

Howe, Susan. *The Birth-mark: Unsettling the Wilderness in American Literary History.* Hanover: UP of New England, 1993.

Howe, Susan. "Encloser." In Bernstein, *Politics of Poetic Form* 175–96.

Howe, Susan. *My Emily Dickinson.* Berkeley: North Atlantic, 1985.

Hows, John W. S., ed. *Golden Leaves from the American Poets.* New York: Bunce and Huntington, 1865.

Hudgins, Andrew. "Contemporary Poetry: Four Anthologies." *Missouri Review* 1 (1989): 197–216.

Hunt, Erica. "Notes for an Oppositional Poetics." In Bernstein, *Politics of Poetic Form* 197–212.

Hutner, Gordon. "Reviewing America: John Crowe Ransom's *Kenyon Review*." *American Quarterly* 44 (1992): 101-14.

Huyssen, Andreas. *After the Great Divide: Modernism, Mass Culture, Postmodernism.* Bloomington: Indiana UP, 1986.

Ignatow, David. "An Interview with David Ignatow." With Leif Sjoberg. *Contemporary Literature* 28 (1987): 143-62.

Inman, P. "From *Ocker*." In Silliman, *In the American Tree* 336-40.

Inman, P. "One to One." In Bernstein, *Politics of Poetic Form* 221-25.

Jameson, Fredric. *The Political Unconscious: Narrative as a Socially Symbolic Act.* Ithaca: Cornell UP, 1981.

Jameson, Fredric. "Postmodernism and Consumer Society." In Foster 111-25.

Jameson, Fredric. "Postmodernism, or The Cultural Logic of Late Capitalism." *New Left Review* 146 (1984): 53-92.

Jarrell, Randall. *Poetry and the Age.* New York: Vintage, 1953.

Johnson, Carol. "John Berryman and Mistress Bradstreet: A Relation of Reason." *Essays in Criticism* 14 (1964): 388-96.

Jones, LeRoi. "An Interview on *Yugen*." With David Ossman. In Anderson and Kinzie 317-23.

Kalaidjian, Walter. *Languages of Liberation: The Social Text in Contemporary American Poetry.* New York: Columbia UP, 1989.

Keese, John, ed. *The Poets of America.* 2 vols. Vol. 1. New York: Samuel Colman, 1840-42.

Kelly, Ernece B., ed. *Searching for America.* Urbana, IL: National Council of Teachers of English, 1972.

Kenner, Hugh. "The Making of the Modernist Canon." In von Hallberg, *Canons* 363-75.

Kenner, Hugh. "Subways to Parnassus." *Poetry* 84 (1954): 43-53.

Kermode, Frank. *An Appetite for Poetry.* Cambridge: Harvard UP, 1989.

Kermode, Frank. *The Art of Telling: Essays on Fiction.* Cambridge: Harvard UP, 1983.

Kermode, Frank. "Canons." *Dutch Quarterly Review of Anglo-American Letters* 18 (1988): 258-70.

Kermode, Frank. *Forms of Attention.* Chicago: U of Chicago P, 1985.

Kernan, Alvin. *The Imaginary Library: An Essay on Literature and Society.* Princeton: Princeton UP, 1982.

Kettell, Samuel, ed. *Specimens of American Poetry.* 3 vols. Boston: S. G. Goodrich, 1829.

Kinnell, Galway. "From 'The Poetics of the Physical World.'" In Berg and Mezey 133-36.

Kniffel, Leonard. "American Literature—Who's Publishing It?" *Library Journal* (15 Feb. 1987): 103-9.

Koch, Kenneth. *Thank You and Other Poems.* New York: Grove, 1962.

Kostelanetz, Richard. "Conversation with Berryman." *Massachusetts Review* 11 (1970): 340-47.

Kostelanetz, Richard. *The End of Intelligent Writing: Literary Politics in America.* New York: Sheed and Ward, 1974.

Kreymborg, Alfred, ed. *An Anthology of American Poetry: Lyric America, 1630-1930.* New York: Tudor, 1930.

Krieger, Murray. *Words about Words about Words: Theory, Criticism, and the Literary Text.* Baltimore: Johns Hopkins UP, 1988.

Krim, Seymour. "A Backward Glance o'er Beatnik Roads." In Anderson and Kinzie 324-37.

Krupat, Arnold. *The Voice in the Margin: Native American Literature and the Canon.* Berkeley: U of California P, 1989.

Kunitz, Stanley. "The New Books." *Harper's Magazine* 221 (Sept. 1960): 100.

Lauter, Paul. *Canons and Contexts.* New York: Oxford UP, 1991.

Lauter, Paul. "A Small Survey of Introductory Courses in American Literature." *Women's Studies Quarterly* 9.4 (1981): 12.

Lazer, Hank. "The Politics of Form and Poetry's Other Subjects: Reading Contemporary American Poetry." *American Literary History* 2 (1990): 503-27.

Leed, Jacob. "Robert Creeley and *The Lititz Review*: A Recollection with Letters." *Journal of Modern Literature* 5 (1976): 243-59.

Leitch, Vincent B. *American Literary Criticism from the Thirties to the Eighties.* New York: Columbia UP, 1988.

Lewis, R. W. B. *The American Adam: Innocence, Tragedy, and Tradition in the Nineteenth Century.* Chicago: U of Chicago P, 1955.

Lindenberger, Herbert. *The History in Literature: On Values, Genre, Institutions.* New York: Columbia UP, 1990.

Linton, W. J., ed. *Poetry of America: Selections from One Hundred American Poets from 1776 to 1876.* London: George Bell, 1878.

Logan, John. "On Poets and Poetry Today." In Berg and Mezey 235-41.

Long, Augustus White, ed. *American Poems, 1776-1900.* New York: American Book Co., 1905.

Lounsbury, Thomas R., ed. *Yale Book of American Verse.* New Haven: Yale UP, 1912.

Lowell, Amy. "Walt Whitman and the New Poetry." *Yale Review* 16 (1927): 502-19.

Lynes, Russell. "Highbrow, Lowbrow, Middlebrow." *Harper's Magazine* (Feb. 1949): 19-28.

Mac Low, Jackson. "Language-Centered." In Silliman, *In the American Tree* 491-95.

Malone, Marvin. "The Gall of *Wormwood* in Printing over 66 Issues and Still Continuing." In Anderson and Kinzie 389-97.

Marcus, Jane. "Still Practice, A/Wrested Alphabet: Toward a Feminist Aesthetic." In Benstock 79-97.

Margerum, Eileen. "Anne Bradstreet's Public Poetry and the Tradition of Humility." *Early American Literature* 17 (1982): 152-60.

Mariani, Paul. *Dream Song: The Life of John Berryman.* New York: William Morrow, 1990.

Mariani, Paul. *A Usable Past: Essays on Modern and Contemporary Poetry.* Amherst: U of Massachusetts P, 1984.

Mariani, Paul. *William Carlos Williams: A New World Naked.* New York: McGraw-Hill, 1981.

Martin, Jay. *Harvests of Change: American Literature, 1865–1914.* Englewood Cliffs, NJ: Prentice-Hall, 1967.

Martz, William J. *John Berryman.* Minneapolis: U of Minnesota P, 1969.

Matterson, Stephen. *Berryman and Lowell: The Art of Losing.* Totowa, NJ: Barnes and Noble, 1988.

Matthiessen, F. O., ed. *The Oxford Book of American Verse.* New York: Oxford UP, 1950.

May, James Boyer. "On *Trace.*" In Anderson and Kinzie 376–87.

May, James Boyer. *Twigs as Varied Bent.* Corona: Sparrow, 1954.

McCaffery, Steve. "From the Notebooks." In Andrews and Bernstein 159–62.

McCaffery, Steve. "Intraview." In Andrews and Bernstein 189.

McCaffery, Steve. *Panopticon.* Toronto: Blewointment, 1984.

McDowell, Robert. "The Poetry Anthology." *Hudson Review* 42 (1989–90): 594–608.

McGann, Jerome. "Contemporary Poetry, Alternative Routes." In von Hallberg, *Politics and Poetic Value* 253–76.

McQuade, Donald, et al., eds. *The Harper American Literature.* Vol. 2. New York: Harper & Row, 1987; 2d ed. 1993.

Merwin, W. S. *Regions of Memory: Uncollected Prose, 1949–82.* Ed. Ed Folsom and Cary Nelson. Urbana: U of Illinois P, 1987.

Messerli, Douglas, ed. *From the Other Side of the Century: A New American Poetry, 1960–1990.* Los Angeles: Sun and Moon, 1994.

Messerli, Douglas, ed. *"Language" Poetries: An Anthology.* New York: New Directions, 1987.

Middleton, Peter. "The Academic Development of *The Waste Land.*" *Glyph Textual Studies* 1 (1986): 153–80.

Middleton, Peter. "Language Poetry and Linguistic Activism." *Social Text* 25/26 (1990): 242–53.

Middleton, Peter. "On Ice: Julia Kristeva, Susan Howe and Avant-Garde Poetics." In *Contemporary Poetry Meets Modern Theory,* ed. Antony Easthope and John O. Thompson. Toronto: U of Toronto P, 1991. 81–95.

Miles, Barry. *Ginsberg: A Biography.* New York: Simon and Schuster, 1989.

Miller, James E., Jr. "Whitman Then and Now: A Reminiscence." Unpublished paper, 1990.

Miller, Perry. *The New England Mind: The Seventeenth Century.* New York: Macmillan, 1939.

Miller, Perry. *The Raven and the Whale: The War of Wit and Words in the Era of Poe and Melville.* New York: Harcourt and Brace, 1956.

Mirsky, D. S. "Walt Whitman: Poet of American Democracy." Trans. Bernard Guilbert Guerney. *Dialectics* 1 (1937): 11–27.

Mizruchi, Susan. "Cataloguing the Creatures of the Deep: 'Billy Budd, Sailor' and the Rise of Sociology." *Boundary 2* 17 (1990): 272–304.

MLA Committee on Research Activities. "The Aims, Methods, and Materials of Research in the Modern Languages and Literatures." *PMLA* 67 (1952): 3–37.

Moi, Toril. *Sexual/Textual Politics: Feminist Literary Theory*. London: Methuen, 1985.

Molesworth, Charles. *The Fierce Embrace: A Study of Contemporary American Poetry*. Columbia: U of Missouri P, 1979.

Monroe, Harriet, and Alice Corbin Henderson, eds. *The New Poetry: An Anthology*. New York: Macmillan, 1917.

Morris, Adalaide. "Dick, Jane, and American Literature: Fighting with Canons." *College English* 47 (1985): 467–81.

Morris, R. L. "Can Poetry Be Taught?" *Sewanee Review* 47 (1939): 89–94.

Morsberger, Robert E. "Segregated Surveys: American Literature." *Negro American Literature Forum* 4 (1970): 3–8.

Mott, Frank Luther. *Golden Multitudes: The Story of Best Sellers in the United States*. New York: Macmillan, 1947.

Mott, Frank Luther. *A History of American Magazines, 1741–1850*. New York: D. Appleton, 1930.

Mott, Frank Luther. *A History of American Magazines, 1865–1885*. Cambridge: Harvard UP, 1938.

Murphy, James F. *The Proletarian Moment: The Controversy over Leftism in Literature*. Urbana: U of Illinois P, 1991.

Myers, John A., Jr. "Modern Criticism and the Teaching of Poetry in the Schools." In *The Teacher and American Literature*, ed. Lewis Leary. Champaign: National Council of Teachers of English, 1965. 57–63.

Nathanson, Tenney. "Collage and Pulverization in Contemporary American Poetry: Charles Bernstein's *Controlling Interests*." *Contemporary Literature* 33 (1992): 302–18.

Nelson, Cary. "Multiculturalism without Guarantees: From Anthologies to Social Text." *Journal of the Midwest Modern Language Association* 26.1 (1993): 47–57.

Nelson, Cary. *Repression and Recovery: Modern American Poetry and the Politics of Cultural Memory, 1910–1945*. Madison: U of Wisconsin P, 1989.

Nemoianu, Virgil. "Literary Canons and Social Value Options." In *The Hospitable Canon: Essays on Literary Play, Scholarly Choice, and Popular Pressures*, ed. Nemoianu and Robert Royal. Philadelphia: John Benjamins, 1991. 215–47.

Newcomb, John Timberman. "Canonical Ahistoricism vs. Histories of Canons: Towards Methodological Dissensus." *South Atlantic Review* 54 (1989): 3–20.

Newcomb, John Timberman. *Wallace Stevens and Literary Canons*. Jackson: UP of Mississippi, 1992.

Nielsen, Aldon Lynn. *Reading Race: White American Poets and the Racial Discourse in the Twentieth Century*. Athens: U of Georgia P, 1988.

Norris, Ken. *The Little Magazine in Canada, 1925–1980: Its Role in the Development of Modernism and Post-Modernism in Canadian Poetry.* N.p.: ECW, 1984.

Novik, Mary. *Robert Creeley: An Inventory, 1945–1970.* Kent: Kent State UP, 1973.

O'Connor, William Van. "The Expense of Conventions." *Poetry* 76 (1950): 118–20.

Ohmann, Richard. *English in America: A Radical View of the Profession.* New York: Oxford UP, 1976.

Ohmann, Richard. *Politics of Letters.* Middletown: Wesleyan UP, 1987.

Olson, Charles. *The Collected Poems of Charles Olson.* Ed. George F. Butterick. Berkeley: U of California P, 1987.

Olson, Charles. *Human Universe and Other Essays.* Ed. Donald Allen. New York: Grove, 1967.

Olson, Charles. *Selected Writings.* Ed. Robert Creeley. New York: New Directions, 1966.

Olson, Charles. "This Is Yeats Speaking." *Partisan Review* 13 (1946):139–42.

Olson-Creeley Correspondence. Charles Olson and Robert Creeley: The Complete Correspondence. Ed. George F. Butterick and Richard Blevins. 9 vols. to date. Santa Barbara and Santa Rosa: Black Sparrow, 1980–.

Oppen, George. Interview. In *The Contemporary Writer: Interviews with Sixteen Novelists and Poets,* ed. L. S. Dembo and Cyrena Pondrom. Madison: U of Wisconsin P, 1970.

Ostricker, Alicia Suskin. *Stealing the Language: The Emergence of Women's Poetry in America.* London: Women's Press, 1987.

Pack, Robert. "Introduction." In *New Poets of England and America,* ed. Donald Hall and Robert Pack. 2d sel. New York: New American Library, 1962. 177–83.

Palgrave, Francis Turner, ed. *The Golden Treasury.* London: Macmillan, 1861.

Palmer, Michael. "Counter-Poetics and Current Practice." *Pavement* 7 (1986): 1–21.

Palmer, Michael. " 'Dear Lexicon': An Interview with Michael Palmer." With Benjamin Hollander and David Levi Strauss. *Acts* 5 (1986): 8–36.

Palmer, Michael. "An Interview with Michael Palmer." With Keith Tuma. *Contemporary Literature* 30 (1989): 1–12.

Palmer, Michael. "Some Notes on Shelley, Poetics and the Present." *Sulfur* 33 (1993): 273–81.

Parrinder, Patrick. *Authors and Authority: English and American Criticism, 1750–1990.* New York: Columbia UP, 1991.

Parrington, Vernon Louis. *Main Currents in American Thought: An Interpretation of American Literature from the Beginnings to 1920.* Vol. 3. New York: Harcourt, Brace, 1930.

Pattee, Fred Lewis. "Anthologies of American Literature before 1861." *Colophon* 4, pt. 16 (1934). N. pag.

Pattee, Fred Lewis. *The Feminine Fifties.* New York: D. Appleton-Century, 1940.

Pattee, Fred Lewis. *The New American Literature, 1890-1930*. New York: Century, 1930.

Patterson, Annabel. "Couples, Canons, and the Uncouth: Spenser-and-Milton in Educational Theory." *Critical Inquiry* 16 (1990): 773-93.

Paul, Sherman. *Olson's Push: Origin, Black Mountain, and Recent American Poetry*. Baton Rouge: Louisiana State UP, 1978.

Pearce, Roy Harvey. *The Continuity of American Poetry*. Princeton: Princeton UP, 1961.

Percy, Thomas, ed. *Reliques of Ancient English Poetry*. 1765. 2d ed. London: J. Dodsley, 1767.

Perelman, Bob. "Language Writing and Audience." Unpublished essay, 1988.

Perloff, Marjorie. *The Dance of the Intellect: Studies in the Poetry of the Pound Tradition*. New York: Cambridge UP, 1985.

Phelps, Wallace [William Phillips], and Philip Rahv. "Criticism." *Partisan Review* 2.7 (1935): 16-25.

Phillips, William. Contribution to "The Changing Culture of the University" symposium. *Partisan Review* 58 (1991): 381.

Phillips, William. "On *Partisan Review*." In Anderson and Kinzie 130-41.

Pinsky, Robert. *The Situation of Poetry: Contemporary Poetry and Its Traditions*. Princeton: Princeton UP, 1976.

Pochmann, Henry, and Gay Wilson Allen, eds. *Introduction to Masters of American Literature*. Carbondale: Southern Illinois UP, 1969.

Poe, Edgar Allan. "Griswold's American Poetry." *Boston Miscellany* 2 (1842): 218-21.

Pollack, Felix. "An Interview on Little Magazines." With Mark Olson, John Judson, and Richard Boudreau. In Anderson and Kinzie 34-49.

Porter, Katherine Anne. "The Situation in American Writing: Seven Questions." *Partisan Review* 6.4 (1939): 36-39.

Pound, Ezra. *ABC of Reading*. 1934. New York: New Directions, 1960.

Pound, Ezra. *Selected Prose, 1909-1965*. Ed. William Cookson. New York: New Directions, 1973.

Price, Kenneth M. *Whitman and Tradition: The Poet in His Century*. New Haven: Yale UP, 1990.

Pritchard, William H. "English Studies, Now and Then." In Graff and Gibbons 198-206.

Quartermain, Peter. *Disjunctive Poetics: From Gertrude Stein and Louis Zukofsky to Susan Howe*. New York: Cambridge UP, 1992.

Quiller-Couch, Sir Arthur, ed. *The Oxford Book of English Verse, 1250-1918*. New York: Clarendon P, 1939.

Radway, Janice A. *Reading the Romance: Women, Patriarchy, and Popular Literature*. Chapel Hill: U of North Carolina P, 1984.

Rahv, Philip. *Essays on Literature and Politics, 1932-1972*. Ed. Arabel J. Porter and Andrew J. Dvosin. Boston: Houghton Mifflin, 1978.

Rahv, Philip. "Paleface and Redskin." *Kenyon Review* 1 (1939): 251-56.

Ransom, John Crowe. "The Bases of Criticism." *Sewanee Review* 52 (1944): 556-71.

Ransom, John Crowe. "Mr. Tate and the Professors." *Kenyon Review* 2 (1940): 348-50.

Ransom, John Crowe. "The Poetry of 1900-1950." *Kenyon Review* 13 (1951): 445-54.

Ransom, John Crowe. *Selected Letters of John Crowe Ransom*. Ed. Thomas Daniel Young and George Core. Baton Rouge: Louisiana State UP, 1985.

Ransom, John Crowe. "Strategy for English Studies." *Southern Review* 6 (1940): 226-35.

Ransom, John Crowe. "The Teaching of Poetry." *Kenyon Review* 1 (1939): 81-83.

Ransom, John Crowe. "These Little Magazines." *American Scholar* 15 (1946): 550-51.

Ransom, John Crowe. *The World's Body*. 1938. Port Washington, NY: Kennikat, 1964.

Rasula, Jed. "The Politics of, The Politics in." In von Hallberg, *Politics and Poetic Value* 315-22.

Read, Thomas Buchanan. *The Female Poets of America*. Philadelphia: E. H. Butler, 1849.

Reichert, John. *Making Sense of Literature*. Chicago: U of Chicago P, 1977.

Reinfeld, Linda. *Language Poetry: Writing as Rescue*. Baton Rouge: Lousiana State UP, 1992.

Reising, Russell J. *The Unusable Past: Theory and the Study of American Literature*. New York: Methuen, 1986.

Rich, Adrienne. *On Lies, Secrets, and Silence: Selected Prose, 1966-1978*. New York: W. W. Norton, 1979.

Rickert, Edith, and Jessie Paton, eds. *American Lyrics*. Garden City, NY: Doubleday, Page, 1912.

Ricks, Christopher. "What is at stake in the 'battle of the books'?" *New Criterion* 8 (1989): 40-44.

Ridge, Lola. *Sun-Up and Other Poems*. New York: B. W. Huebsch, 1920.

Riding, Laura, and Robert Graves. *A Survey of Modernist Poetry*. London: W. Heinemann, 1927.

Robinson, Charles. "Academia and the Little Magazine." In Anderson and Kinzie 27-33.

Rodden, John. *The Politics of Literary Reputation: The Making and Claiming of "St. George" Orwell*. New York: Oxford UP, 1989.

Rosenfeld, Alvin H. "Anne Bradstreet's 'Contemplations': Patterns of Form and Meaning." In *Critical Essays on Anne Bradstreet*, ed. Patti Cowell and Ann Stanford. Boston: G. K. Hall, 1983. 123-36.

Ross, Andrew. "The New Sentence and the Commodity Form: Recent American Writing." In *Marxism and the Interpretation of Culture*, ed. Cary Nelson and Lawrence Grossberg. Urbana: U of Illinois P, 1988. 361-80.

Rossetti, William Michael. *The Diary of W. M. Rossetti, 1870-1873*. Ed. Odette Bornand. Oxford: Oxford UP, 1977.

Rothenberg, Jerome, and Pierre Joris, eds. *Poems for the Millennium: The University of California Book of Modern Poetry*. Berkeley: U of California P, forthcoming.

Rukeyser, Muriel. *The Collected Poems of Muriel Rukeyser*. New York: McGraw-Hill, 1982.

Said, Edward. *The World, the Text, and the Critic*. Cambridge: Harvard UP, 1983.

Santayana, George. *The Genteel Tradition: Nine Essays by George Santayana*. Ed. Douglas L. Wilson. Cambridge: Harvard UP, 1967.

Scholes, Robert. *Textual Power: Literary Theory and the Teaching of English*. New Haven: Yale UP, 1985.

Schwartz, Leonard H. *Creating Faulkner's Reputation: The Politics of Modern Literary Criticism*. Knoxville: U of Tennessee P, 1988.

Schweitzer, Ivy. *The Work of Self-Representation: Lyric Poetry in Colonial New England*. Chapel Hill: U of N. Carolina P, 1991.

Scott, Bonnie Kime, ed. *The Gender of Modernism: A Critical Anthology*. Bloomington: Indiana UP, 1990.

Seymour-Smith, Martin. "Review of *Collected Poems: (1934-1953)*, by Dylan Thomas." *Black Mountain Review* 1.1 (1954): 57-58.

Shapiro, Karl. "An Interview on *Poetry*." With Michael Anania and Ralph J. Mills, Jr. In Anderson and Kinzie 196-215.

Showalter, Elaine. "Women's Time, Women's Space: Writing the History of Feminist Criticism." In Benstock 30-44.

Shusterman, Richard. *Pragmatist Aesthetics: Living Beauty, Rethinking Art*. Cambridge, MA: Basil Blackwell, 1992.

Silliman, Ron. "Canons and Institutions: New Hope for the Disappeared." In Bernstein, *Politics of Poetic Form* 149-74.

Silliman, Ron. "Disappearance of the Word, Appearance of the World." In Andrews and Bernstein 121-32.

Silliman, Ron. "If by 'Writing' We Mean Literature (if by 'literature' we mean poetry (if . . .)). . . ." In Andrews and Bernstein 167-68.

Silliman, Ron. *The New Sentence*. New York: Roof, 1987.

Silliman, Ron. *Paradise*. Providence: Burning Deck, 1985.

Silliman, Ron. "Poets and Intellectuals." *Temblor* 9 (1989): 122-24.

Silliman, Ron, ed. *In the American Tree: Language, Realism, Poetry*. Orono, ME: National Poetry Foundation, 1986.

Silliman, Ron, Carla Harryman, Lyn Hejinian, Steve Benson, Bob Perelman, and Barrett Watten. "Aesthetic Tendency and the Politics of Poetry: A Manifesto." *Social Text* 19/20 (1988): 261-75.

Simpson, Lewis P., ed. *The Federalist Literary Mind: Selections from the "Monthly Anthology and Boston Review," 1803-1811, Including Documents Relating to the Boston Athenaeum*. Baton Rouge: Louisiana State UP, 1962.

Smith, Barbara Herrnstein. *Contingencies of Value: Alternative Perspectives for Critical Theory*. Cambridge: Harvard UP, 1988.

Smith, Bernard. *Forces in American Criticism: A Study in the History of American Literary Thought*. New York: Harcourt, Brace, 1939.

Smith, Elihu Hubbard, ed. *American Poems, Selected and Original.* Vol. 1. Litch-
    field, CT: Collier and Buel, 1793. Reprint. Ed. William K. Bottorff.
    Gainesville, FL: Scholars' Facsimiles and Reprints, 1966.
Snyder, John Edwin. "Walt Whitman's Woman." *Socialist Woman* (Feb. 1909): 7.
Sorrentino, Gilbert. "*Neon, Kulchur,* etc." In Anderson and Kinzie 298–316.
Souster, Raymond. "Some Afterthoughts on *Contact* Magazine." In Gnarowski
    1–2.
[Spargo, John?]. "Greeting." *Comrade* (Oct. 1901): [12].
Spears, Monroe K. "The Present Function of the Literary Quarterlies." *Texas
    Quarterly* 3.1 (1960): 33–50.
Spenser, Benjamin T. *The Quest for Nationality: An American Literary Companion.*
    Syracuse: Syracuse UP, 1957.
Spengemann, William C. *A Mirror for Americanists: Reflections on the Idea of
    American Literature.* Hanover: UP of New England, 1989.
Spier, Leonard. "Walt Whitman." *International Literature* (Sept. 1935): 72–89.
Spier, Leonard. "What We Need." *Rebel Poet* (Oct.–Dec. 1931): 9.
Spivak, Gayatri Chakravorty. "The Making of Americans, the Teaching of
    English, and the Future of Culture Studies." *New Literary History* 21 (1990):
    781–98.
Stafford, John. *The Literary Criticism of "Young America": A Study in the Relation-
    ship of Politics and Literature, 1837–1850.* Berkeley: U of California P, 1952.
Stanford, Ann. *Anne Bradstreet: The Worldly Puritan. An Introduction to the Poetry.*
    New York: Burt Franklin, 1974.
Stange, G. Robert. "1887 and the Making of the Victorian Canon." *Victorian
    Poetry* 25 (1987): 151–68.
Stedman, Edmund Clarence, ed. *An American Anthology, 1787–1900.* Boston:
    Houghlin and Mifflin: 1900.
Stefanile, Felix. "The Imagination of the Amateur." *The American Literary
    Anthology/1: The First Annual Collection of the Best from the Literary Maga-
    zines.* New York: Farrar, Straus and Giroux, 1968. 337–60.
Stefanile, Felix. "The Little Magazine Today." In Anderson and Kinzie 648–63.
Stevens, Wallace. *Letters of Wallace Stevens.* Sel. and ed. Holly Stevens. New
    York: Knopf, 1981.
Stevenson, Philip. "Walt Whitman's Democracy." *New Masses* (14 June 1938):
    129–33.
Suleiman, Susan Rubin. *Subversive Intent: Gender, Politics, and the Avant-Garde.*
    Cambridge: Harvard UP, 1990.
Swallow, Alan. "Postwar Little Magazines." *Prairie Schooner* 23 (1949): 152–57.
Tanselle, G. Thomas. "Two Early Letters of Ezra Pound." *American Literature*
    34 (1962): 114–19.
Tate, Allen. *Essays of Four Decades.* New York: William Morrow, 1970.
Tate, Allen. *The Forlorn Demon: Didactic and Critical Essays.* Chicago: Regnery,
    1953.
Tate, Allen. *Memoirs and Opinions, 1926–1974.* Chicago: Swallow, 1975.

Tate, Allen. *The Poetry Reviews of Allen Tate, 1924–1944*. Ed. Ashley Brown and Frances Neel Cheney. Baton Rouge: Louisiana State UP, 1983.

Tate, Allen. *Reactionary Essays on Poetry and Ideas*. New York: Scribner, 1936.

Tate, Allen. *Reason in Madness: Critical Essays*. 1941. Freeport, NY: Books for Libraries, 1968.

Tate, Allen. "Remarks on the Southern Religion." *I'll Take My Stand: The South and the Agrarian Tradition*. 1930; New York: Harper, 1962. 155–75.

Tate, Allen. "The Situation in American Writing: Seven Questions." *Partisan Review* 6.4 (1939): 28–30.

Tate, Allen. "The Unliteral Imagination; or, I, Too, Dislike It." *Southern Review*, n.s. 1 (1965): 530.

Taylor, Gary. *Reinventing Shakespeare: A Cultural History, From the Restoration to the Present*. New York: Oxford UP, 1989.

Teres, Harvey. "Remaking Marxist Criticism: *Partisan Review*'s Eliotic Leftism, 1934–1936." *American Literature* 64 (1992): 127–53.

Thomas, Harry, ed. *Berryman's Understanding: Reflections on the Poetry of John Berryman*. Boston: Northeastern UP, 1988.

Thomas, Wright, and Stuart Gerry Brown. *Reading Poems: An Introduction to Critical Study*. New York: Oxford UP, 1941.

Thornbury, Charles. "John Berryman and the 'Majestic Shade' of W. B. Yeats." In *Yeats: An Annual of Critical and Textual Studies*, ed. George Bornstein and Richard J. Finneran. Ithaca: Cornell UP, 1985. 121–72.

Tompkins, Jane P. *Sensational Designs: The Cultural Work of American Fiction, 1790–1860*. New York: Oxford UP, 1985.

Tomsich, John. *A Genteel Endeavor: American Culture and Politics in the Gilded Age*. Stanford: Stanford UP, 1971.

Torgersen, Eric. "Cold War in Poetry: Notes of a Conscientious Objector." *American Poetry Review* (July–Aug. 1982): 31–35.

Toynbee, Philip. "Berryman's Songs." In Thomas 133–38.

Trilling, Lionel. *The Liberal Imagination: Essays on Literature and Society*. 1950. Garden City, NY: Doubleday, 1953.

Trilling, Lionel. *Speaking of Literature and Society*. Ed. Diana Trilling. New York: Harcourt Brace Jovanovich, 1980.

Tuckerman, H. T. "The Poetry of Bryant." *United States Magazine and Democratic Review* 16 (Feb. 1845): 185–91.

Untermeyer, Louis, ed. *American Poetry from the Beginning to Whitman*. New York: Harcourt and Brace, 1931.

Untermeyer, Louis, ed. *Early American Poets*. 1952. Freeport, NY: Books for Libraries, 1970.

Van Brunt, H. L. "The Property of Love: Little Magazines in the Seventies." *Smith* 17 (1974): 180–84.

Van Doren, Mark. "Walt Whitman, Stranger." *American Mercury* 35 (1935): 277–84.

Van Wienen, Mark. "Taming the Socialist: Carl Sandburg's *Chicago Poems* and Its Critics." *American Literature* 63 (1991): 89–103.

Vendler, Helen. "The Literature of Contemporary America: Poetry." In McQuade et al. 1st ed. 2737–44; 2d ed. 2393–96.

Vendler, Helen. "The Literature of Postwar America: Poetry/1940–1973." In McQuade et al. 1st ed. 2243–54.

Vendler, Helen. *The Music of What Happens: Poems, Poets, Critics.* Cambridge: Harvard UP, 1988.

Vendler, Helen. *Part of Nature, Part of Us: Modern American Poets.* Cambridge: Harvard UP, 1980.

Vendler, Helen, ed. *The Harvard Book of Contemporary American Poetry.* Cambridge: Harvard UP, 1985.

Von Hallberg, Robert. "American Poet-Critics since 1945." In *Reconstructing American Literary History,* ed. Sacvan Bercovitch. Cambridge: Harvard UP, 1986. 280–99.

Von Hallberg, Robert. *American Poetry and Culture, 1945–1980.* Cambridge: Harvard UP, 1985.

Von Hallberg, Robert. "Introduction." In *Canons* 1–4.

Von Hallberg, Robert, ed. *Canons.* Chicago: U of Chicago P, 1984.

Von Hallberg, Robert, ed. *Politics and Poetic Value.* Chicago: U of Chicago P, 1987.

Waggoner, Hyatt H. *American Poets from the Puritans to the Present.* Rev. ed. Baton Rouge: Louisiana State UP, 1984.

Walker, Cheryl. *The Nightingale's Burden: Women Poets and American Culture before 1900.* Bloomington: Indiana UP, 1982.

Walker, David. *The Transparent Lyric: Reading and Meaning in the Poetry of Stevens and Williams.* Princeton: Princeton UP, 1984.

Wallace, Ronald, ed. *Vital Signs: Contemporary American Poetry from the University Presses.* Madison: U of Wisconsin P, 1989.

Warren, Robert Penn. "The Situation in American Writing: Seven Questions (Part 2)." *Partisan Review* 6.5 (1939): 112–13.

Warren, Robert Penn. *New and Selected Essays.* New York: Random House, 1989.

Warren, Robert Penn. "Poets and Scholars." *Nation* (8 Aug. 1942): 137.

Warren, Robert Penn. "The Present State of Poetry III. In the United States." *Kenyon Review* 1 (1939): 384–98.

Warren, Robert Penn. Untitled statement in *Wilson Library Bulletin* 13 (1939): 652.

Watkins, Evan. "Reproduction, Reading, and Resistance." *American Literary History* 2 (1990): 550–63.

Watten, Barrett. "Barrett Watten on Poetry and Politics: An Interview by George Hartley." *Sulfur* 21 (1988): 196–207.

Watten, Barrett. "Method and $L=A=N=G=U=A=G=E$." In Silliman, *In the American Tree* 599–612.

Watten, Barrett. " 'X.' " In Messerli, *"Language" Poetries* 131–35.

Watts, Emily Stipes. *The Poetry of American Women from 1632 to 1945.* Austin: U of Texas P, 1977.

Webster, Grant. *The Republic of Letters: A History of Postwar American Literary Opinion*. Baltimore: Johns Hopkins UP, 1979.

Weinberger, Eliot. "Final Response." *Sulfur* 22 (1988): 199–202.

Weinberger, Eliot. "[Letter to Michael Davidson]." *Sulfur* 22 (1988): 180–86.

Weinberger, Eliot, ed. *American Poetry since 1950: Innovators and Outsiders*. New York: Marsilio, 1993.

Weiss, Theodore. *The Man from Porlock: Engagements, 1944–1981*. Princeton: Princeton UP, 1982.

Wellek, René. "The New Criticism: Pro and Contra." *Critical Inquiry* 4 (1978): 611–24.

Wellek, René. "Respect for Tradition." *TLS* (10 Dec. 1982): 1356.

Wetherbee, Winthrop. "*Poeta che mi quidi*: Dante, Lucan, and Virgil." In von Hallberg, *Canons* 131–48.

Wexler, Joyce Piell. *Laura Riding's Pursuit of Truth*. Athens: Ohio UP, 1979.

White, Elizabeth Wade. Review of *Homage to Mistress Bradstreet*. *New England Quarterly* 29 (1956): 545–48.

Whittemore, Reed. *The Boy from Iowa: Poems and Essays*. New York: Macmillan, 1962.

Whittemore, Reed. *Little Magazines*. Minneapolis: U of Minnesota P, 1963.

Whittier, John Greenleaf, ed. *Songs of Three Centuries*. Boston: J. R. Osgood, 1875.

Williams, Raymond. *Marxism and Literature*. New York: Oxford UP, 1977.

Williams, William Carlos. *The Autobiography of William Carlos Williams*. 1951. New York: New Directions, 1967.

Wilson, Edmund. *Letters on Literature and Politics, 1912–1972*. Ed. Elena Wilson. New York: Farrar, Straus and Giroux, 1977.

Wimsatt, W. K. *Hateful Contraries: Studies in Literature and Criticism*. Lexington: U of Kentucky P, 1965.

Wimsatt, W. K. *The Verbal Icon: Studies in the Meaning of Poetry*. 1954. New York: Farrar, Straus, and Cudahy, 1960.

Winters, Yvor. *The Function of Criticism: Problems and Exercises*. Denver: Swallow, 1957.

Winters, Yvor. *In Defense of Reason*. Chicago: Swallow, 1947.

Winters, Yvor. *Maule's Curse: Seven Studies in the History of American Obscurantism*. Norfolk, CT: New Directions, 1938.

Winters, Yvor. "The Poet and the University: A Reply." *Poetry* 75 (1949): 304–9.

Winters, Yvor. *The Uncollected Essays and Reviews of Yvor Winters*. Ed. Francis Murphy. Chicago: Swallow, 1973.

Wolpert, J. F. "Notes on the American Intelligentsia." *Partisan Review* 14 (1947): 472–85.

Wood, James Playsted. *Magazines in the United States: Their Social and Economic Influence*. 2d ed. New York: Ronald, 1956.

Woodcock, George. "Old and New Oxford Books: The Idea of an Anthology."
   Sewanee Review 82 (1974): 119–30.
Yau, John. "Neither Us nor Them." *American Poetry Review* (Mar.–Apr. 1994):
   45–54.
Yingling, Thomas E. *Hart Crane and the Homosexual Text: New Thresholds, New
   Anatomies*. Chicago: U of Chicago P, 1990.
Zetzel, James E. G. "Re-creating the Canon: Augustan Poetry and the Alex-
   andrian Past." In von Hallberg, *Canons* 107–29.

Index

Aaron, Daniel, 94, 95
Aesthetic model of canon formation: xv, xvi, 41, 45-57, 69, 145, 184-85n6; Helen Vendler's version of, 46-51, 52, 53; limitations of, 47-57, 183n3; unacknowledged institutional elements in, 49-51, 52, 53, 55-56; Hugh Kenner's version of, 51-52; Harold Bloom's version of, 53-57
Aiken, Conrad, 22-26 *passim*
Allen, Donald M., 28, 29, 32, 34, 36, 125, 126
Allen, Gay Wilson, 29, 112
Allen, William G., 27
Alsop, Richard, 11, 15
Althusser, Louis, 154, 157
Altieri, Charles, 46, 114, 152, 153
American Anthology, 1787-1900 (ed. Stedman), 7, 19-21
American Poems, Selected and Original (ed. Smith), 4, 8-11
American Poetry since 1950 (ed. Weinberger), 31-33, 179n24-25
Ammons, A. R., 54
Anderson, Margaret, 120
Andrews, Bruce, 149, 155, 160, 165, 166, 168
Anthologies: of American women poets, 7, 14, 174n9; of African-American poetry, 7, 27-28, 29, 179n23; textbook, of poetry, 8, 36-40; of English poetry, 9, 13, 174n6, 176n17, 178n20; of American literature, 110-12, 197n34
Anthologies of American poetry: xvi, 3-40 *passim*; conflicting editorial principles in, 4, 6, 9-10, 36-39; historicizing as editorial motive in, 4, 9, 11-16, 24, 29; preservation as editorial motive in, 4-6, 8-11, 12,

29, 174n4, 179n22; literary nationalism in, 5-6, 9, 11-16 *passim*, 17, 22-23, 29, 175-76n14; moralizing as editorial motive in, 6, 14-16, 174n8; women poets in, 7, 14, 37, 173n3, 179n25, 179-80n26; regional, 7, 174-75n9, 182n31; universal excellence as criterion in, 7-8, 16-18, 29; regional bias in, 11, 14, 174-75n9; differences from English anthologies, 13, 16, 174n6; newness/modernity as criterion in, 21-23, 177n18; African-American poets in, 25, 27, 29-30, 37, 38, 173-74n3, 179n25, 179-80n26, identity-based, 29, 30, 178n21; mainstream survey, 35, 182n32, 182-83n33
Arac, Jonathan, 56, 103, 107
Arnold, Matthew, 11, 54, 103
Arpin, Gary, 59
Arvin, Newton, 94, 95
Ashbery, John, xvii, 35, 56, 140, 144
Auden, W. H., 88, 116, 118

Babbitt, Irving, 73, 81
Baker, Howard, 105, 106
Baraka, Amiri, 31, 35, 37, 153. *See also* Jones, LeRoi
Barlow, Joel, 9, 10, 11, 15
Barone, Dennis, 33
Barrett, William, 80, 84
Barthes, Roland, 155-56, 169
Bartlett, Lee, 153, 161
Baudelaire, Charles, 67
Bawer, Bruce, 64
Beach, Christopher, 136
Beardsley, Monroe, 76
Bee, Susan, 165
Belitt, Ben, 117
Bellamy, Edward, 94
Bennett, David, 127

235

The Wisconsin Project on American Writers

Frank Lentricchia, General Editor

Lionel Trilling: The Work of Liberation
   Daniel T. O'Hara

Visionary Compacts: American Renaissance Writings in Cultural Context
   Donald E. Pease

"A White Heron" and the Question of Minor Literature
   Louis A. Renza

The Theoretical Dimensions of Henry James
   John Carlos Rowe

Chicano Narrative: The Dialectics of Difference
   Ramón Saldívar

Greek Mind/Jewish Soul: The Conflicted Art of Cynthia Ozick
   Victor Strandberg

The Dickinson Sublime
   Gary Lee Stonum

The American Evasion of Philosophy: A Genealogy of Pragmatism
   Cornel West

Specifying: Black Women Writing the American Experience
   Susan Willis

American Sublime: The Genealogy of a Poetic Genre
   Rob Wilson